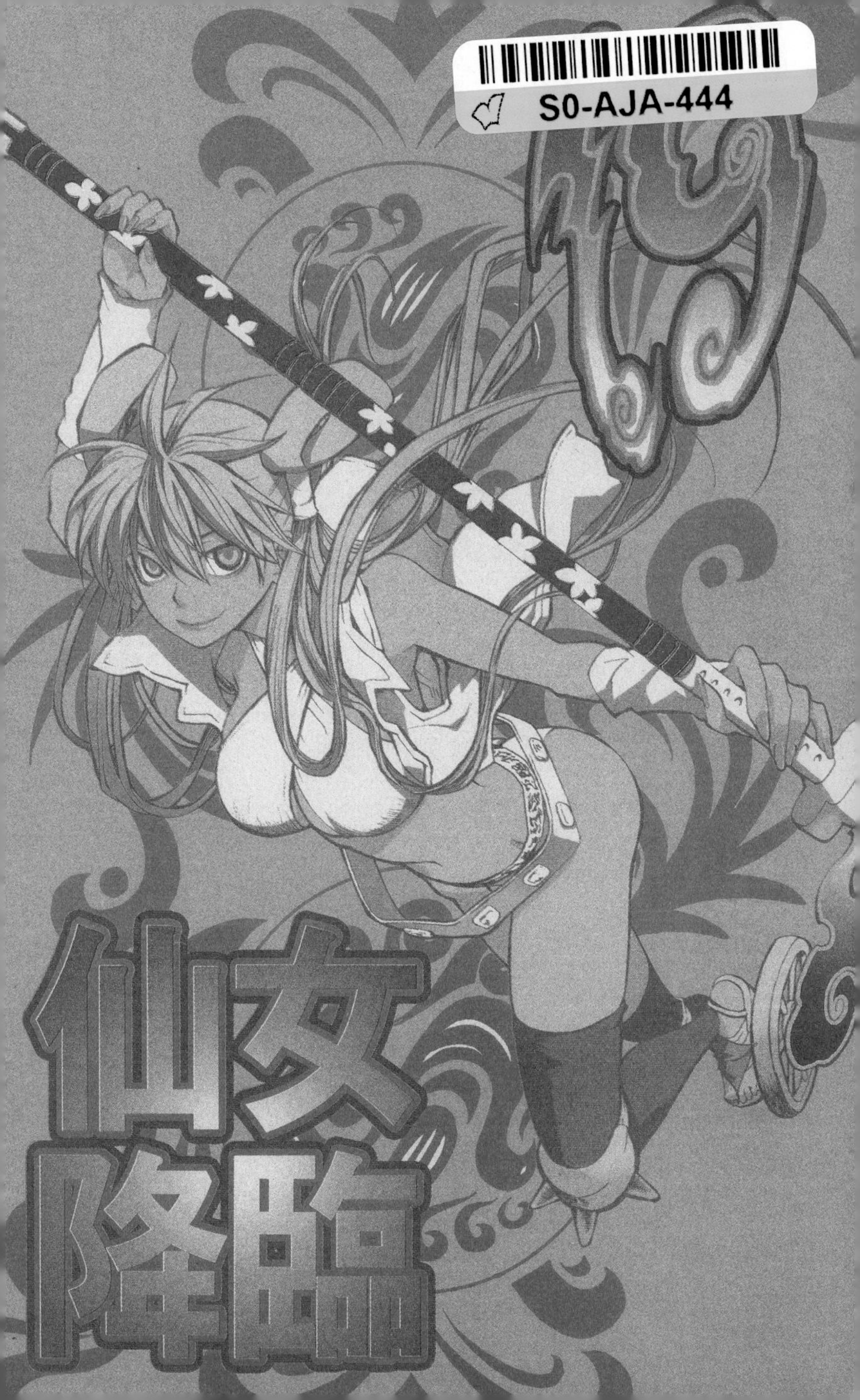
仙女
降臨

Faeries' Landing Volume 19
Created by You Hyun

Translation - Woo Sok Park
English Adaptation - Hyun Joo Kim
Copy Editor - Jessica Chavez
Retouch and Lettering - Star Print Brokers
Production Artist - Jennifer Sanchez
Graphic Designer - Monalisa De Asis

Editor - Hyun Joo Kim
Digital Imaging Manager - Chris Buford
Pre-Production Supervisor - Lucas Rivera
Production Manager - Elisabeth Brizzi
Managing Editor - Vy Nguyen
Creative Director - Anne Marie Horne
Editor-in-Chief - Rob Tokar
Publisher - Mike Kiley
President and C.O.O. - John Parker
C.E.O. and Chief Creative Officer - Stu Levy

A  Manga

TOKYOPOP Inc.
5900 Wilshire Blvd. Suite 2000
Los Angeles, CA 90036

E-mail: info@TOKYOPOP.com
Come visit us online at www.TOKYOPOP.com

ISBN: 978-1-4278-1237-7

First TOKYOPOP printing: June 2008
10 9 8 7 6 5 4 3 2 1
Printed in the USA

Faeries' Landing

Volume 19

By

You Hyun

TOKYOPOP®

HAMBURG // LONDON // LOS ANGELES // TOKYO

From the Realm of Avalon

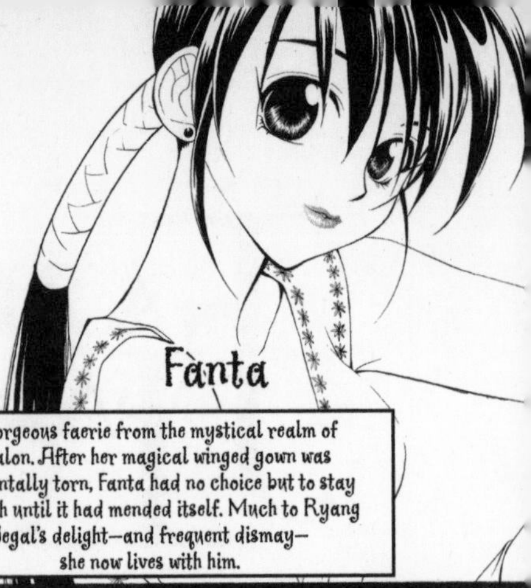

Fanta

A gorgeous faerie from the mystical realm of Avalon. After her magical winged gown was accidentally torn, Fanta had no choice but to stay on earth until it had mended itself. Much to Ryang Jegal's delight—and frequent dismay—she now lives with him.

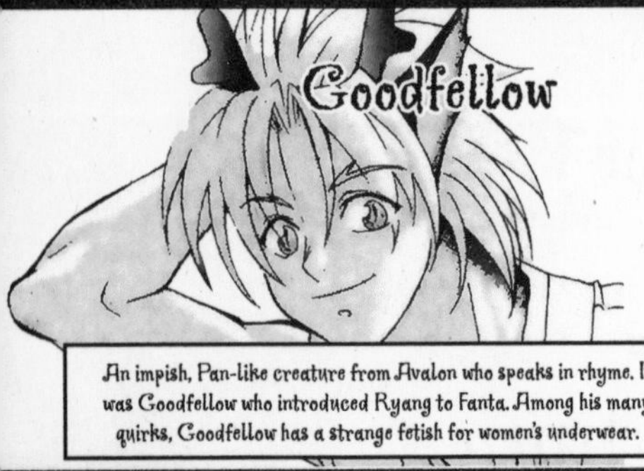

Goodfellow

An impish, Pan-like creature from Avalon who speaks in rhyme. It was Goodfellow who introduced Ryang to Fanta. Among his many quirks, Goodfellow has a strange fetish for women's underwear.

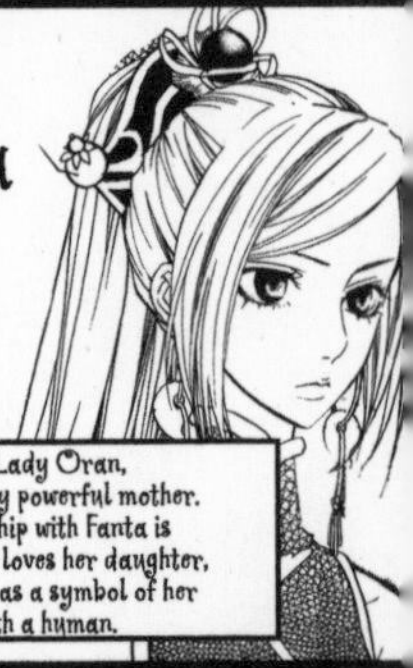

Oreadia

Also known as Lady Oran, Oreadia is Fanta's very powerful mother. Oreadia's relationship with Fanta is complicated. While she loves her daughter, she also resents Fanta as a symbol of her indiscretion with a human.

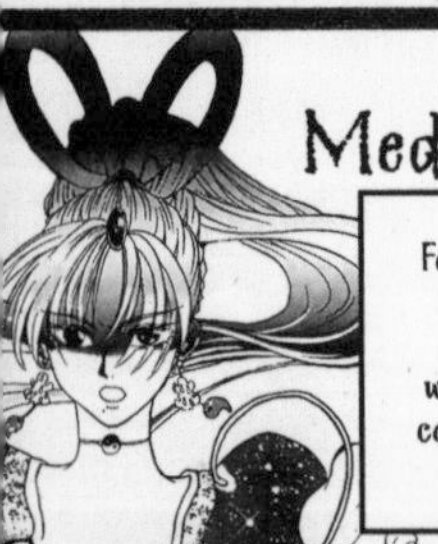

Medea

Fanta's devious and ambitious rival. Medea aspires to be the Queen of Avalon and was the faerie responsible for condemning Ryang to a string of 108 bad relationships.

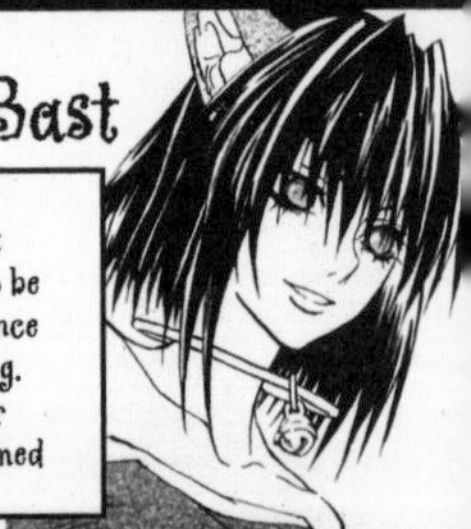

Bast

This southern-drawl-sporting cat goddess has proven to be one nasty little nuisance for Fanta and Ryang. Bast is working for Oreadia and has teamed up with Yuri Kim.

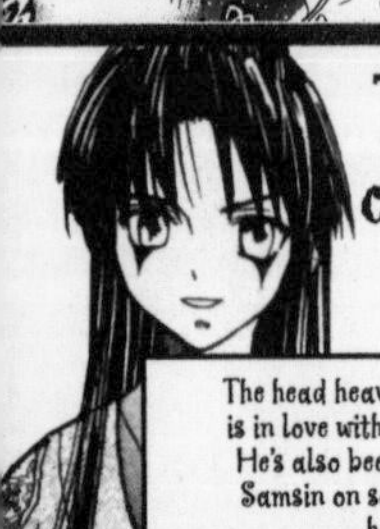

The King of Avalon

The head heavenly honcho. The King of Avalon is in love with Fanta, much to Medea's dismay. He's also been secretly conspiring with Lady Samsin on something nasty, but what that is has yet to be revealed.

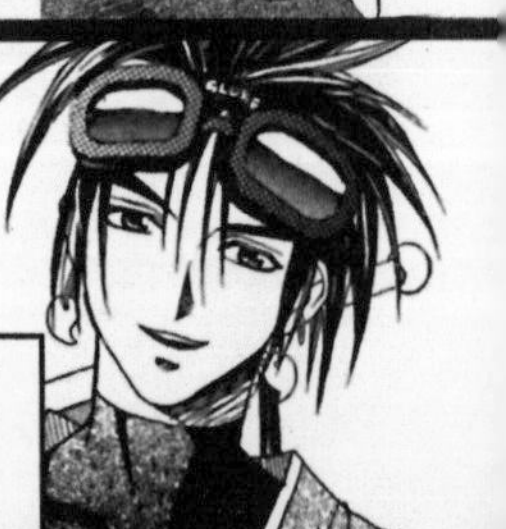

Pain

A flamboyant faerie in every sense of the word, Pain is Avalon's royal inspector and Fanta's brother.

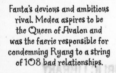

Lady Samsin

At 5,000 years old, Samsin is the oldest of the gods. She oversees all the births in Avalon and lately has been seen conspiring with the King of Avalon. To what ends, however, is unknown.

Charon

As the right-hand man of the King of Avalon, Charon overlooks all the important administrative duties in Avalon. He's also Medea's older brother.

Spirit Forces

These three elemental spirits live in Ryang's skateboard. (Don't ask.) They answer to the names Zero, Gabija and Nyrckes, except when Ryang's calling them. Then they don't answer at all.

Camaxtli and Nina

These two siblings are the royal guards of the King of Avalon. Camaxtli, aka Max, is somewhat feather-brained, but luckily for him and all of Avalon, Nina is by his side to guide him straight..

From the Realm of Man

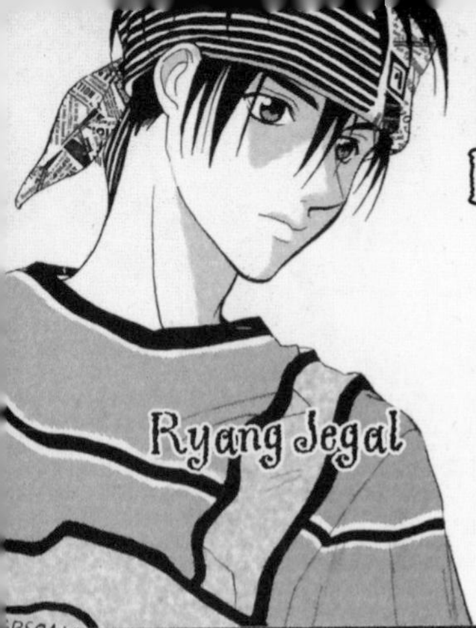

Ryang Jegal

Our hapless bandanna-wearing human protagonist. Ryang's been harboring Fanta, a fetching faerie who's been grounded on earth. Due to a magical curse, Ryang must suffer through 108 doomed relationships. And you thought YOU were unlucky in love...

Mungyeong Seong

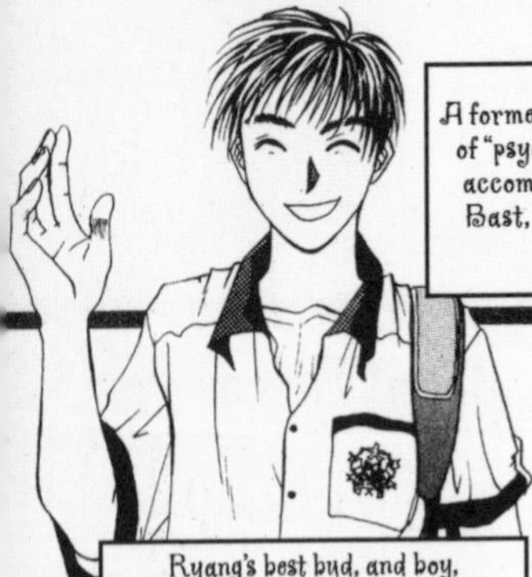

Ryang's best bud, and boy, is he ever a sucker for pretty girls. Lately, Mungyeong's been feeling a bit jealous that every girl in school seems to be falling for Ryang.

Yuri Kim

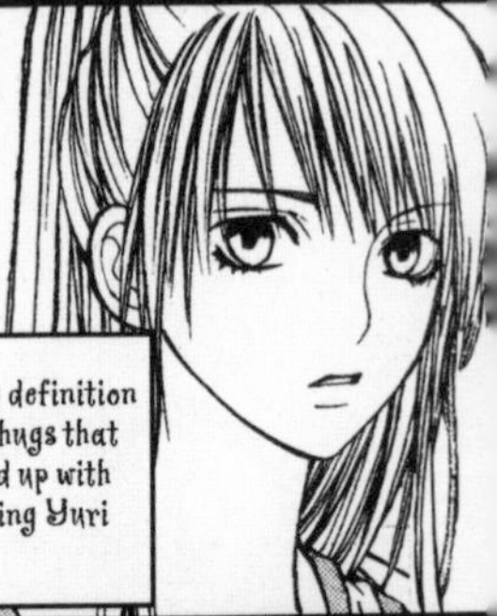

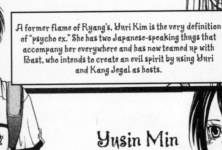

A former flame of Ryang's, Yuri Kim is the very definition of "psycho ex." She has two Japanese-speaking thugs that accompany her everywhere and has now teamed up with Bast, who intends to create an evil spirit by using Yuri and Kang Jegal as hosts.

Yusin Min

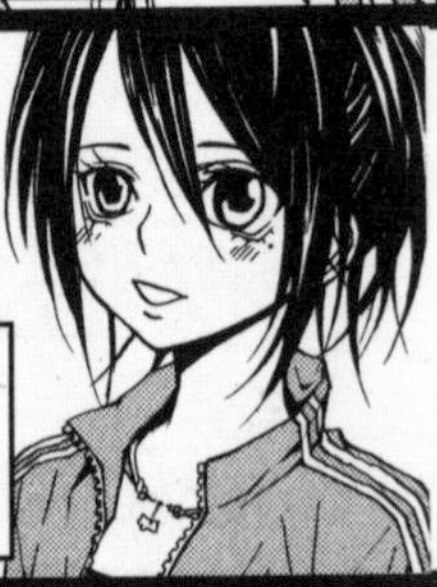

Gracing us again with her presence, Yusin is the only girl from Ryang's 108 evil affinity fiasco who ended up really falling for him.

Hun Jegal and Taeyeong

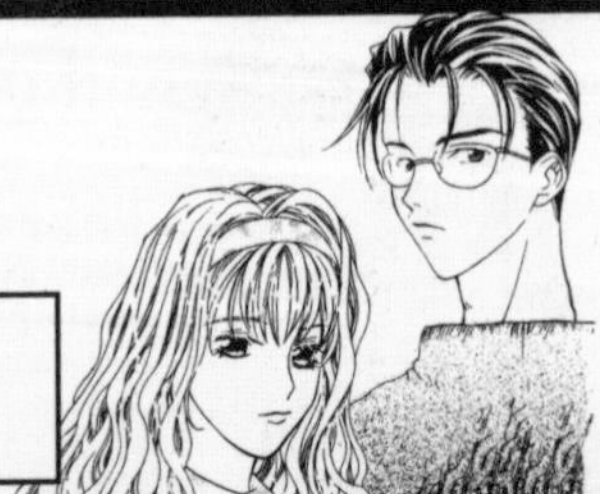

Hun is Ryang's older brother, and Taeyeong is Hun's lovely wife. Ryang currently lives with them.

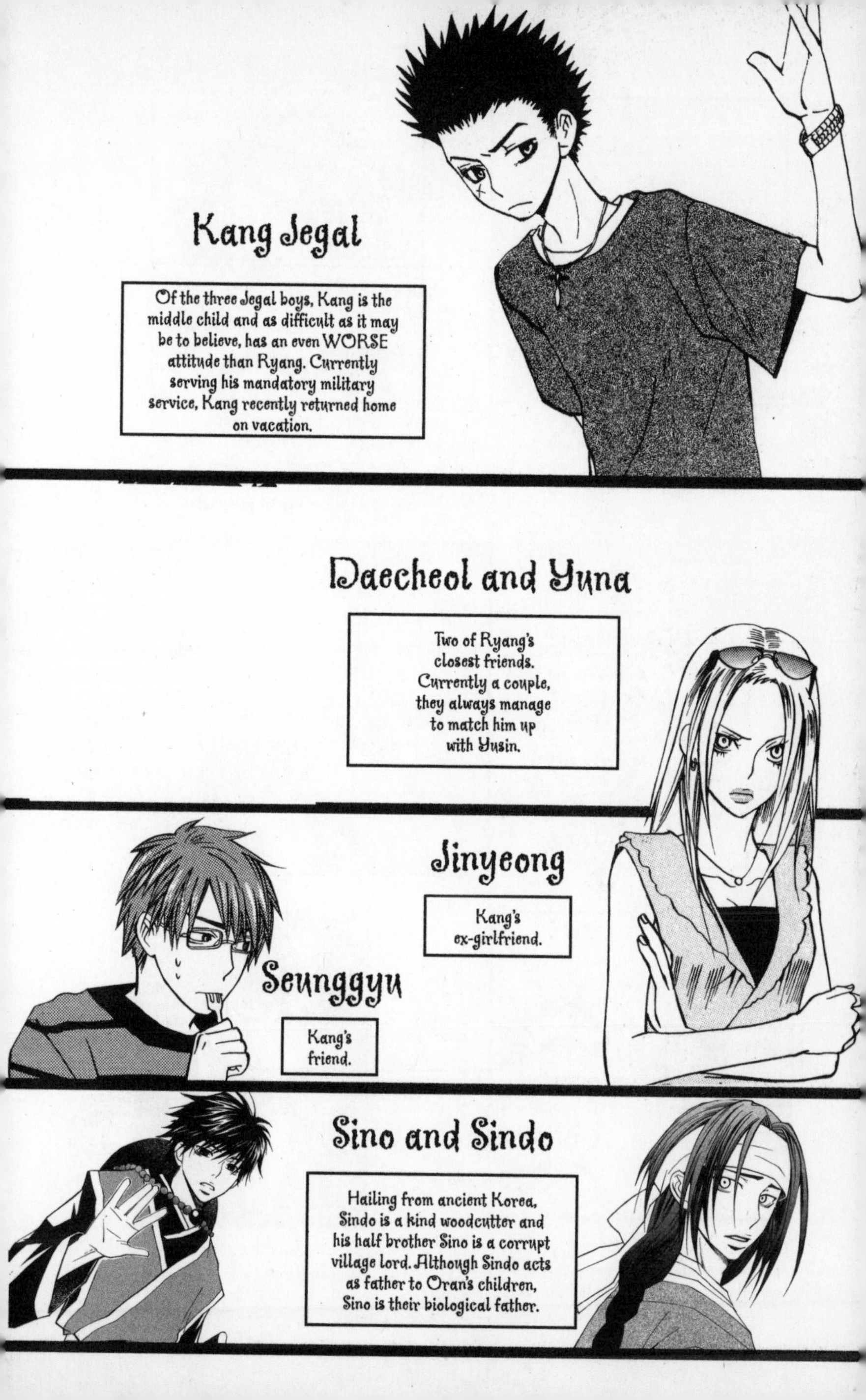
Kang Jegal
Of the three Jegal boys, Kang is the middle child and as difficult as it may be to believe, has an even WORSE attitude than Ryang. Currently serving his mandatory military service, Kang recently returned home on vacation.
Daecheol and Yuna
Two of Ryang's closest friends. Currently a couple, they always manage to match him up with Yusin.
Jinyeong
Kang's ex-girlfriend.
Seunggyu
Kang's friend.
Sino and Sindo
Hailing from ancient Korea, Sindo is a kind woodcutter and his half brother Sino is a corrupt village lord. Although Sindo acts as father to Oran's children, Sino is their biological father.

STORY SO FAR...

Meet Ryang, an average, everyday high school student. Ryang lives in Faeries' Landing, a small suburban town in Korea.

One day, Ryang met Fanta, a powerful (and pretty cute) faerie. Fanta wants nothing more than to experience human life, and since meeting Ryang, she has—as his roommate.

Ryang has a problem. After he accidentally confused a faerie serum with eye drops, he found himself cursed. Any girl he looks in the eye becomes a host for an "evil affinity." This is destined to happen 108 times in his life.

If that weren't bad enough, Fanta finds out her mother, Oreadia, has been trying to kill her.

To understand why her mother seems to hate her and her father, Fanta casts a spell to send Ryang and her back in time to when her parents first met.

There they meet Sindo, the woodcutter Oreadia is destined to marry, and his evil brother, Sino. As the head honcho of the village, Sino is used to having everything his way.

Sino rapes Oreadia when she descends to Earth, but kindhearted Sindo takes her in as Oran after he finds her passed out without her memory or winged gown.

Sindo, Oran and their son Pain form a small but happy family. That is, until Sino switches bodies with Sindo to rape Oran again and impregnate her with Fanta.

Oran's memories and coldness are restored as she calls for her robe. Regaining consciousness as Oreadia, she takes her children away to Avalon but gives Sindo an ultimatum—if he wants to be with his family, he must kill Sino.

Meanwhile, in Avalon, the King turns Charon into the Old Nine-tailed Fox because the prime minister discovers what his king is up to.

The king then holds a banquet for his partner-in-crime, Samsin, and the highlight of the party is the hunt of the Fox. Max, along with some high ranking faeries close in on the creature, not realizing it's really Charon, but they unexpectedly run into Oreadia and Fanta.

Episode 112
Over the Shield of Truth..........................11

Episode 113
Cessation..31

Episode 114
Identity of the Old Nine-Tailed Fox......47

Episode 115
Last Words...73

Episode 116
Brother's Choice....................................89

Episode 117
Freedom...113

Episode 118
Danger in Avalon...................................131

CONTENTS

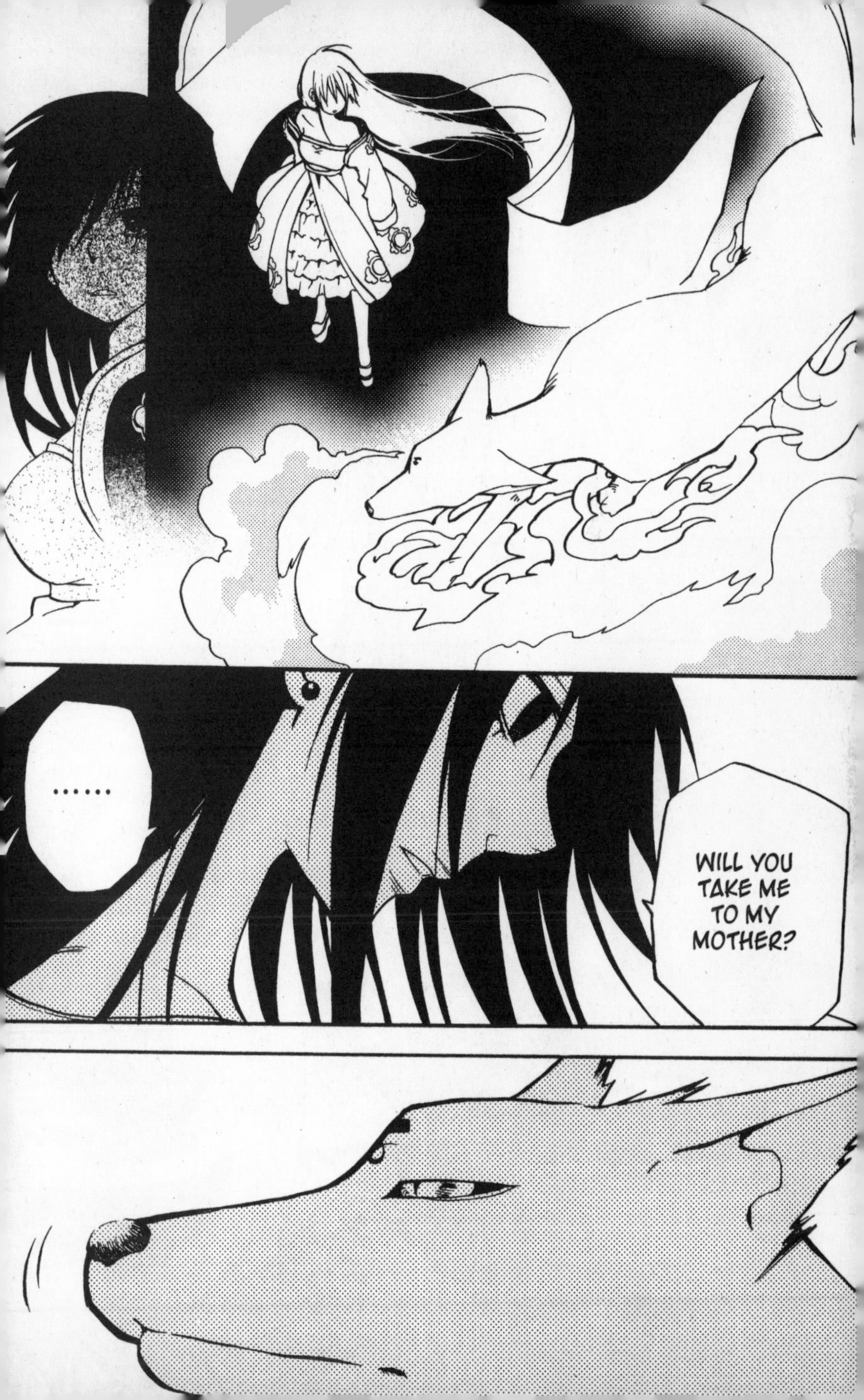

......
WILL YOU TAKE ME TO MY MOTHER?

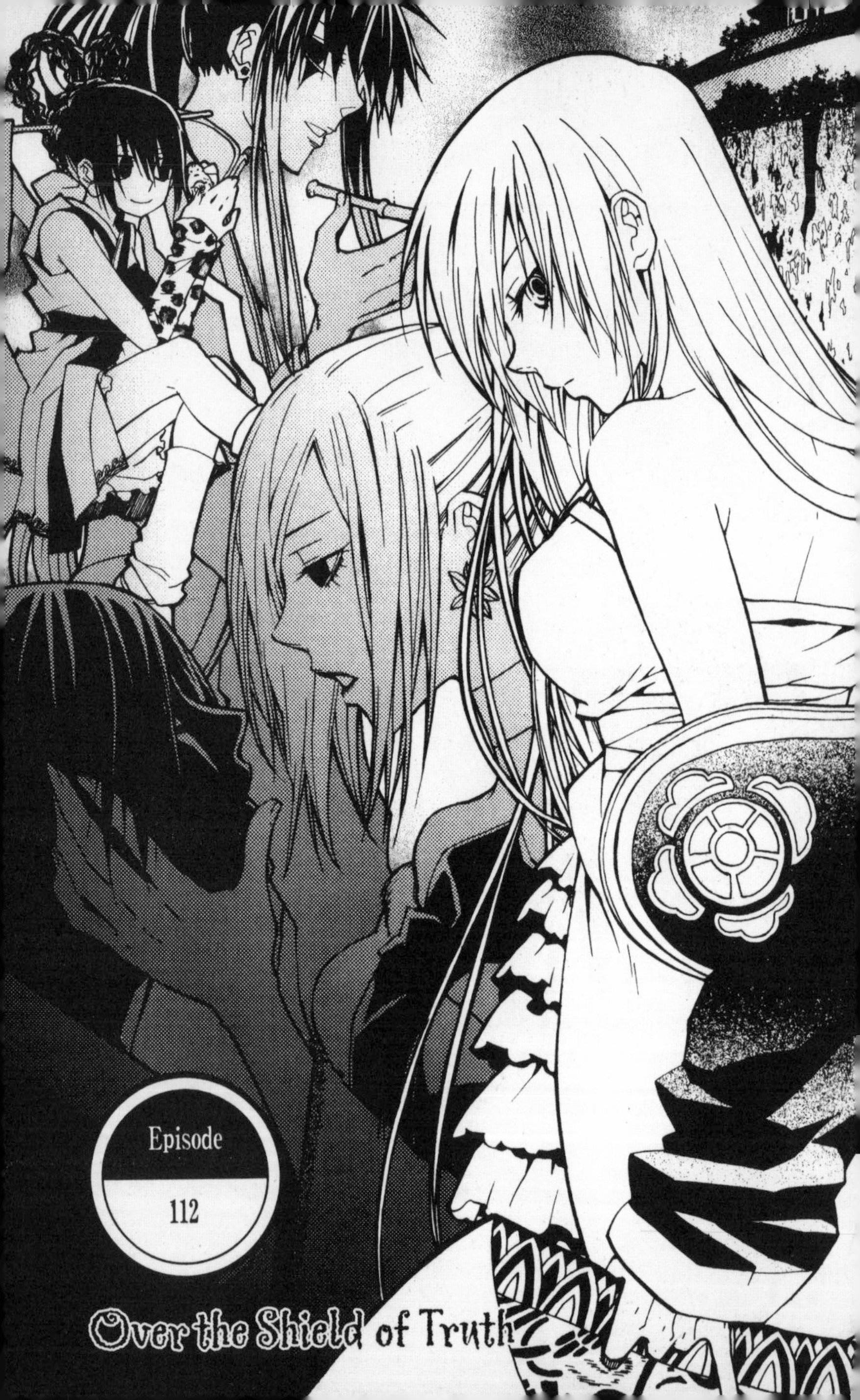
Episode
112
Over the Shield of Truth

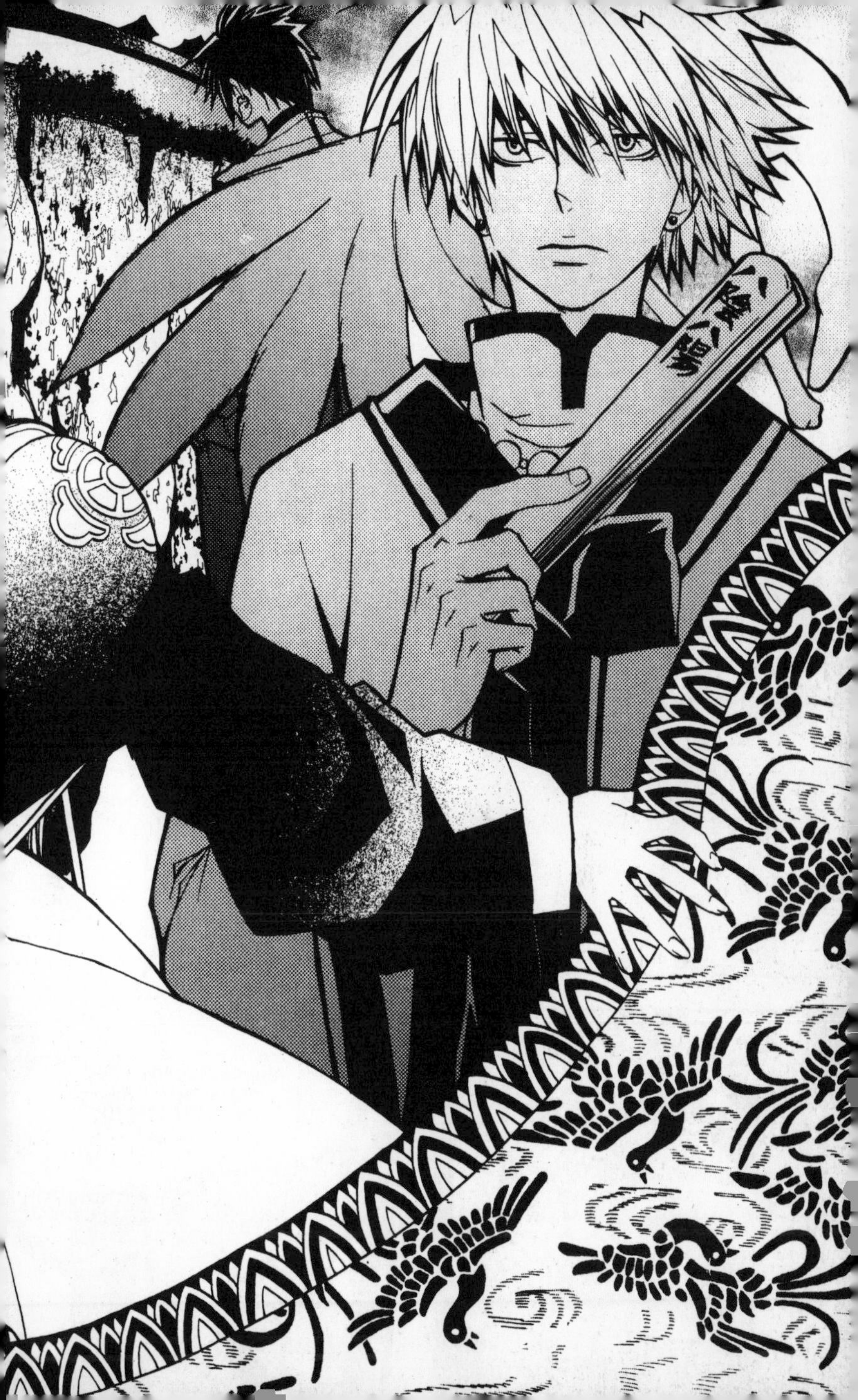

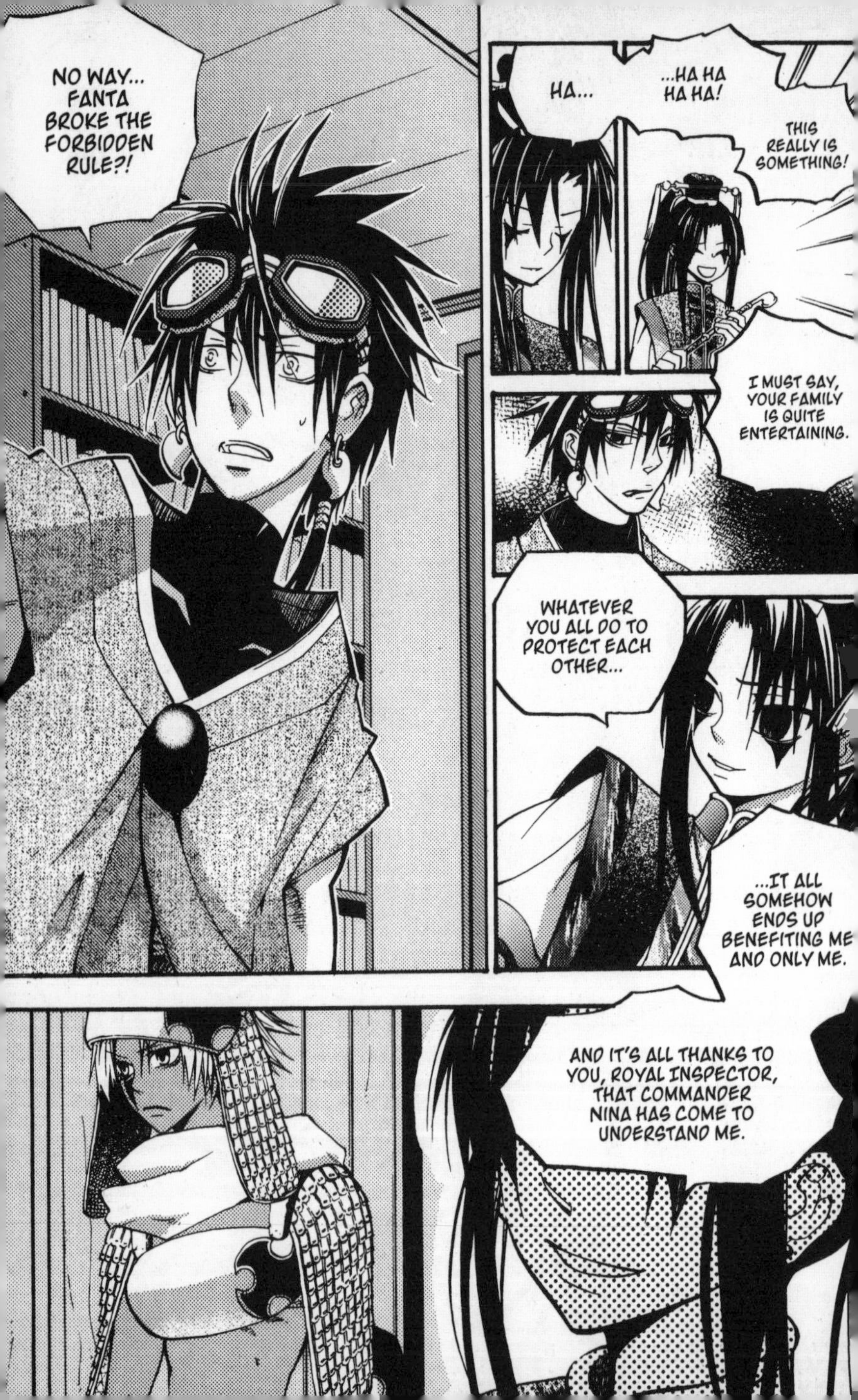
NO WAY... FANTA BROKE THE FORBIDDEN RULE?!
HA...
...HA HA HA HA!
THIS REALLY IS SOMETHING!
I MUST SAY, YOUR FAMILY IS QUITE ENTERTAINING.
WHATEVER YOU ALL DO TO PROTECT EACH OTHER...
...IT ALL SOMEHOW ENDS UP BENEFITING ME AND ONLY ME.
AND IT'S ALL THANKS TO YOU, ROYAL INSPECTOR, THAT COMMANDER NINA HAS COME TO UNDERSTAND ME.

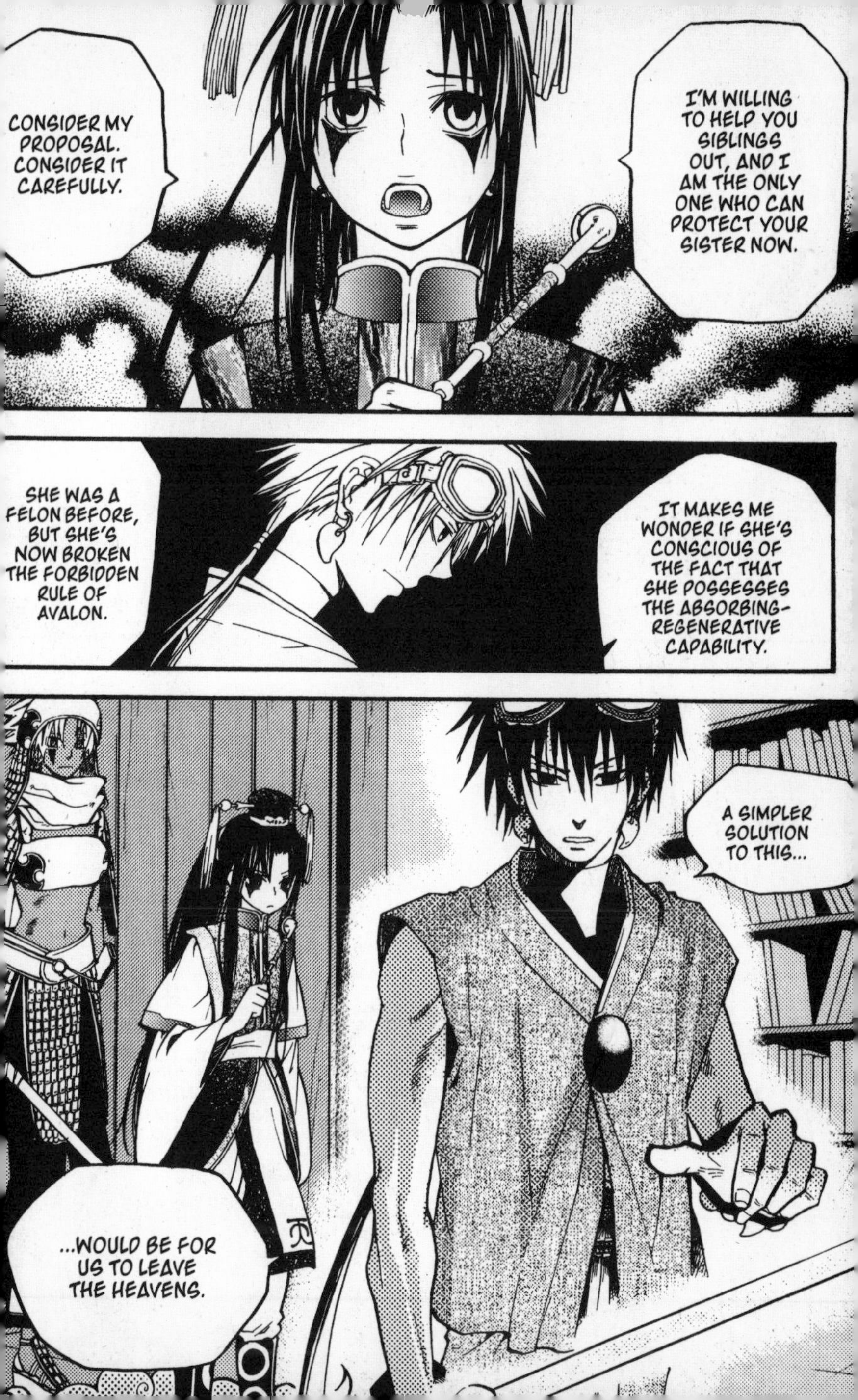
CONSIDER MY PROPOSAL. CONSIDER IT CAREFULLY.
I'M WILLING TO HELP YOU SIBLINGS OUT, AND I AM THE ONLY ONE WHO CAN PROTECT YOUR SISTER NOW.
SHE WAS A FELON BEFORE, BUT SHE'S NOW BROKEN THE FORBIDDEN RULE OF AVALON.
IT MAKES ME WONDER IF SHE'S CONSCIOUS OF THE FACT THAT SHE POSSESSES THE ABSORBING-REGENERATIVE CAPABILITY.
A SIMPLER SOLUTION TO THIS...
...WOULD BE FOR US TO LEAVE THE HEAVENS.

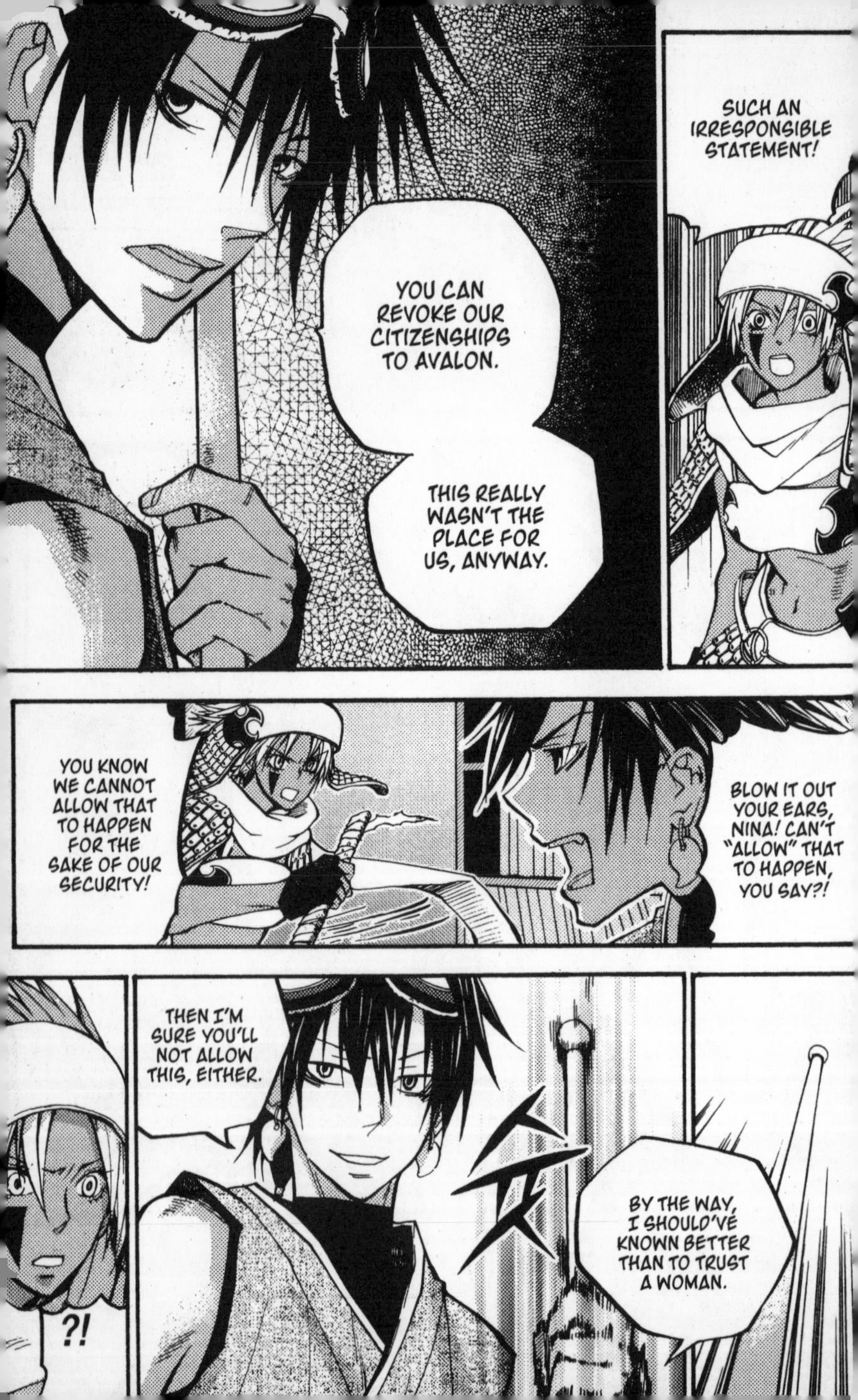
YOU CAN REVOKE OUR CITIZENSHIPS TO AVALON.
THIS REALLY WASN'T THE PLACE FOR US, ANYWAY.
SUCH AN IRRESPONSIBLE STATEMENT!
YOU KNOW WE CANNOT ALLOW THAT TO HAPPEN FOR THE SAKE OF OUR SECURITY!
BLOW IT OUT YOUR EARS, NINA! CAN'T "ALLOW" THAT TO HAPPEN, YOU SAY?!
?!
THEN I'M SURE YOU'LL NOT ALLOW THIS, EITHER.
BY THE WAY, I SHOULD'VE KNOWN BETTER THAN TO TRUST A WOMAN.

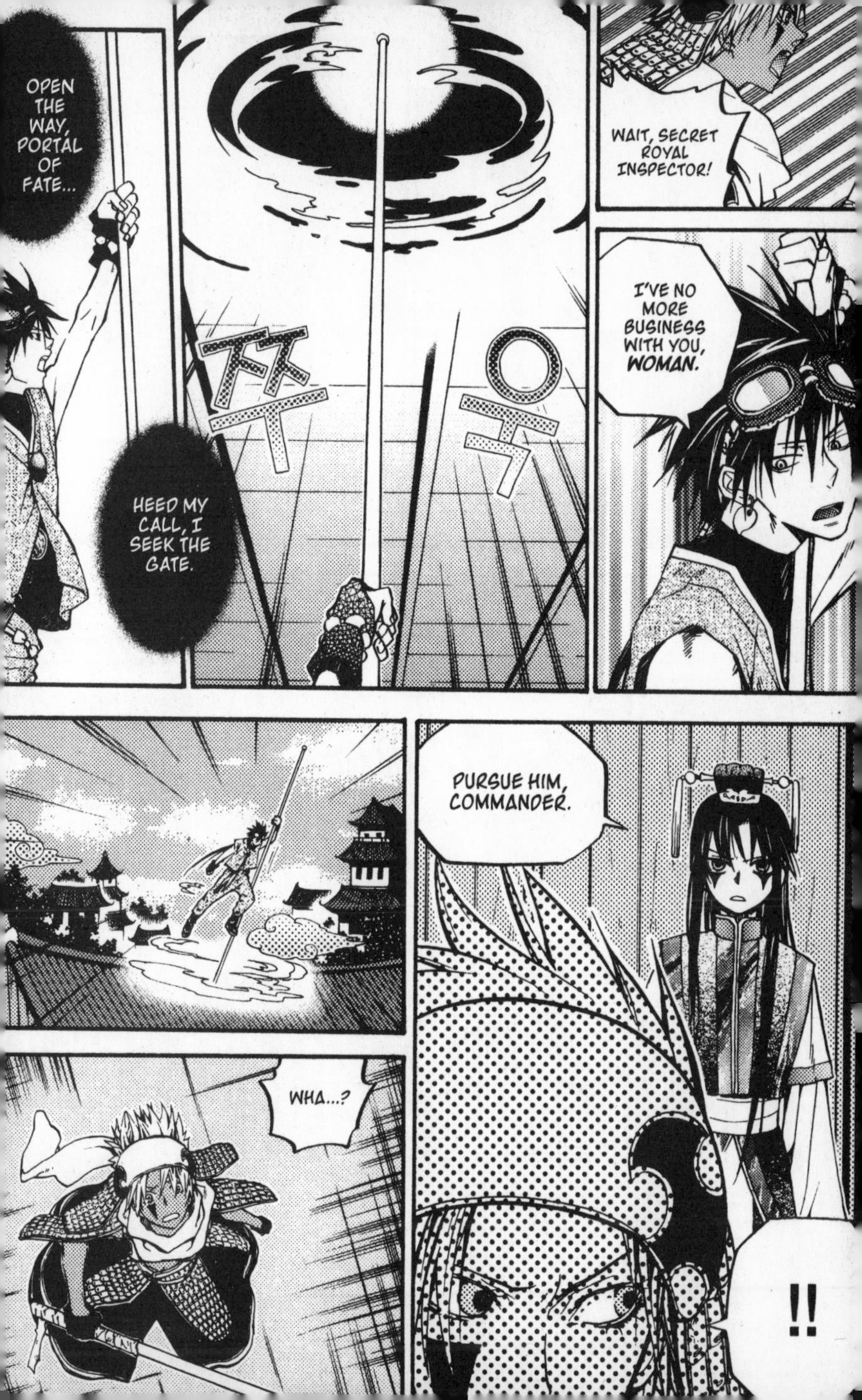
OPEN THE WAY, PORTAL OF FATE...
HEED MY CALL, I SEEK THE GATE.
WAIT, SECRET ROYAL INSPECTOR!
I'VE NO MORE BUSINESS WITH YOU, WOMAN.
WHA...?
PURSUE HIM, COMMANDER.
!!

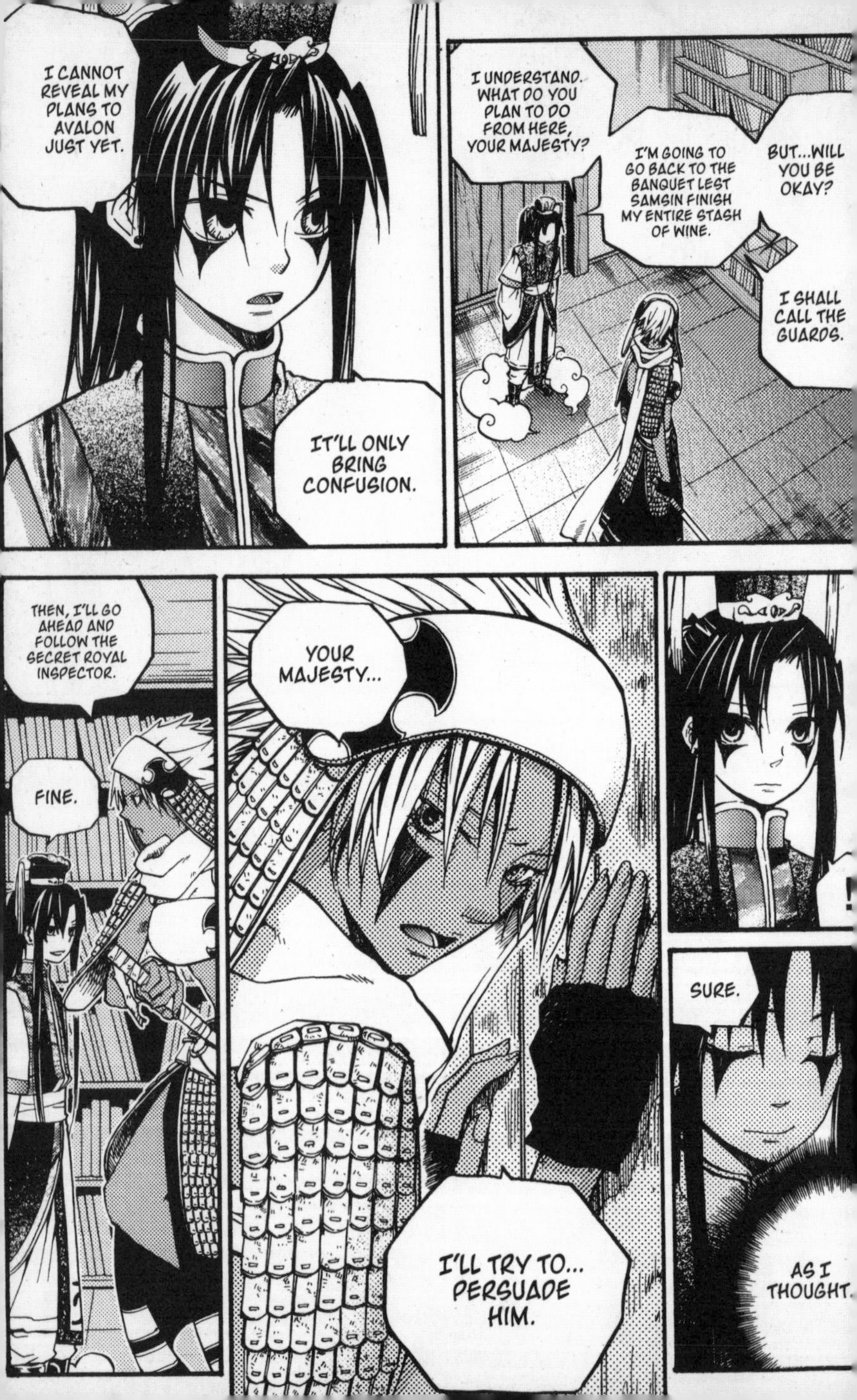
I CANNOT REVEAL MY PLANS TO AVALON JUST YET.
IT'LL ONLY BRING CONFUSION.
I UNDERSTAND. WHAT DO YOU PLAN TO DO FROM HERE, YOUR MAJESTY?
I'M GOING TO GO BACK TO THE BANQUET LEST SAMSIN FINISH MY ENTIRE STASH OF WINE.
BUT...WILL YOU BE OKAY?
I SHALL CALL THE GUARDS.
THEN, I'LL GO AHEAD AND FOLLOW THE SECRET ROYAL INSPECTOR.
FINE.
YOUR MAJESTY...
I'LL TRY TO... PERSUADE HIM.
!
SURE.
AS I THOUGHT.

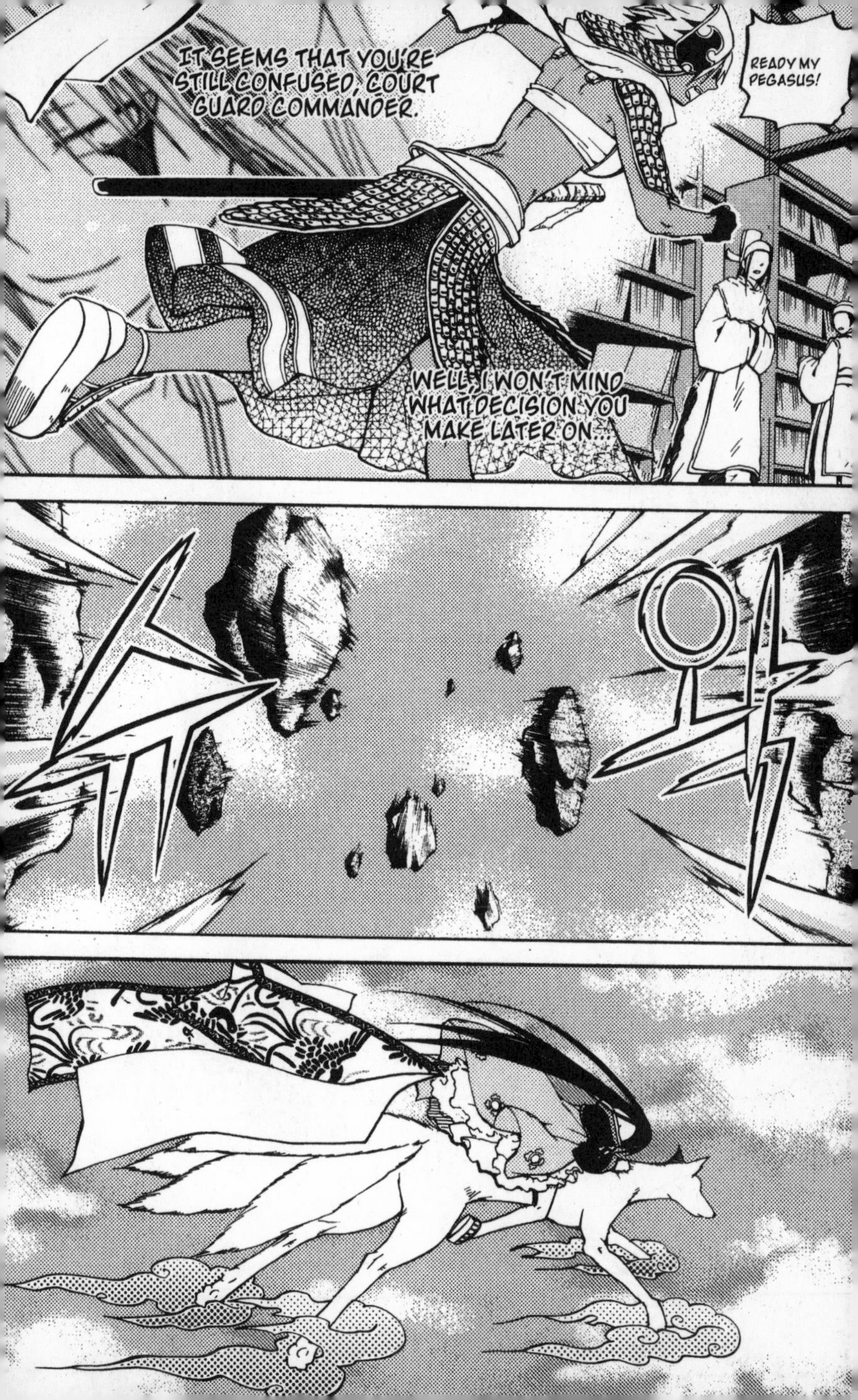
IT SEEMS THAT YOU'RE STILL CONFUSED, COURT GUARD COMMANDER.
READY MY PEGASUS!
WELL, I WON'T MIND WHAT DECISION YOU MAKE LATER ON...

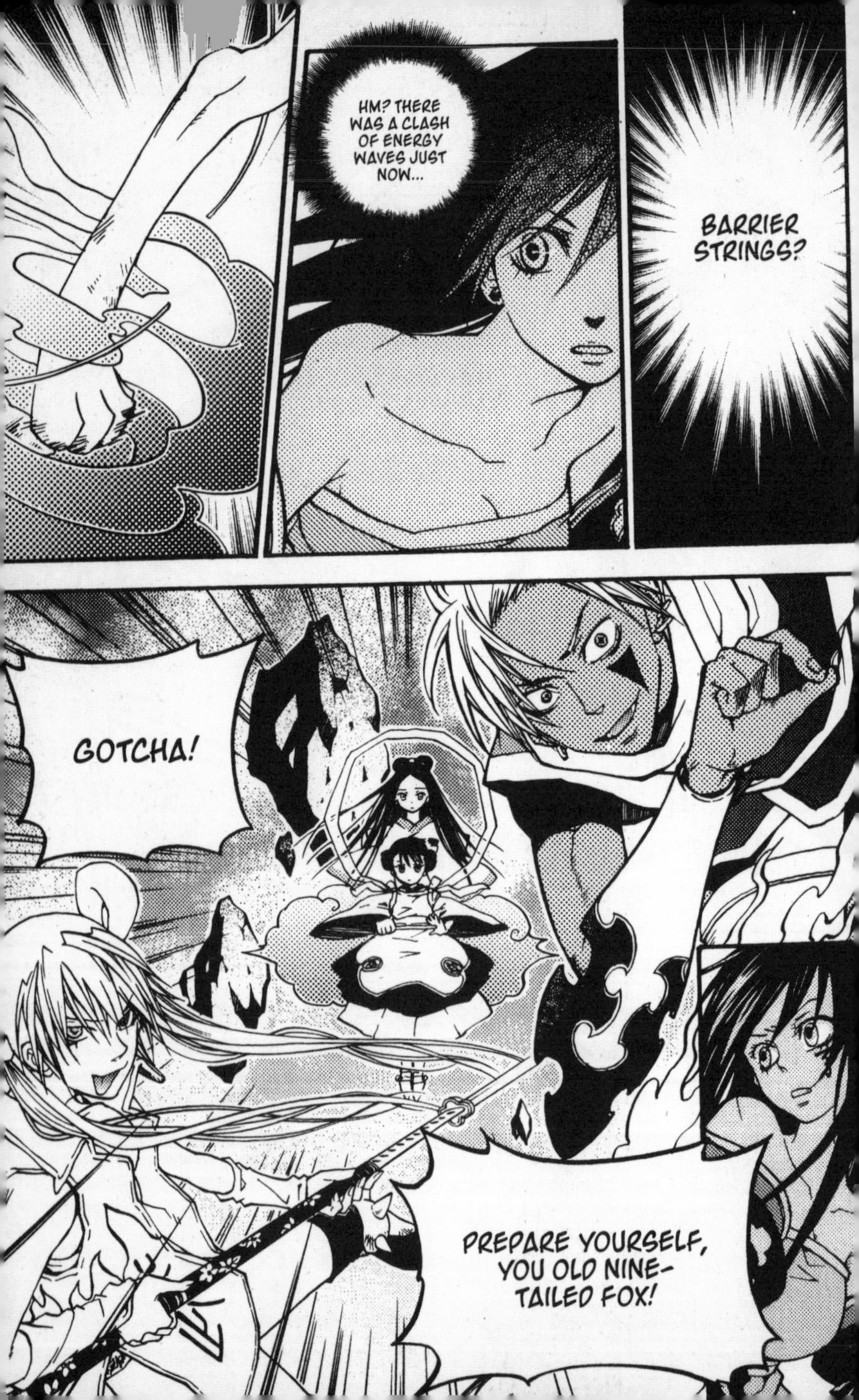
HM? THERE WAS A CLASH OF ENERGY WAVES JUST NOW...
BARRIER STRINGS?
GOTCHA!
PREPARE YOURSELF, YOU OLD NINE-TAILED FOX!

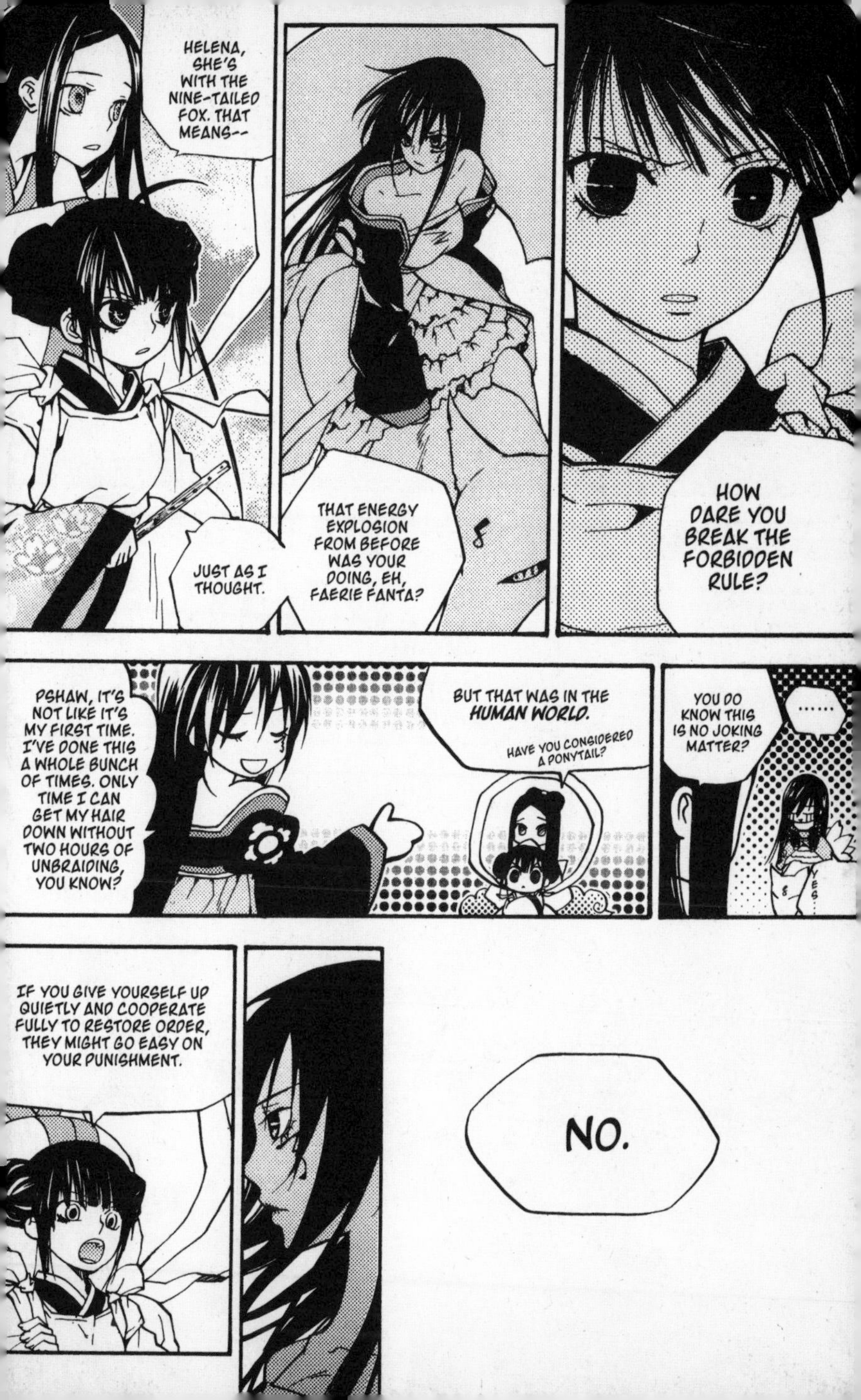
HELENA, SHE'S WITH THE NINE-TAILED FOX. THAT MEANS--
JUST AS I THOUGHT.
THAT ENERGY EXPLOSION FROM BEFORE WAS YOUR DOING, EH, FAERIE FANTA?
HOW DARE YOU BREAK THE FORBIDDEN RULE?
PSHAW, IT'S NOT LIKE IT'S MY FIRST TIME. I'VE DONE THIS A WHOLE BUNCH OF TIMES. ONLY TIME I CAN GET MY HAIR DOWN WITHOUT TWO HOURS OF UNBRAIDING, YOU KNOW?
BUT THAT WAS IN THE *HUMAN WORLD.*
HAVE YOU CONSIDERED A PONYTAIL?
YOU DO KNOW THIS IS NO JOKING MATTER?
....
YES
IF YOU GIVE YOURSELF UP QUIETLY AND COOPERATE FULLY TO RESTORE ORDER, THEY MIGHT GO EASY ON YOUR PUNISHMENT.
NO.

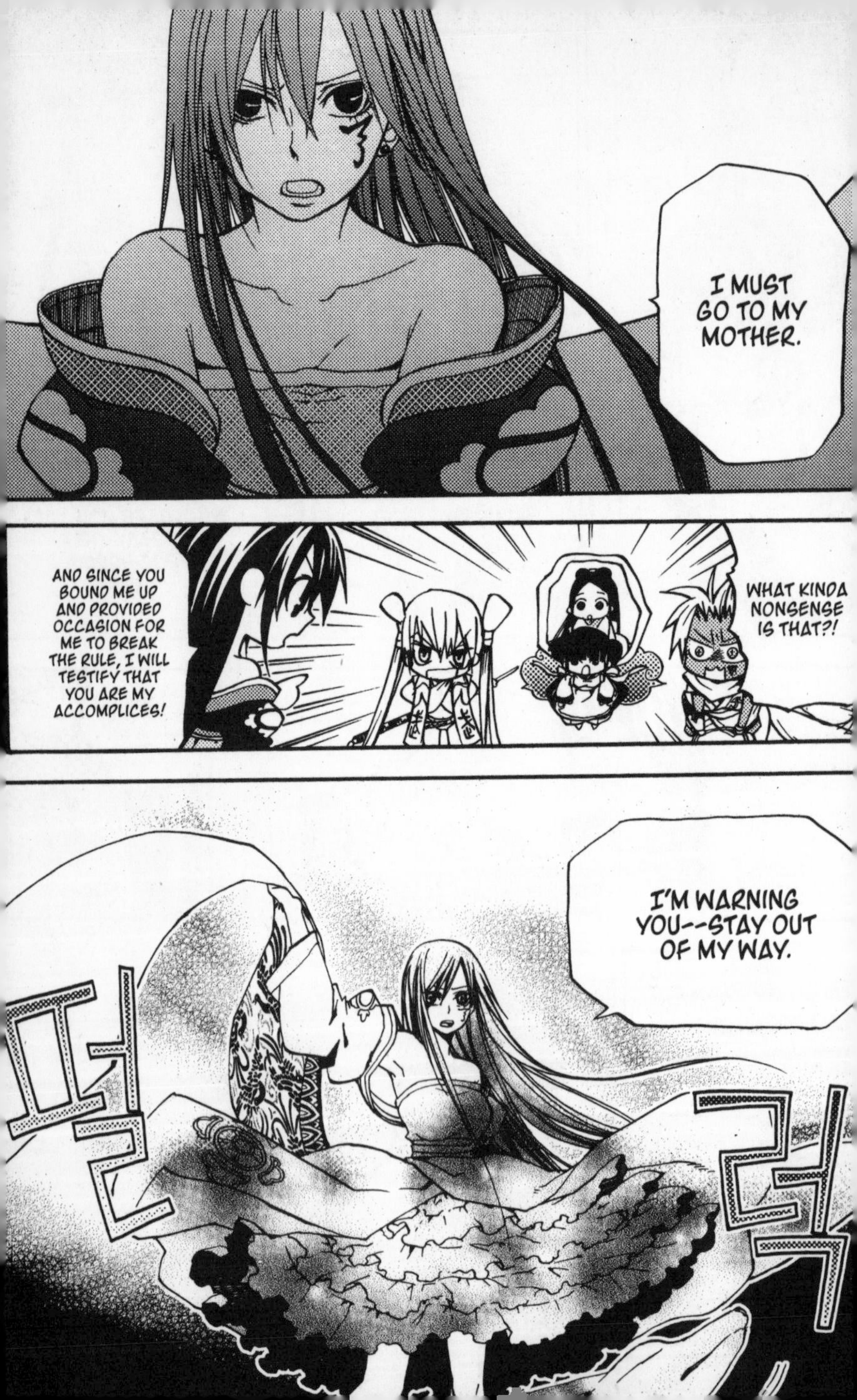
I MUST GO TO MY MOTHER.
AND SINCE YOU BOUND ME UP AND PROVIDED OCCASION FOR ME TO BREAK THE RULE, I WILL TESTIFY THAT YOU ARE MY ACCOMPLICES!
WHAT KINDA NONSENSE IS THAT?!
I'M WARNING YOU--STAY OUT OF MY WAY.

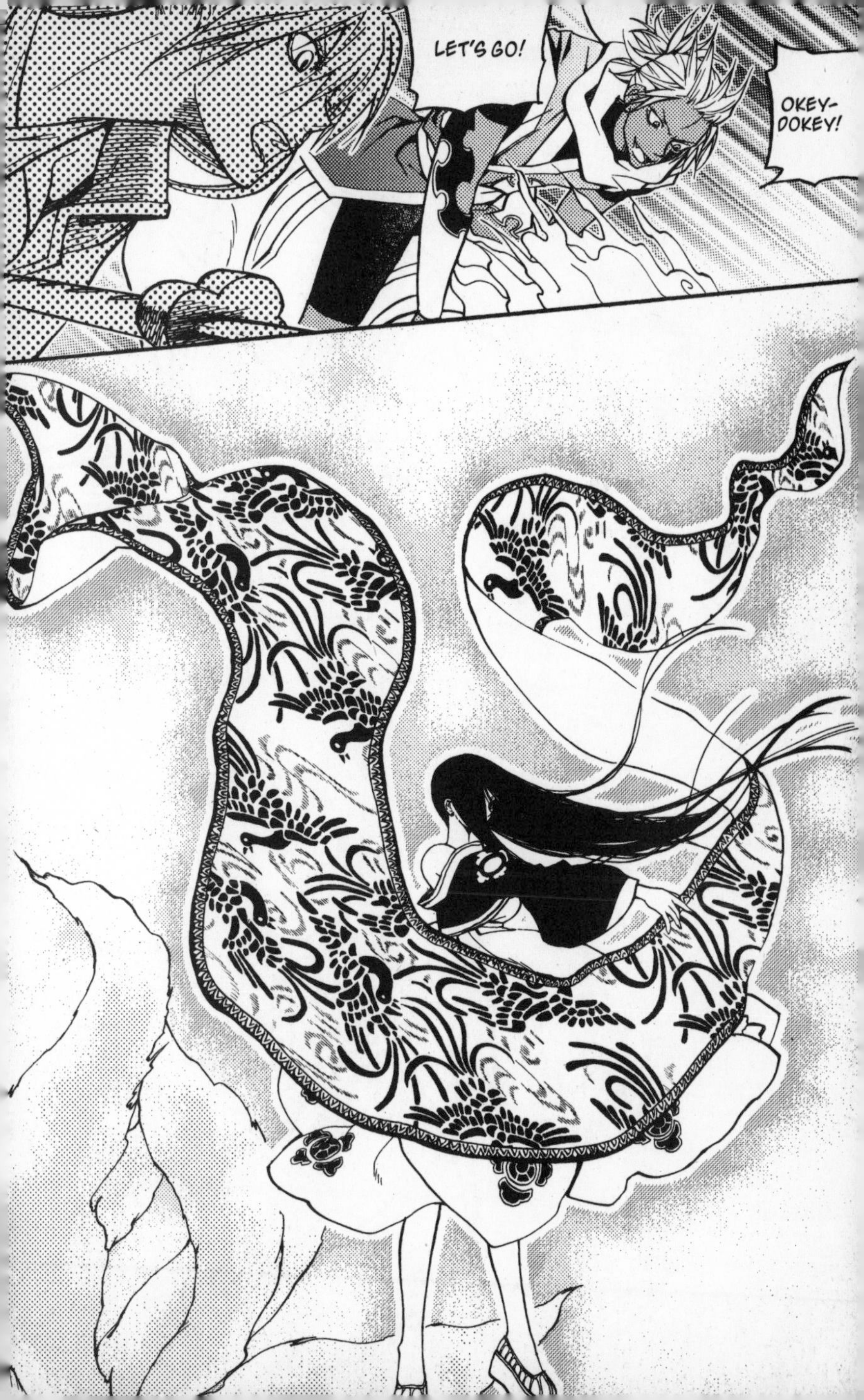
LET'S GO!
OKEY-DOKEY!

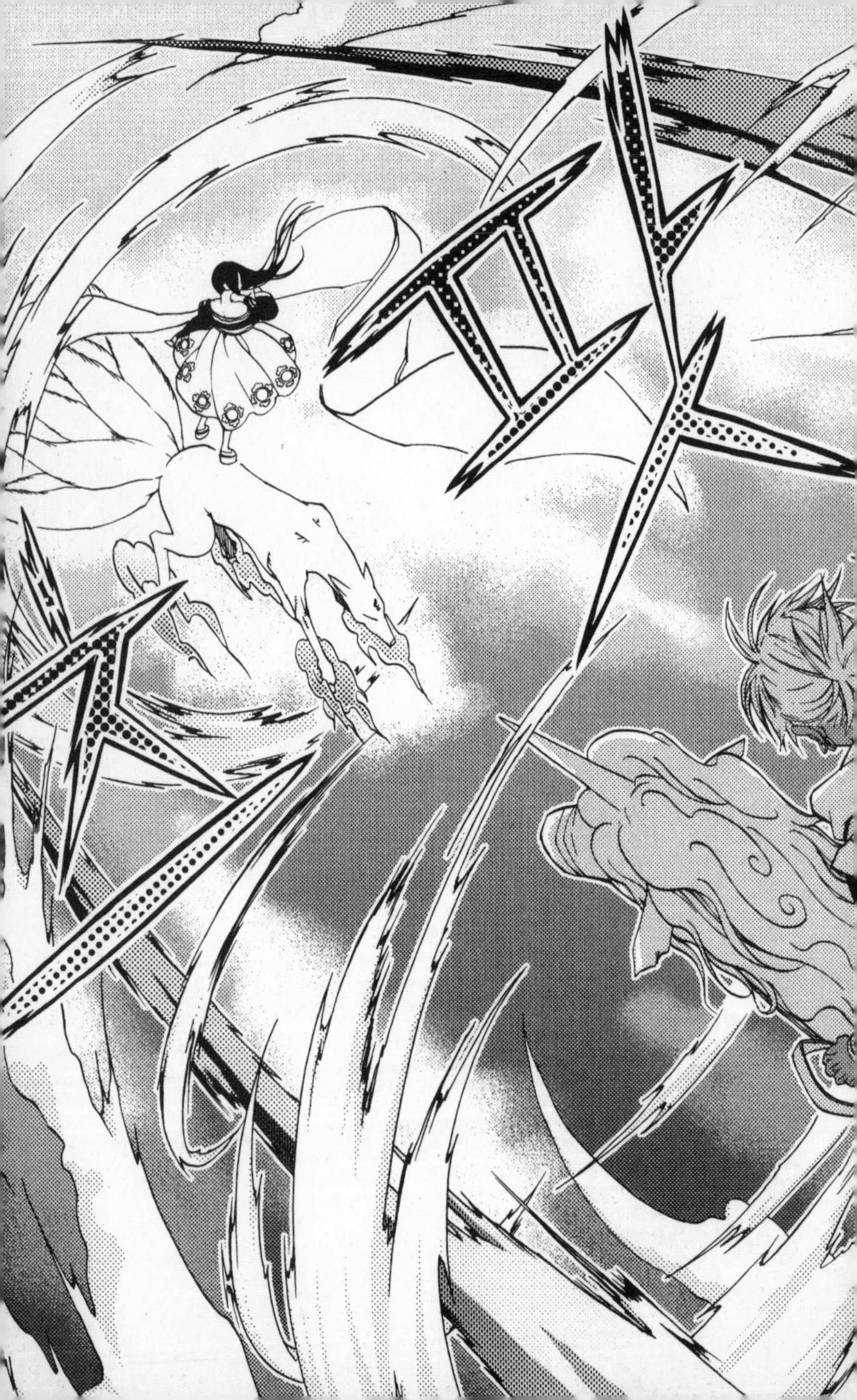

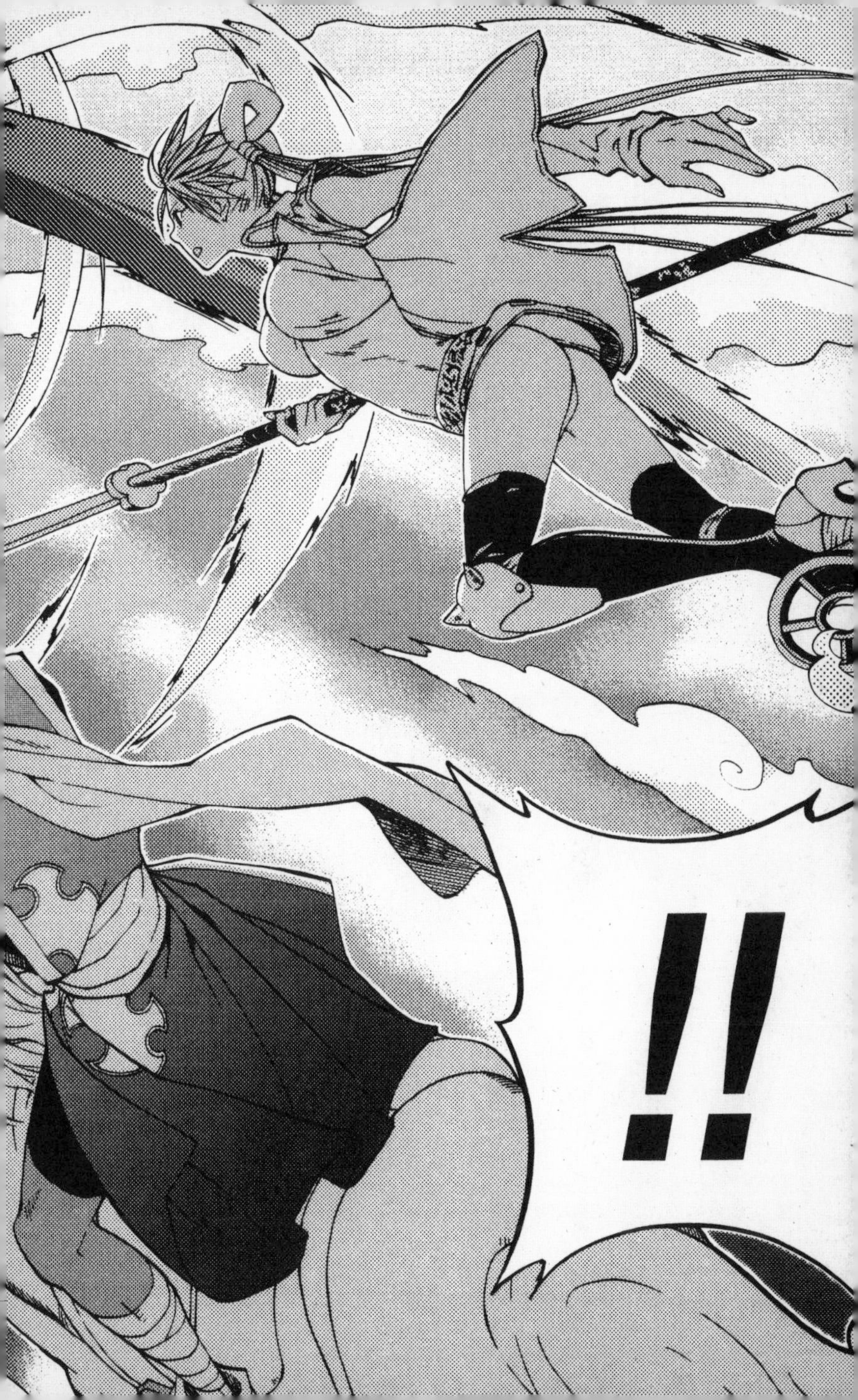
!!

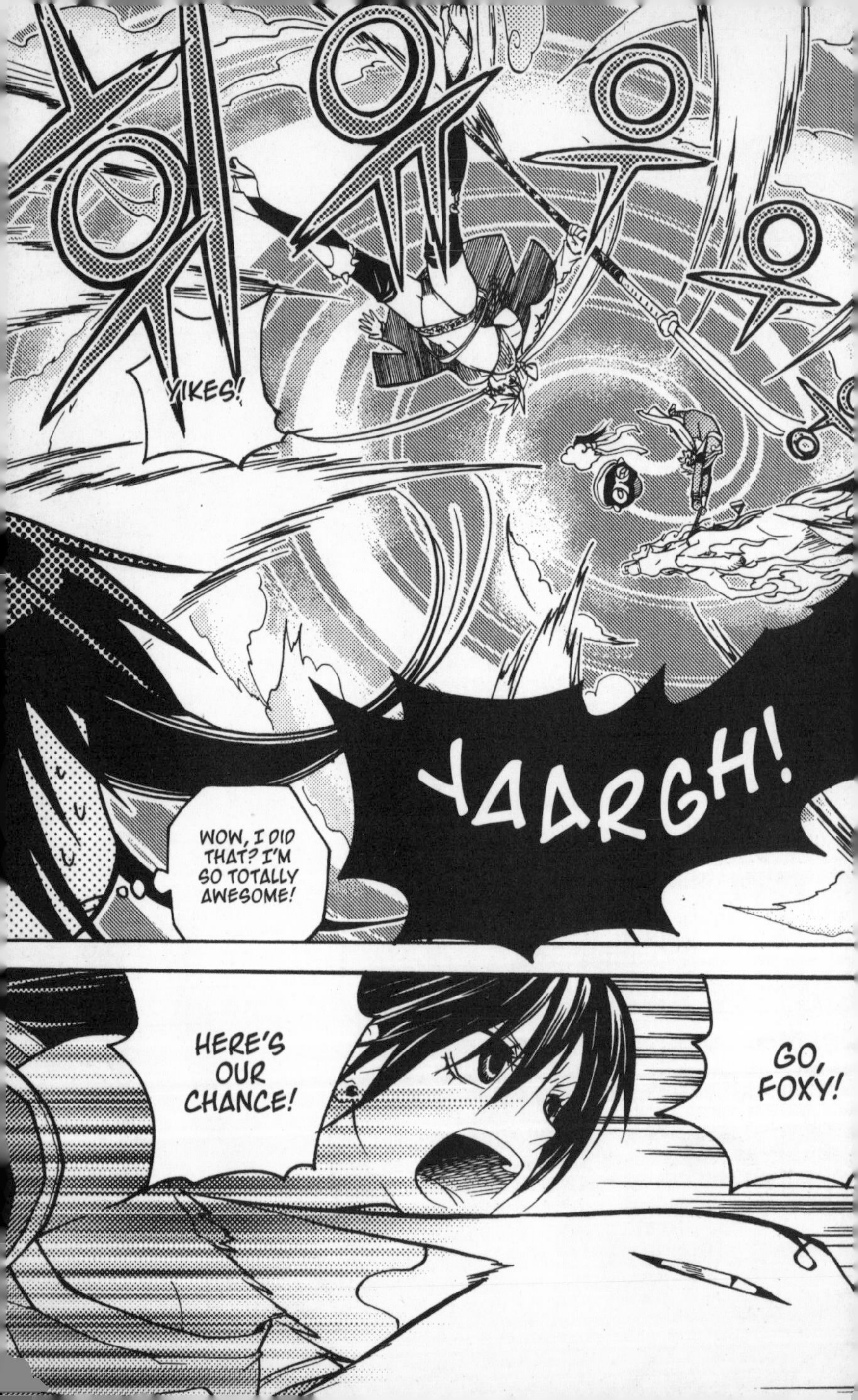

YIKES!
YAARGH!
WOW, I DID THAT? I'M SO TOTALLY AWESOME!
HERE'S OUR CHANCE!
GO, FOXY!

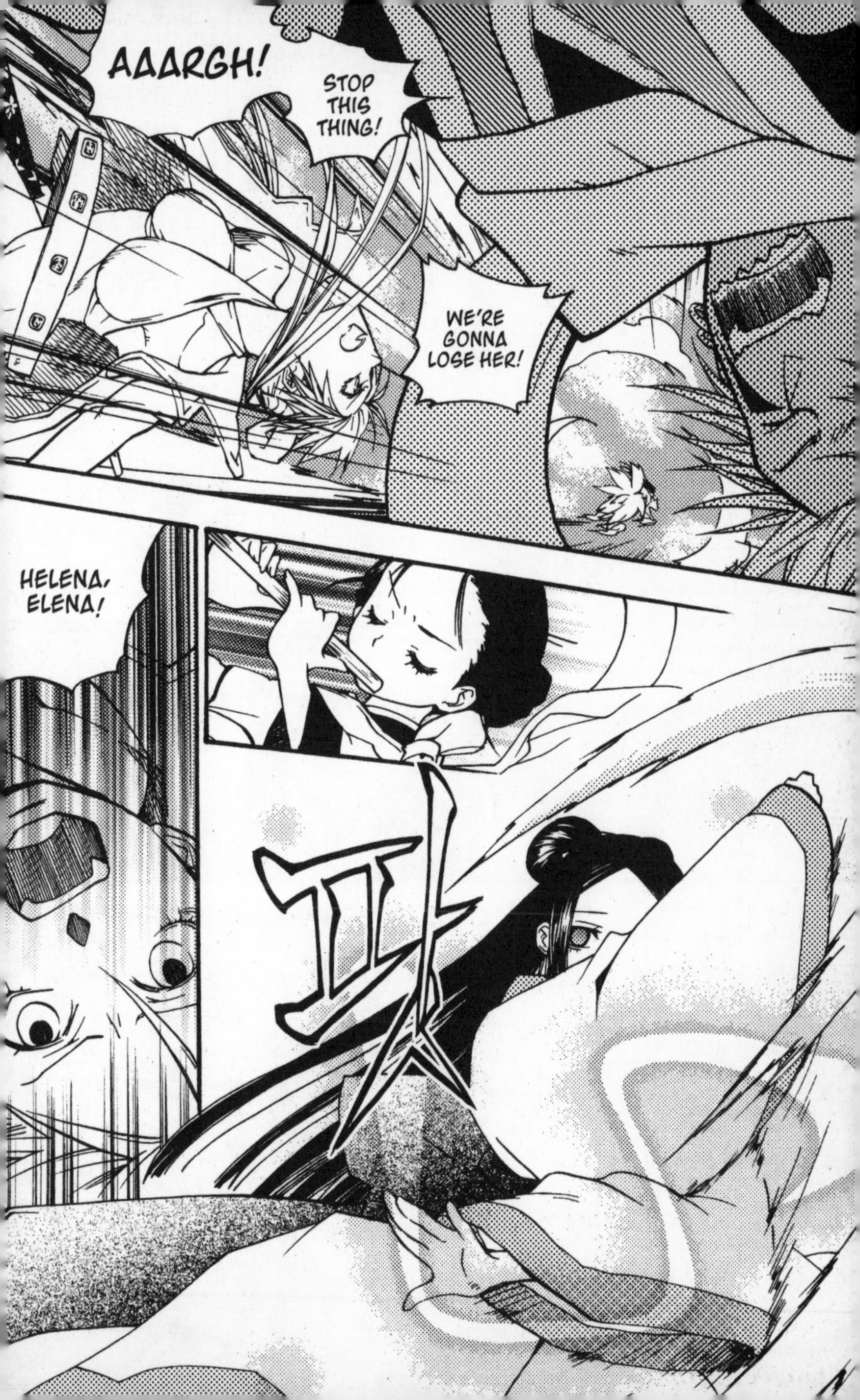
AAARGH!
STOP THIS THING!
WE'RE GONNA LOSE HER!
HELENA, ELENA!

PRRRR

CLUNK

PHEW.
THANKS.
YOU TRULY ARE DA BEST DUO!

HA, YA BETTER REC'NIZE!

WHERE'S FANTA AND THE NINE-TAILED FOX?

THEY'RE NOT FAR AWAY.

WELL THEN, LET'S GET A MOVE ON!

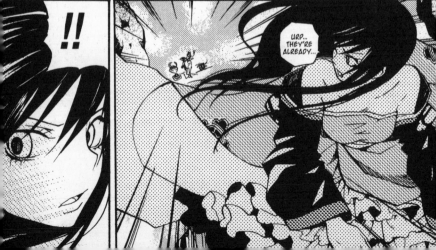

!!

URP... THEY'RE ALREADY...

I BEG YOU!

PLEASE GO FASTER!

OVER THERE!

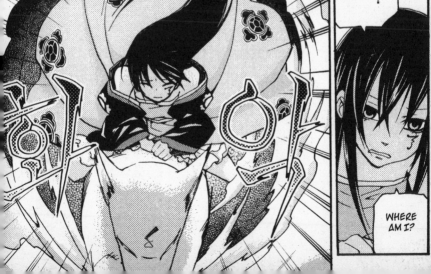

......?

WHERE AM I?

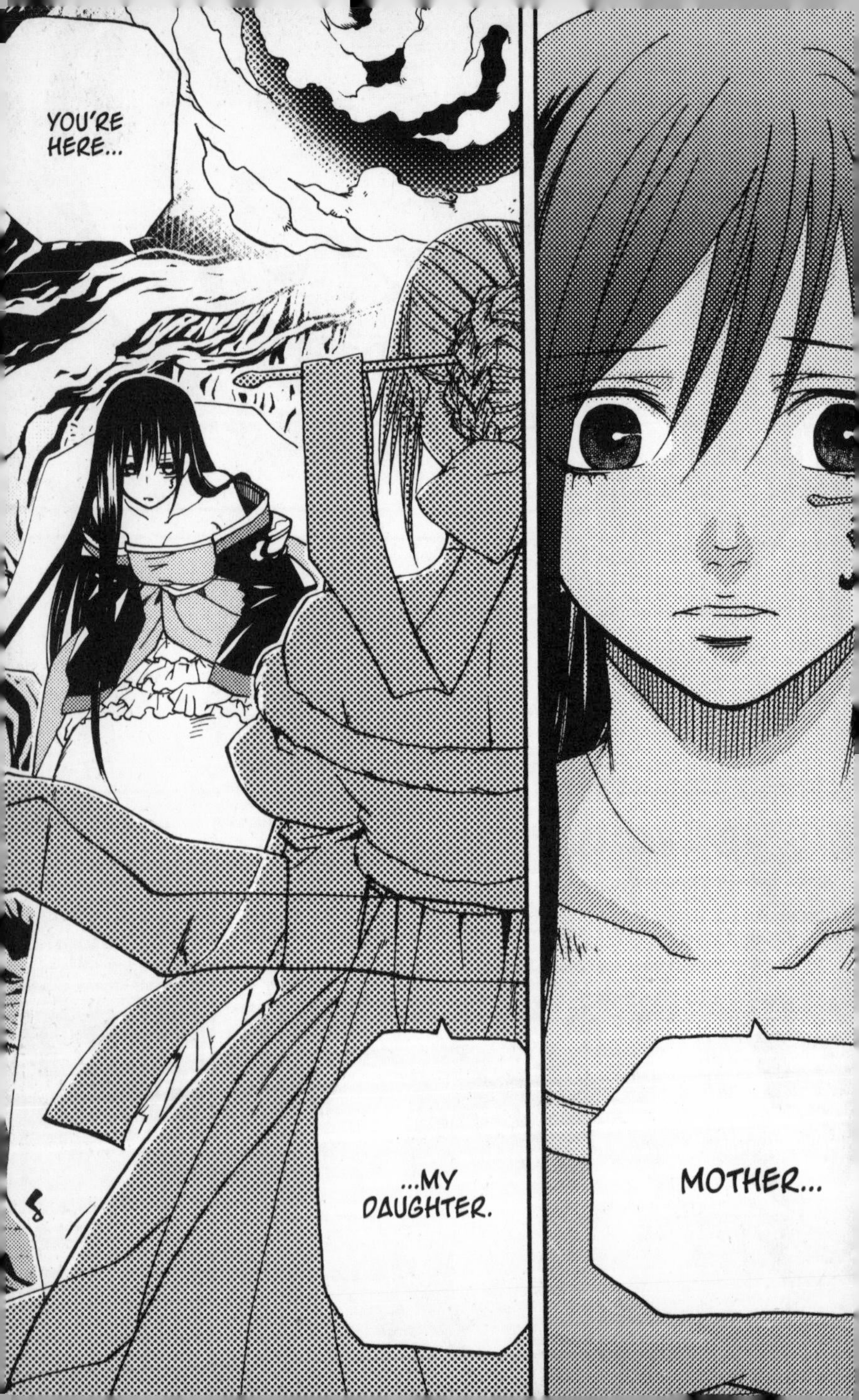
YOU'RE HERE...
...MY DAUGHTER.
MOTHER...

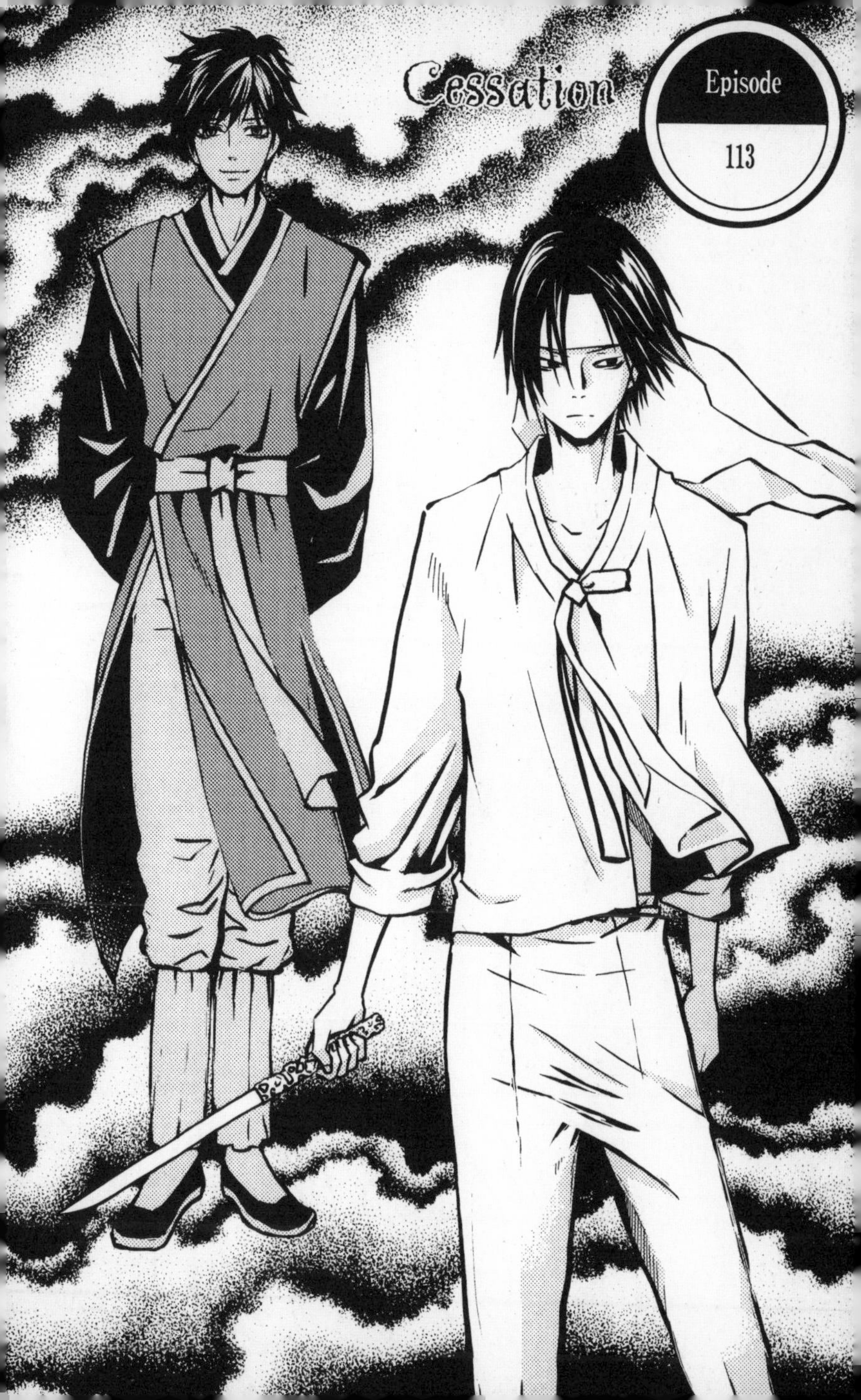
Cessation
Episode
113

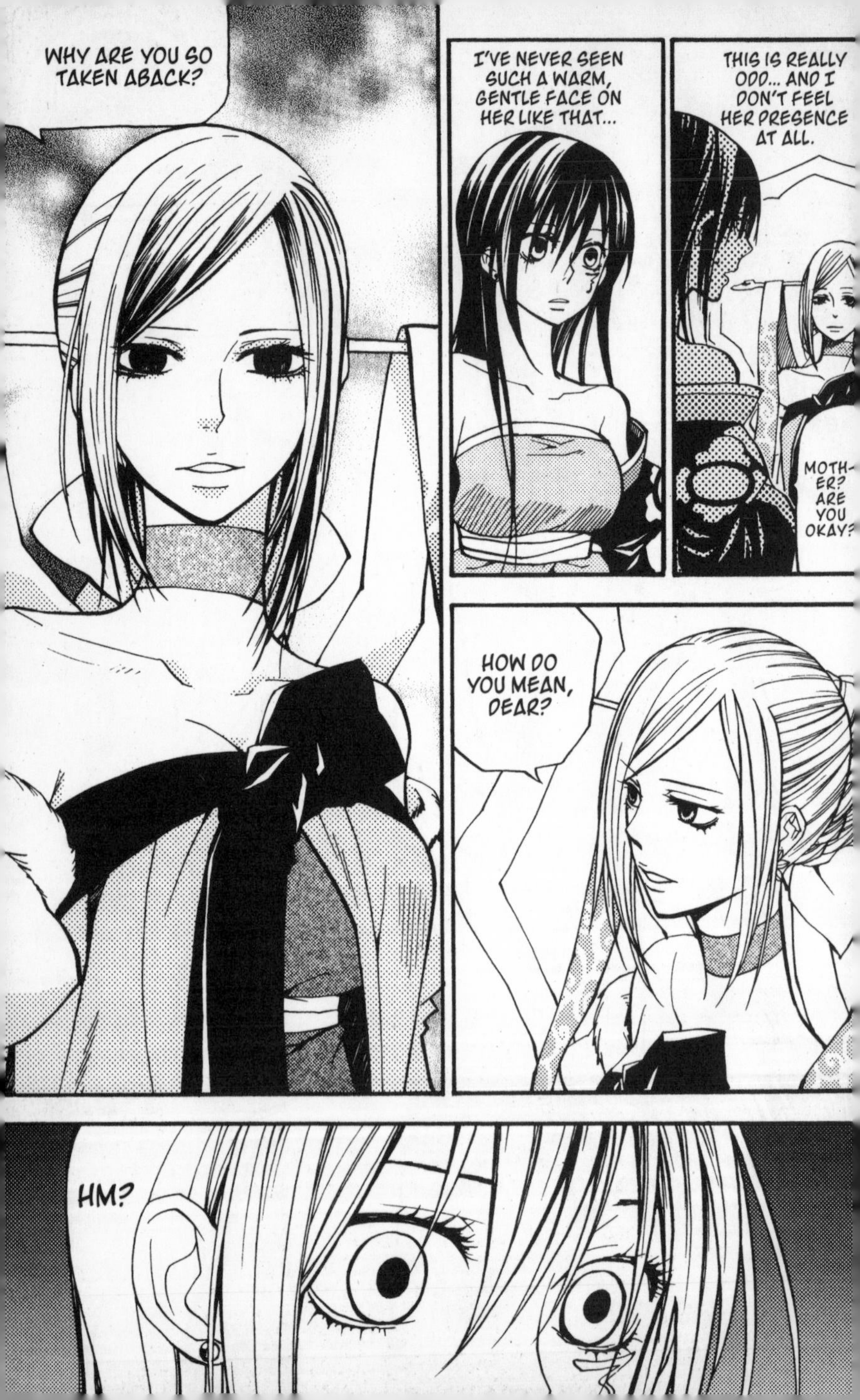

WHY ARE YOU SO TAKEN ABACK?
I'VE NEVER SEEN SUCH A WARM, GENTLE FACE ON HER LIKE THAT...
THIS IS REALLY ODD... AND I DON'T FEEL HER PRESENCE AT ALL.
MOTH-ER? ARE YOU OKAY?
HOW DO YOU MEAN, DEAR?
HM?

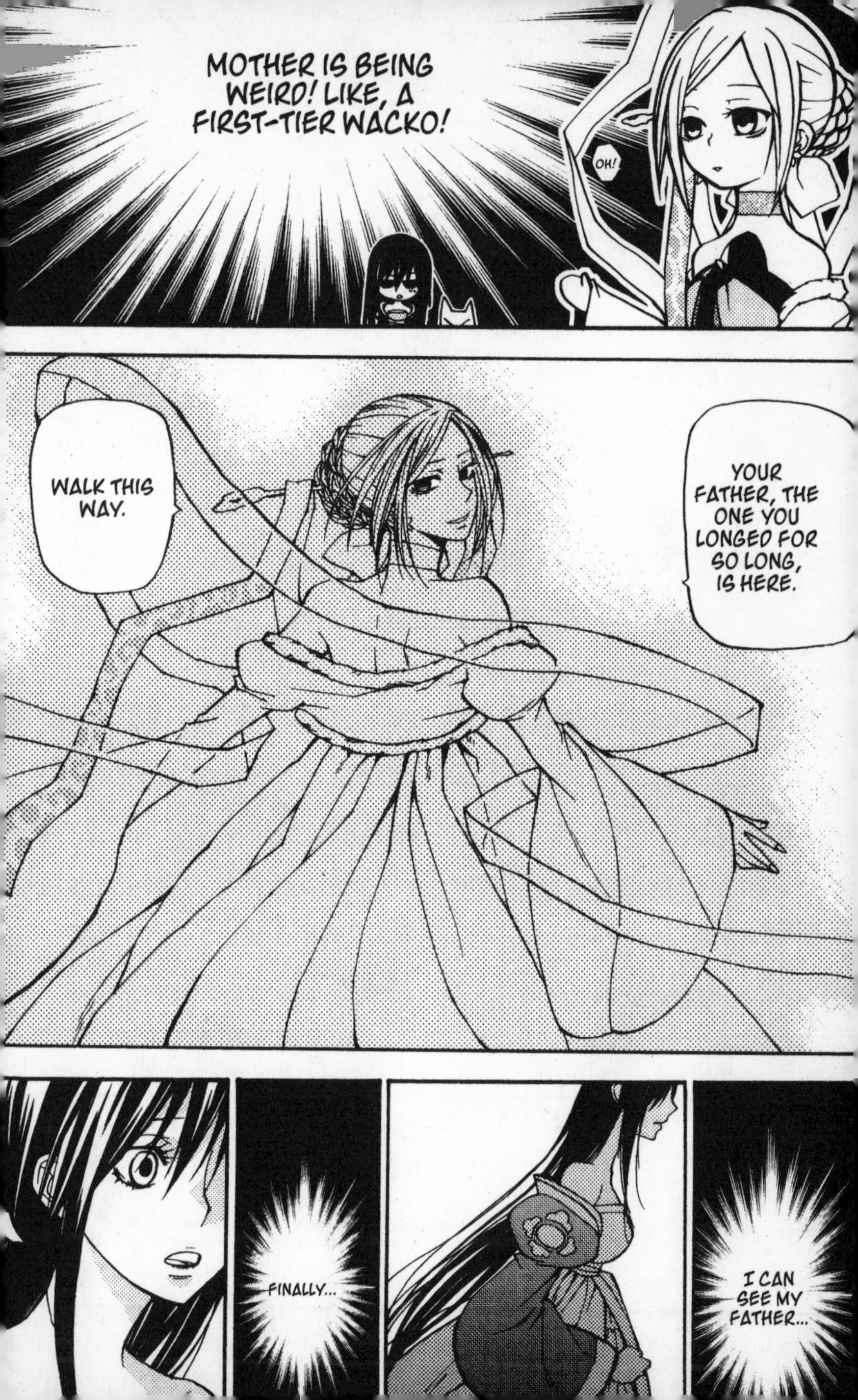
MOTHER IS BEING WEIRD! LIKE, A FIRST-TIER WACKO!
OH!
WALK THIS WAY.
YOUR FATHER, THE ONE YOU LONGED FOR SO LONG, IS HERE.
FINALLY...
I CAN SEE MY FATHER...

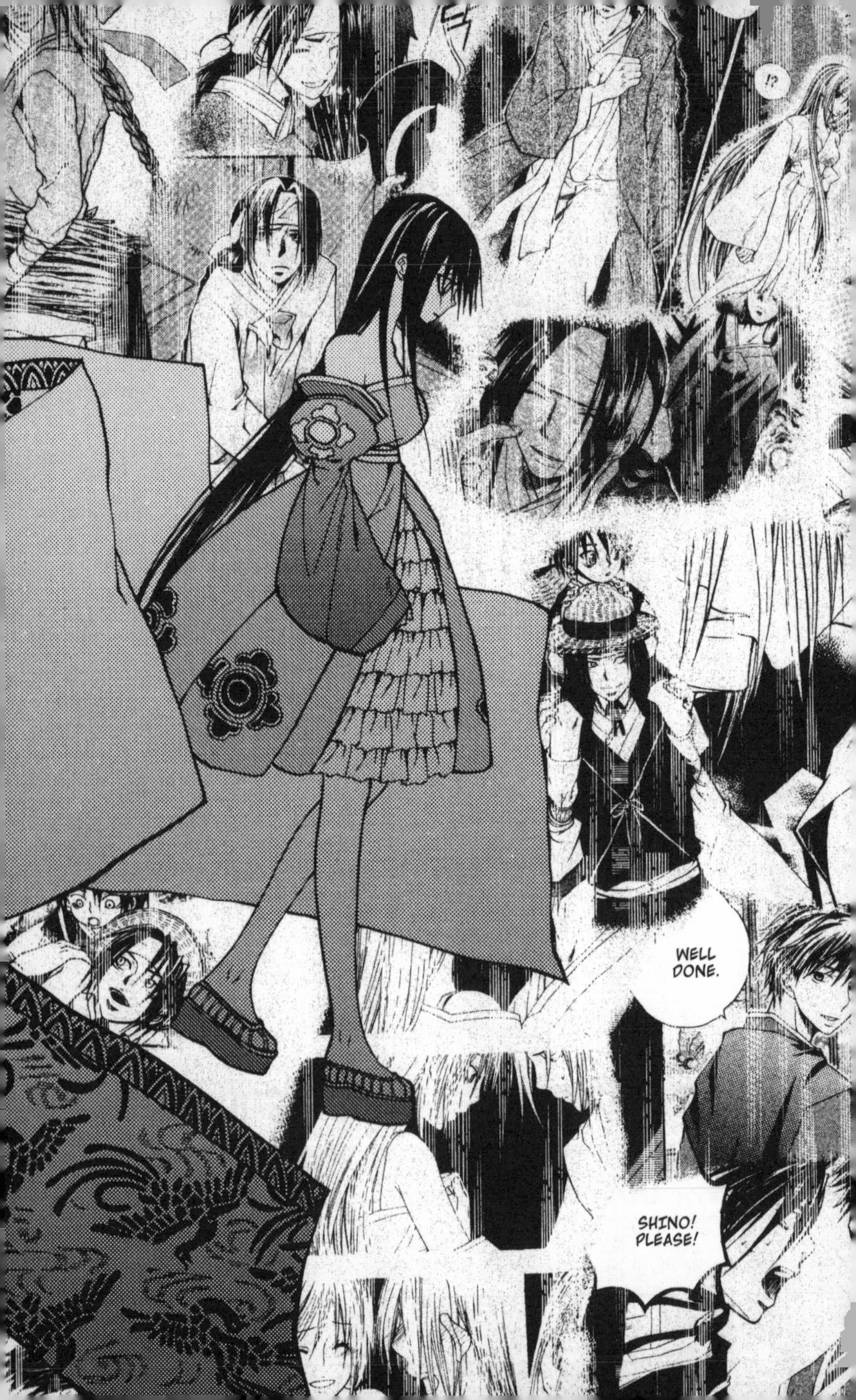
!?
WELL DONE.
SHINO! PLEASE!

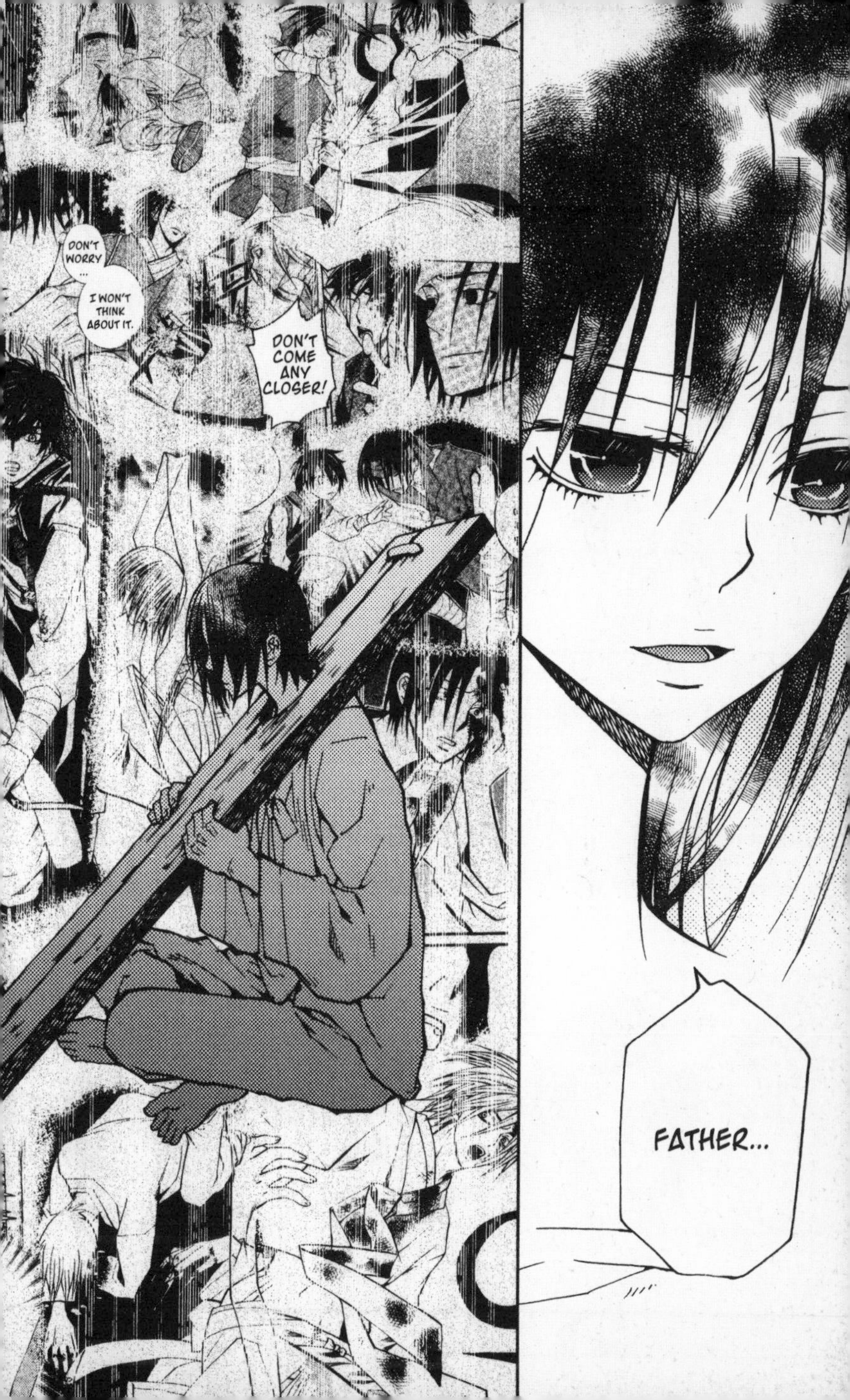
DON'T WORRY ...
I WON'T THINK ABOUT IT.
DON'T COME ANY CLOSER!
FATHER...

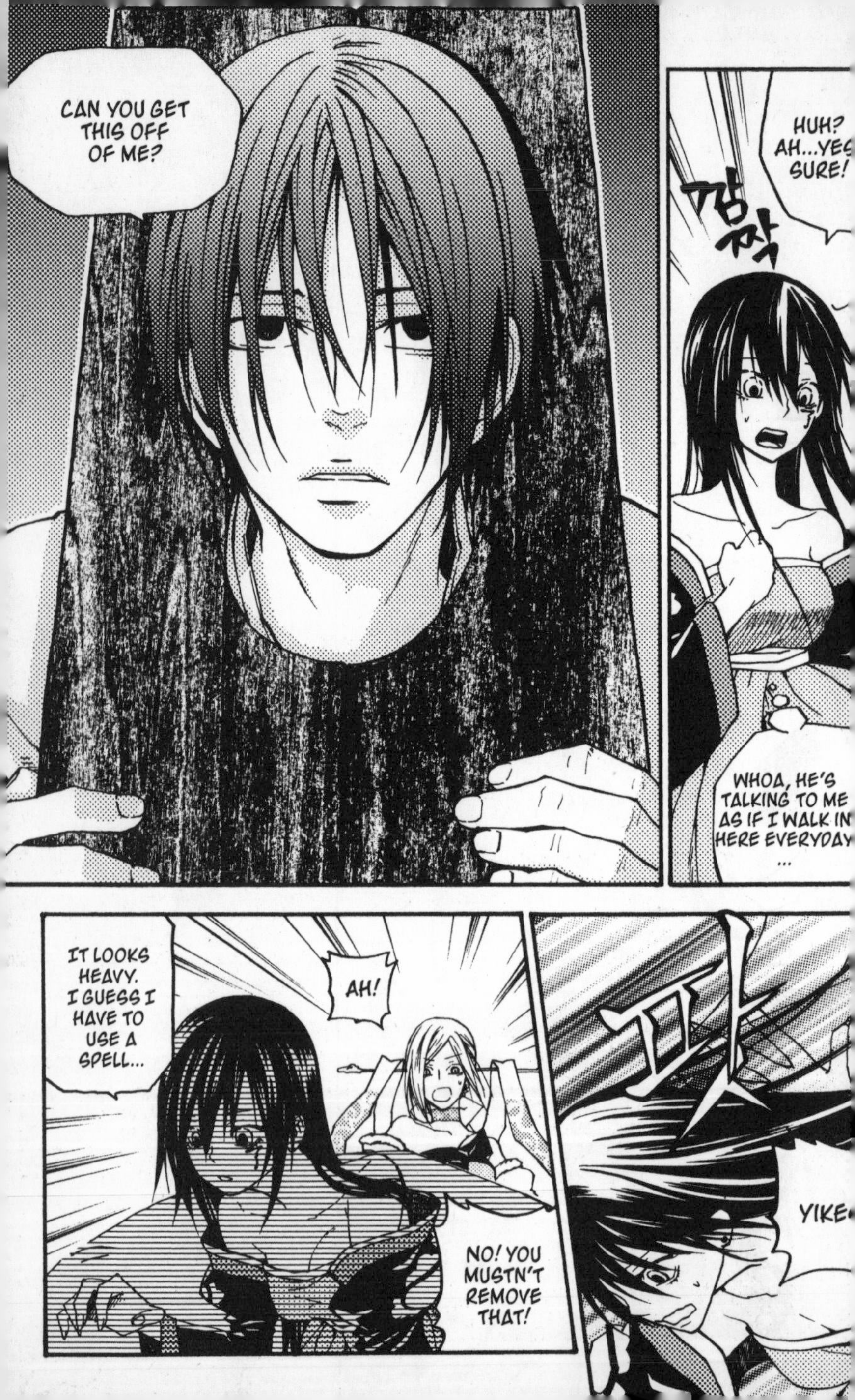
CAN YOU GET THIS OFF OF ME?
HUH? AH...YES SURE!
깜짝
WHOA, HE'S TALKING TO ME AS IF I WALK IN HERE EVERYDAY...
IT LOOKS HEAVY. I GUESS I HAVE TO USE A SPELL...
AH!
NO! YOU MUSTN'T REMOVE THAT!
YIKE

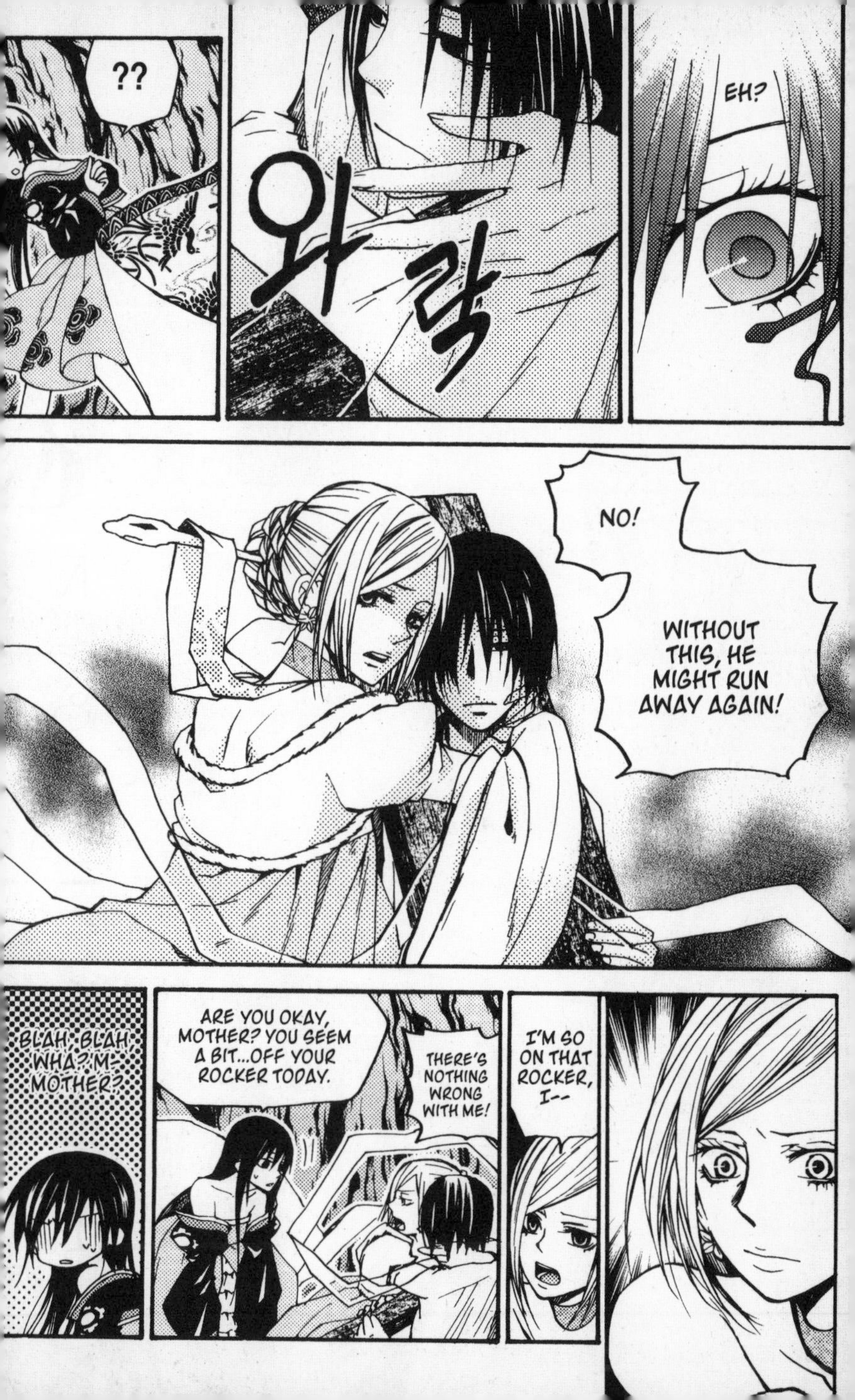
??
와락
EH?
NO!
WITHOUT THIS, HE MIGHT RUN AWAY AGAIN!
BLAH, BLAH, WHA? M-MOTHER?
ARE YOU OKAY, MOTHER? YOU SEEM A BIT...OFF YOUR ROCKER TODAY.
THERE'S NOTHING WRONG WITH ME!
I'M SO ON THAT ROCKER, I--

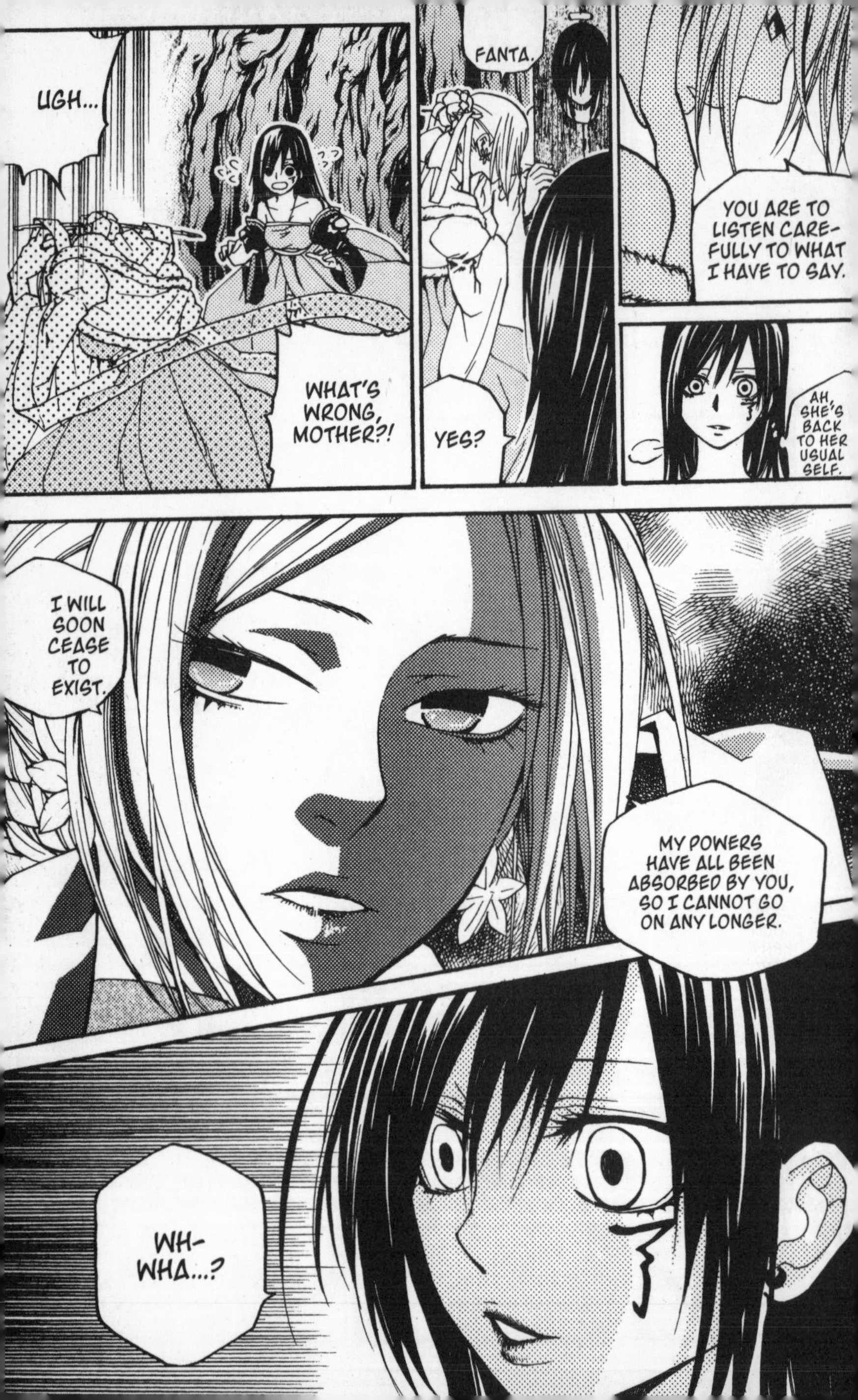
UGH...
WHAT'S WRONG, MOTHER?!
FANTA.
YES?
YOU ARE TO LISTEN CARE-FULLY TO WHAT I HAVE TO SAY.
AH, SHE'S BACK TO HER USUAL SELF.
I WILL SOON CEASE TO EXIST.
MY POWERS HAVE ALL BEEN ABSORBED BY YOU, SO I CANNOT GO ON ANY LONGER.
WH-WHA...?

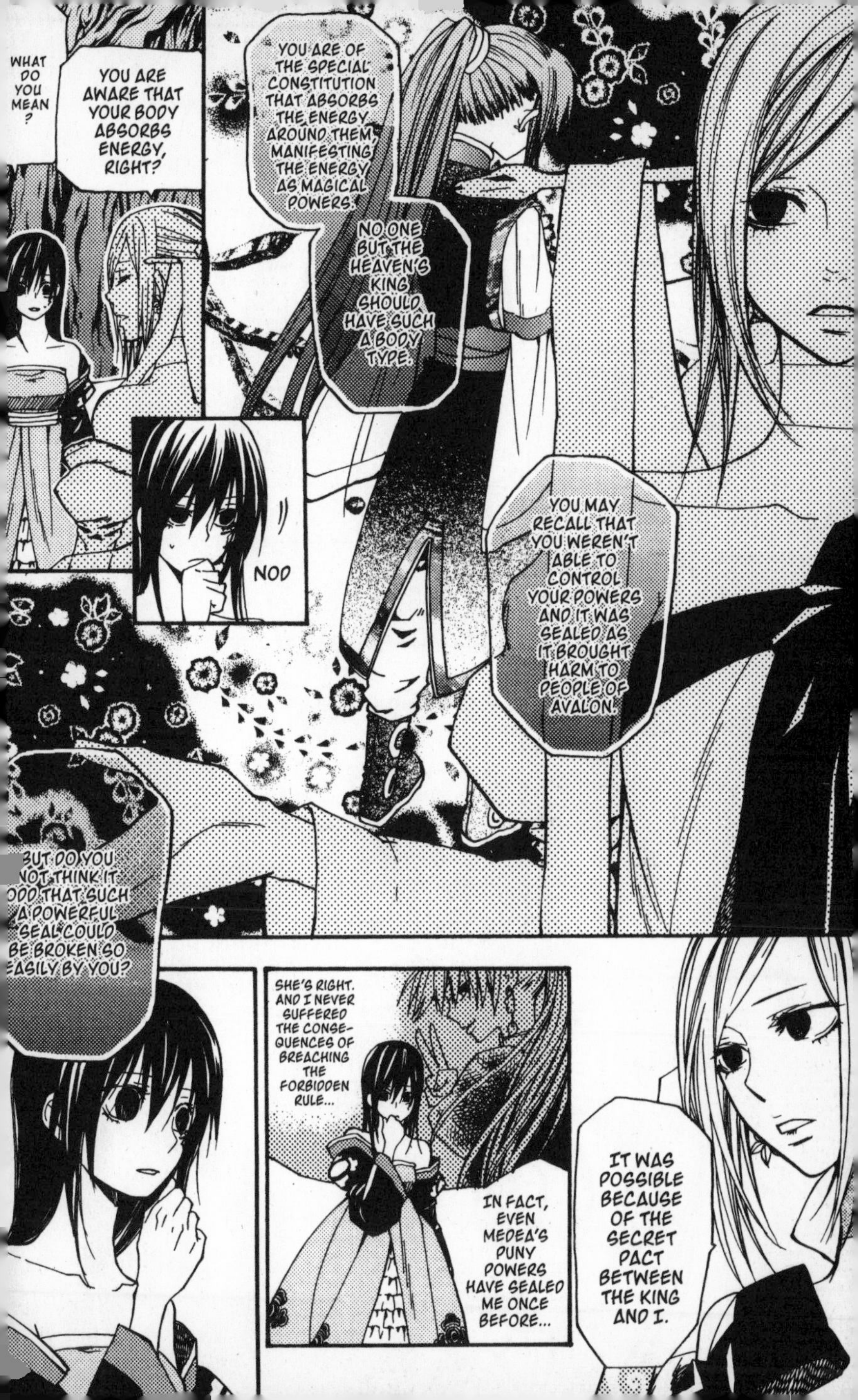

WHAT DO YOU MEAN?
YOU ARE AWARE THAT YOUR BODY ABSORBS ENERGY, RIGHT?
YOU ARE OF THE SPECIAL CONSTITUTION THAT ABSORBS THE ENERGY AROUND THEM, MANIFESTING THE ENERGY AS MAGICAL POWERS.
NO ONE BUT THE HEAVEN'S KING SHOULD HAVE SUCH A BODY TYPE.
NOD
YOU MAY RECALL THAT YOU WEREN'T ABLE TO CONTROL YOUR POWERS AND IT WAS SEALED AS IT BROUGHT HARM TO PEOPLE OF AVALON.
BUT DO YOU NOT THINK IT ODD THAT SUCH A POWERFUL SEAL COULD BE BROKEN SO EASILY BY YOU?
SHE'S RIGHT. AND I NEVER SUFFERED THE CONSE-QUENCES OF BREACHING THE FORBIDDEN RULE...
IN FACT, EVEN MEDEA'S PUNY POWERS HAVE SEALED ME ONCE BEFORE...
IT WAS POSSIBLE BECAUSE OF THE SECRET PACT BETWEEN THE KING AND I.

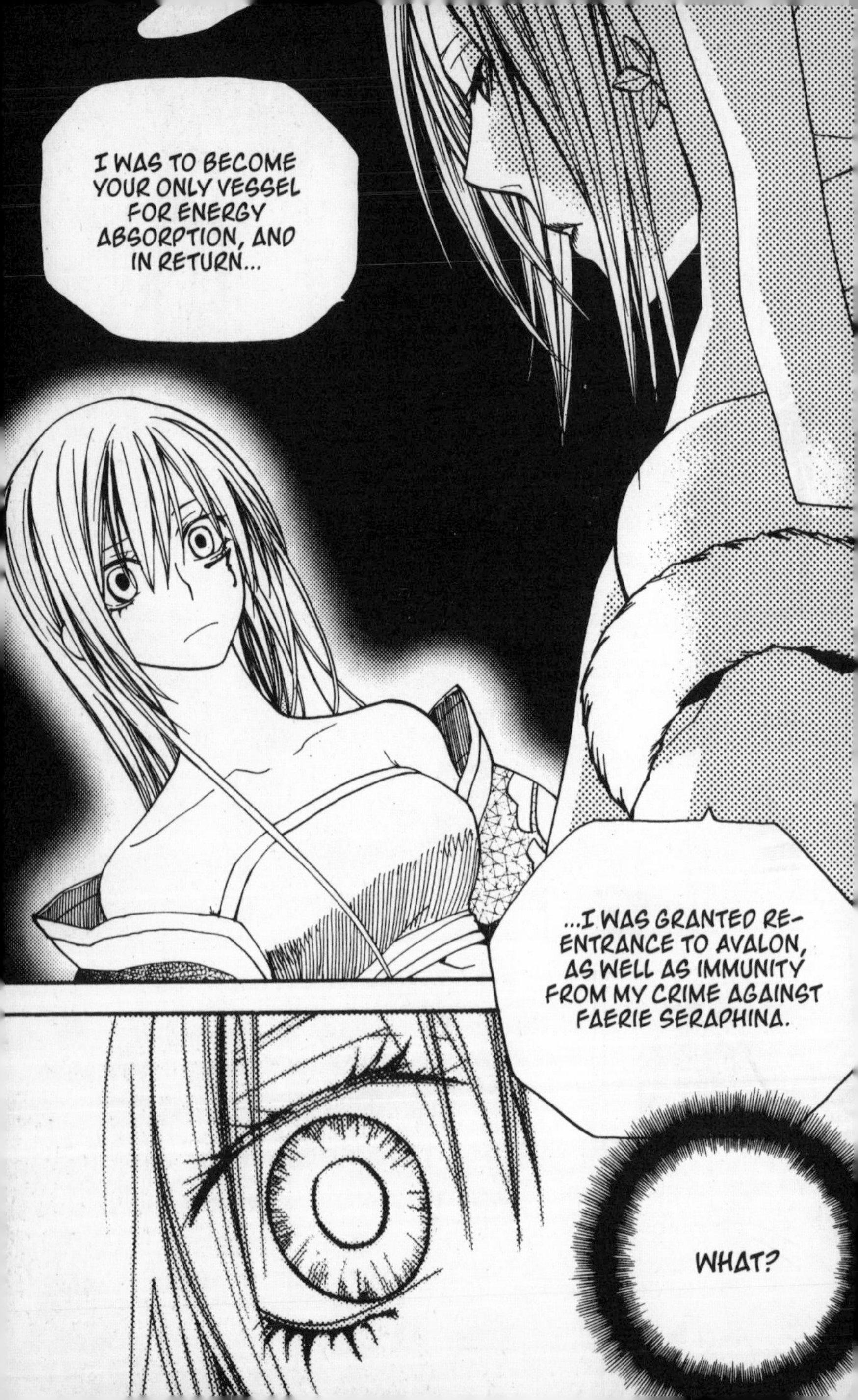
I WAS TO BECOME YOUR ONLY VESSEL FOR ENERGY ABSORPTION, AND IN RETURN...
...I WAS GRANTED RE-ENTRANCE TO AVALON, AS WELL AS IMMUNITY FROM MY CRIME AGAINST FAERIE SERAPHINA.
WHAT?

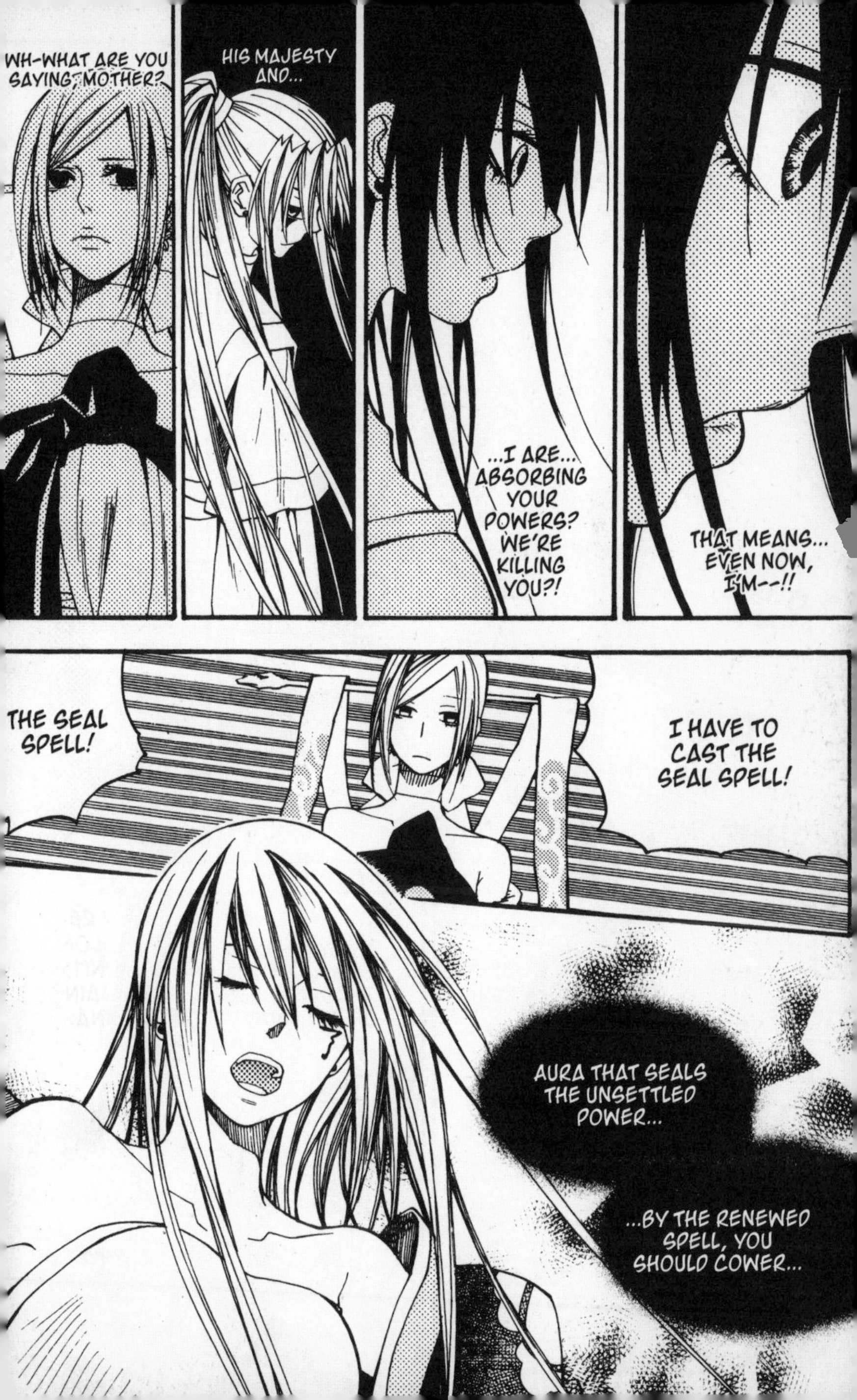
WH-WHAT ARE YOU SAYING, MOTHER?
HIS MAJESTY AND...
...I ARE... ABSORBING YOUR POWERS? WE'RE KILLING YOU?!
THAT MEANS... EVEN NOW, I'M--!!
THE SEAL SPELL!
I HAVE TO CAST THE SEAL SPELL!
AURA THAT SEALS THE UNSETTLED POWER...
...BY THE RENEWED SPELL, YOU SHOULD COWER...

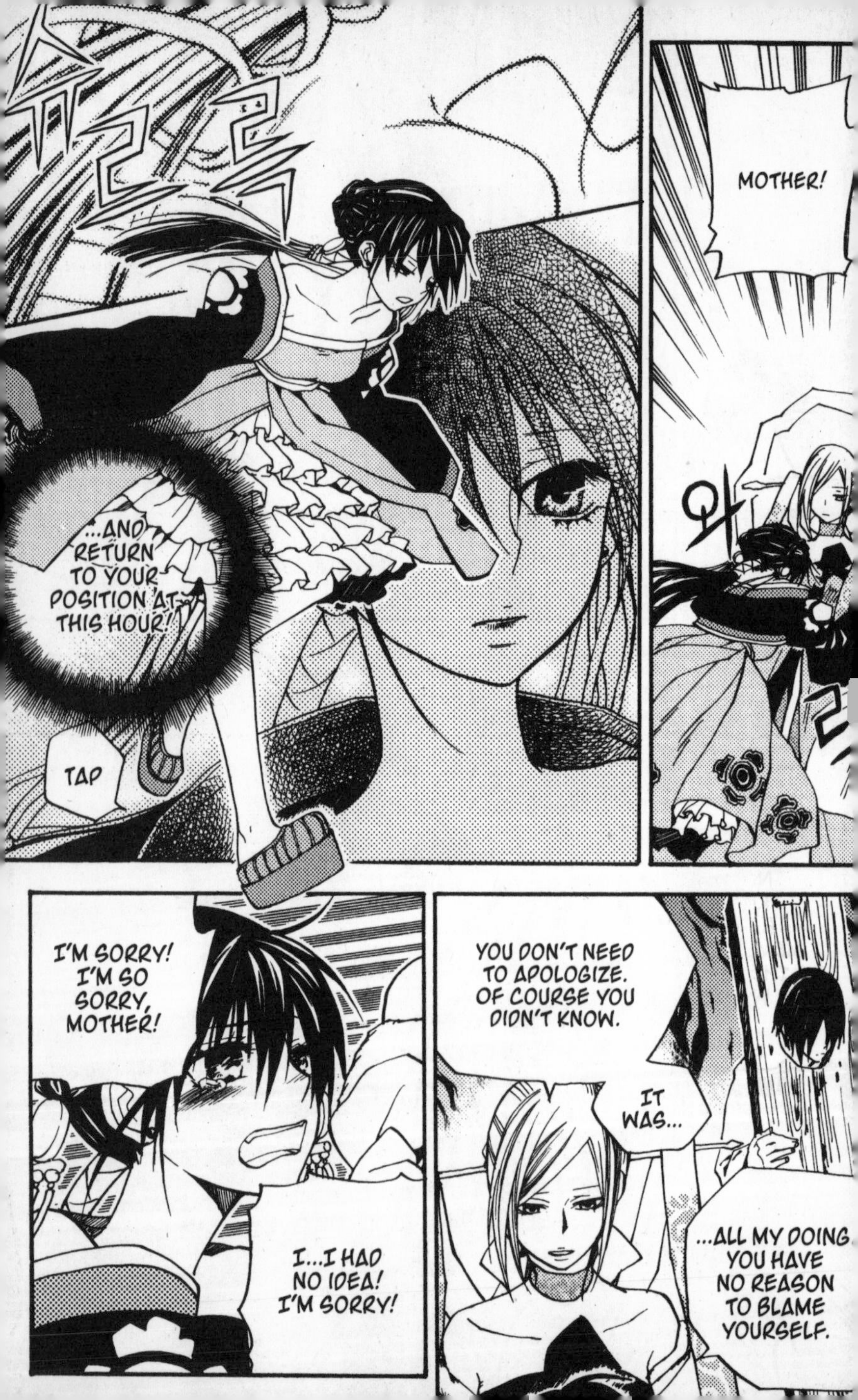
...AND RETURN TO YOUR POSITION AT THIS HOUR!
TAP
MOTHER!
I'M SORRY! I'M SO SORRY, MOTHER!
I...I HAD NO IDEA! I'M SORRY!
YOU DON'T NEED TO APOLOGIZE. OF COURSE YOU DIDN'T KNOW.
IT WAS...
...ALL MY DOING YOU HAVE NO REASON TO BLAME YOURSELF.

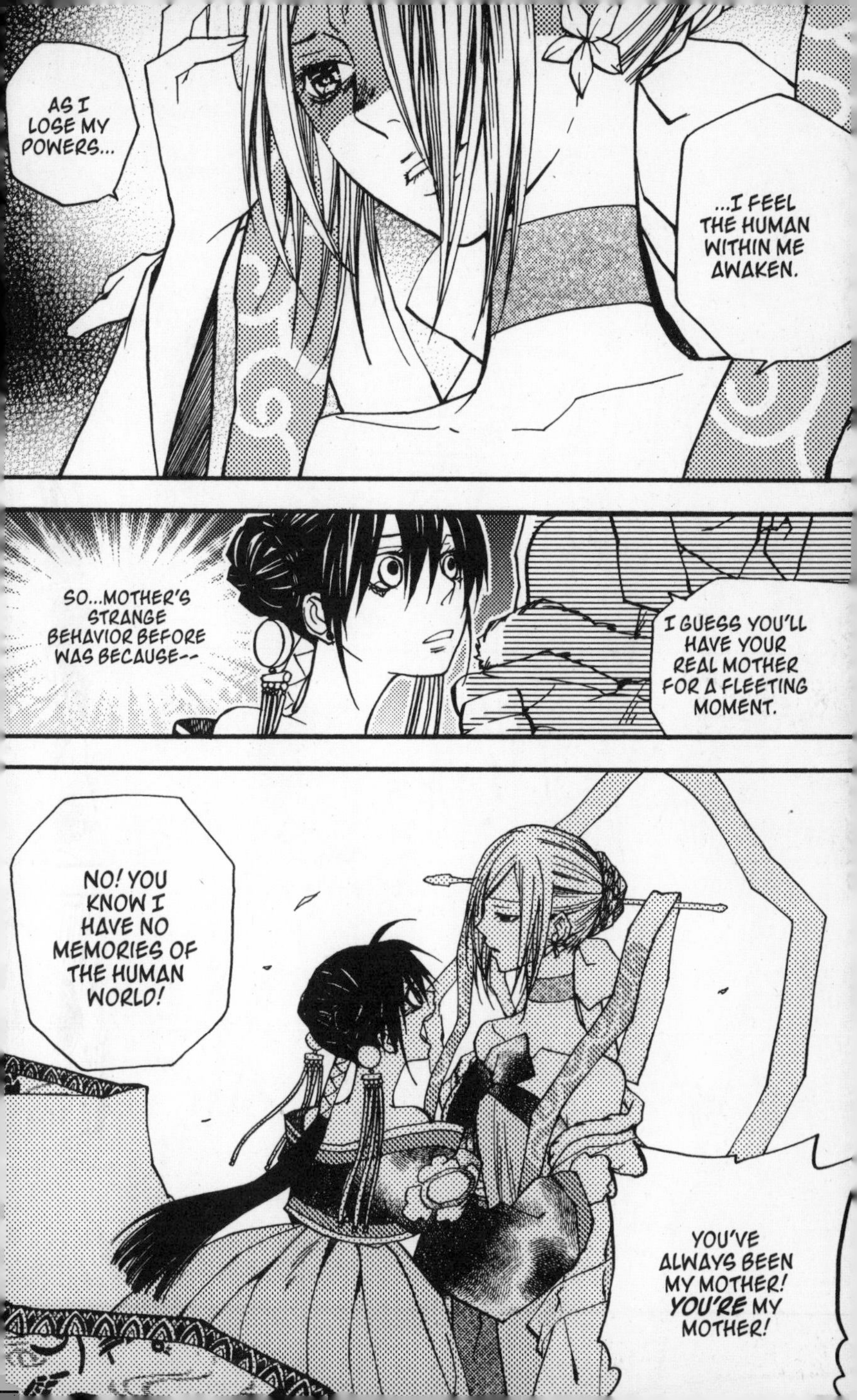
AS I LOSE MY POWERS...
...I FEEL THE HUMAN WITHIN ME AWAKEN.
SO...MOTHER'S STRANGE BEHAVIOR BEFORE WAS BECAUSE--
I GUESS YOU'LL HAVE YOUR REAL MOTHER FOR A FLEETING MOMENT.
NO! YOU KNOW I HAVE NO MEMORIES OF THE HUMAN WORLD!
YOU'VE ALWAYS BEEN MY MOTHER! ***YOU'RE*** MY MOTHER!

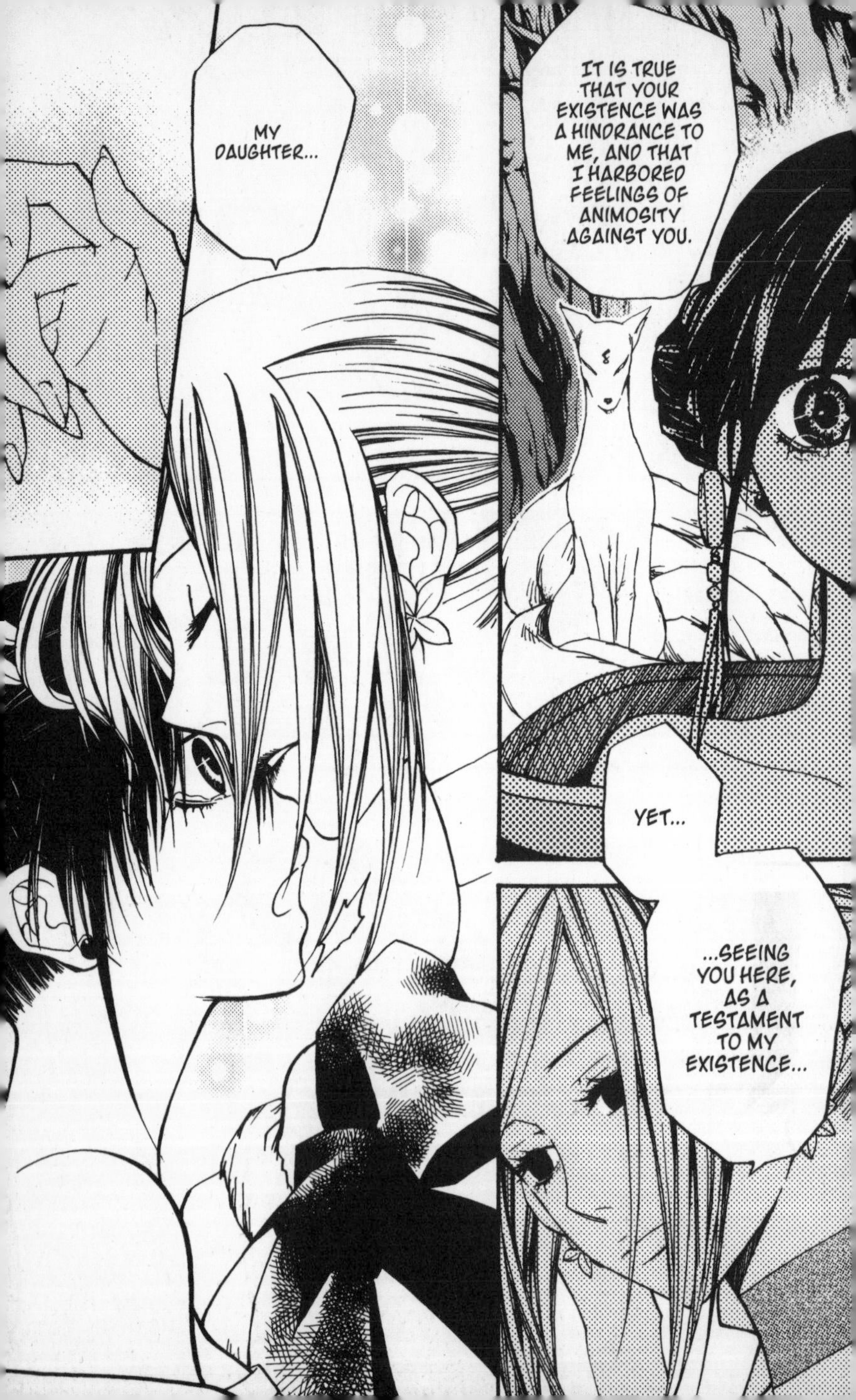
MY DAUGHTER...
IT IS TRUE THAT YOUR EXISTENCE WAS A HINDRANCE TO ME, AND THAT I HARBORED FEELINGS OF ANIMOSITY AGAINST YOU.
YET...
...SEEING YOU HERE, AS A TESTAMENT TO MY EXISTENCE...

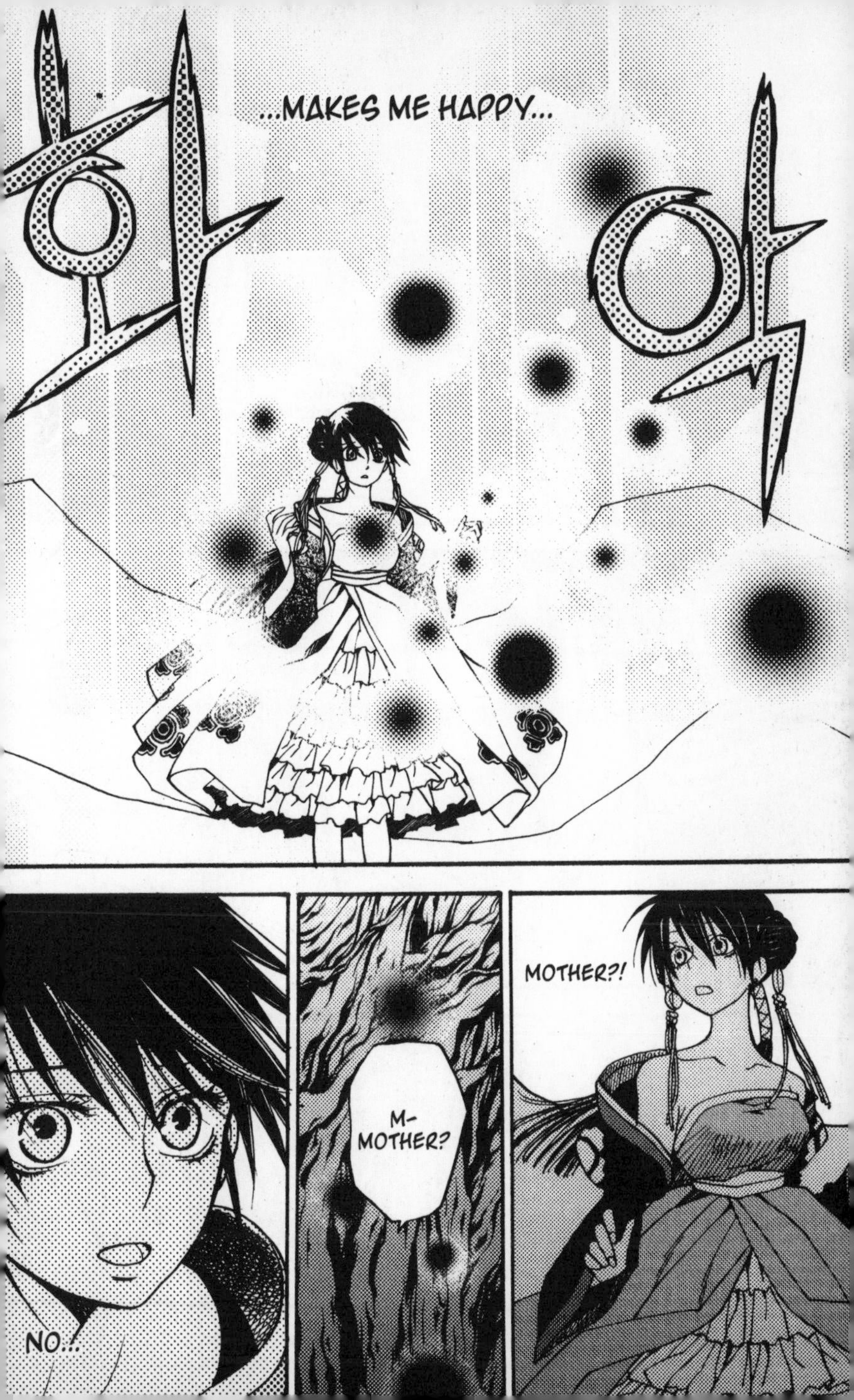

...MAKES ME HAPPY...
화악
NO...
M-
MOTHER?
MOTHER?!

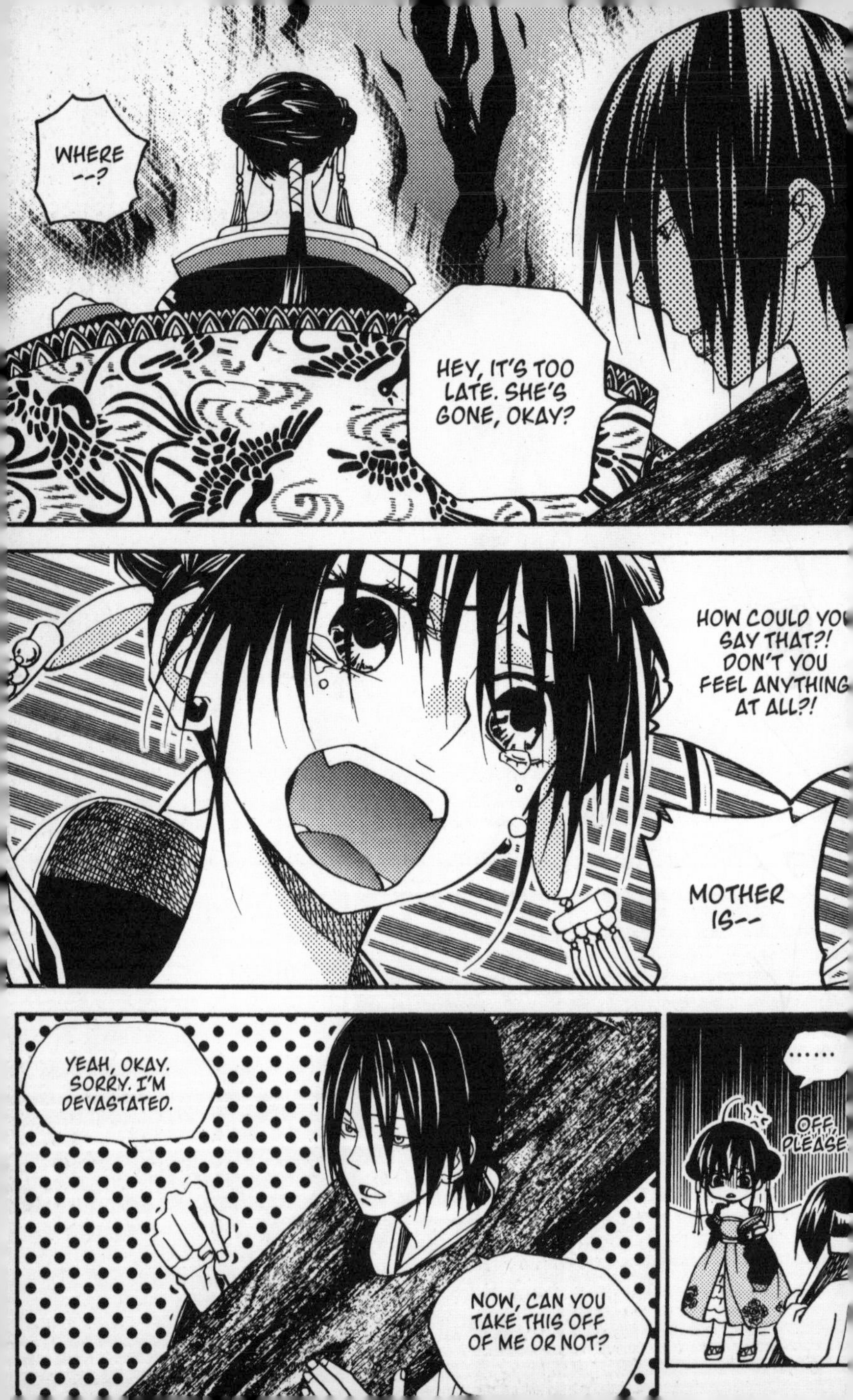
WHERE --?
HEY, IT'S TOO LATE. SHE'S GONE, OKAY?
HOW COULD YOU SAY THAT?! DON'T YOU FEEL ANYTHING AT ALL?!
MOTHER IS--
YEAH, OKAY. SORRY. I'M DEVASTATED.
NOW, CAN YOU TAKE THIS OFF OF ME OR NOT?
......
OFF, PLEASE

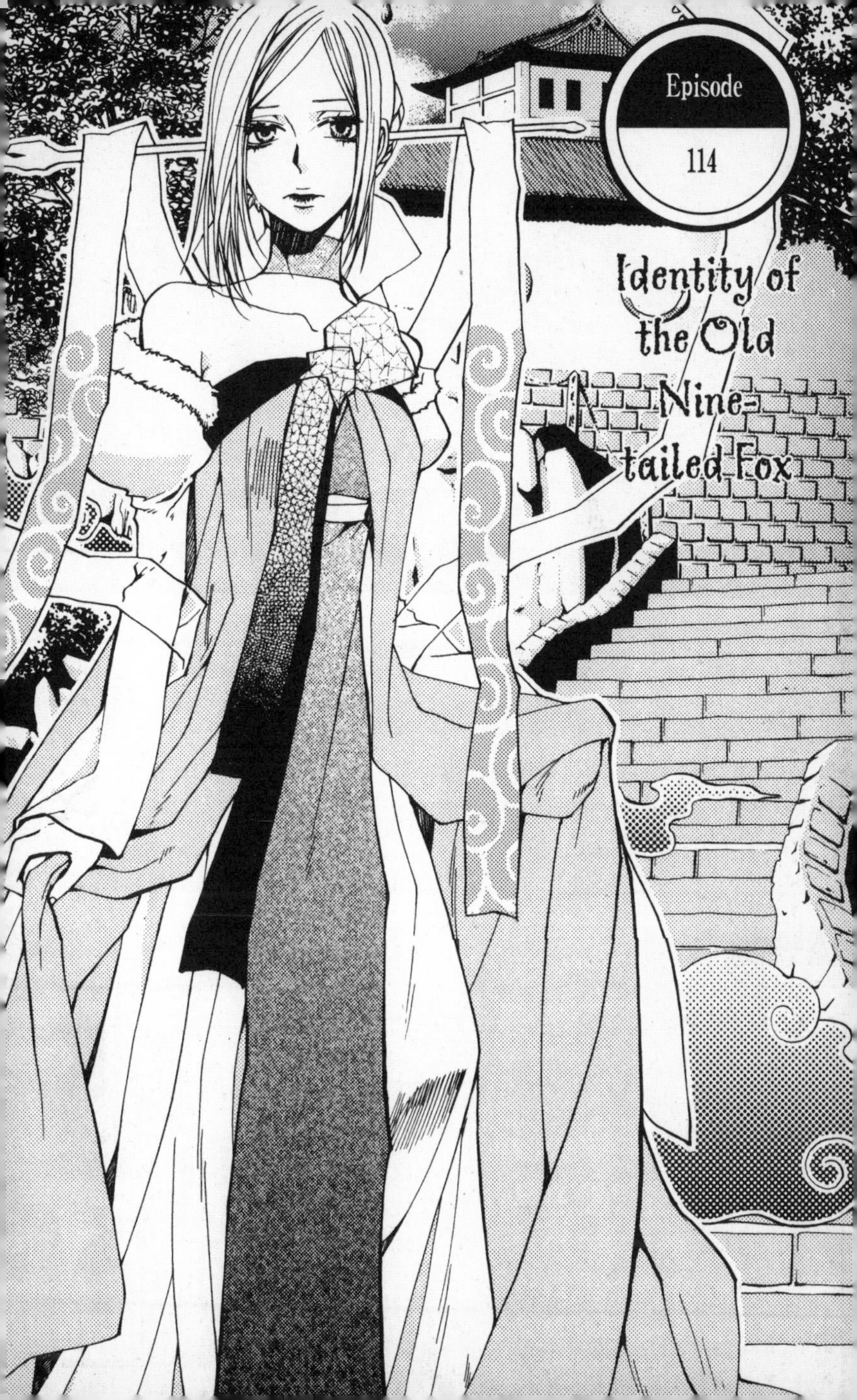
Episode
114
Identity of the Old Nine-tailed Fox

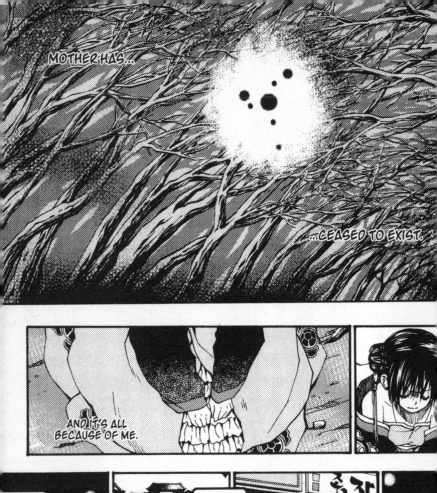

MOTHER HAS...

...CEASED TO EXIST.

AND IT'S ALL BECAUSE OF ME.

CESSATION.

IT'S SOMETHING THAT'S OUTSIDE THE SCOPE OF THE CYCLES OF BIRTH. IT'S A COMPLETE DEATH.

YOU CANNOT EXIST...

...ANYWHERE IN THIS WORLD.

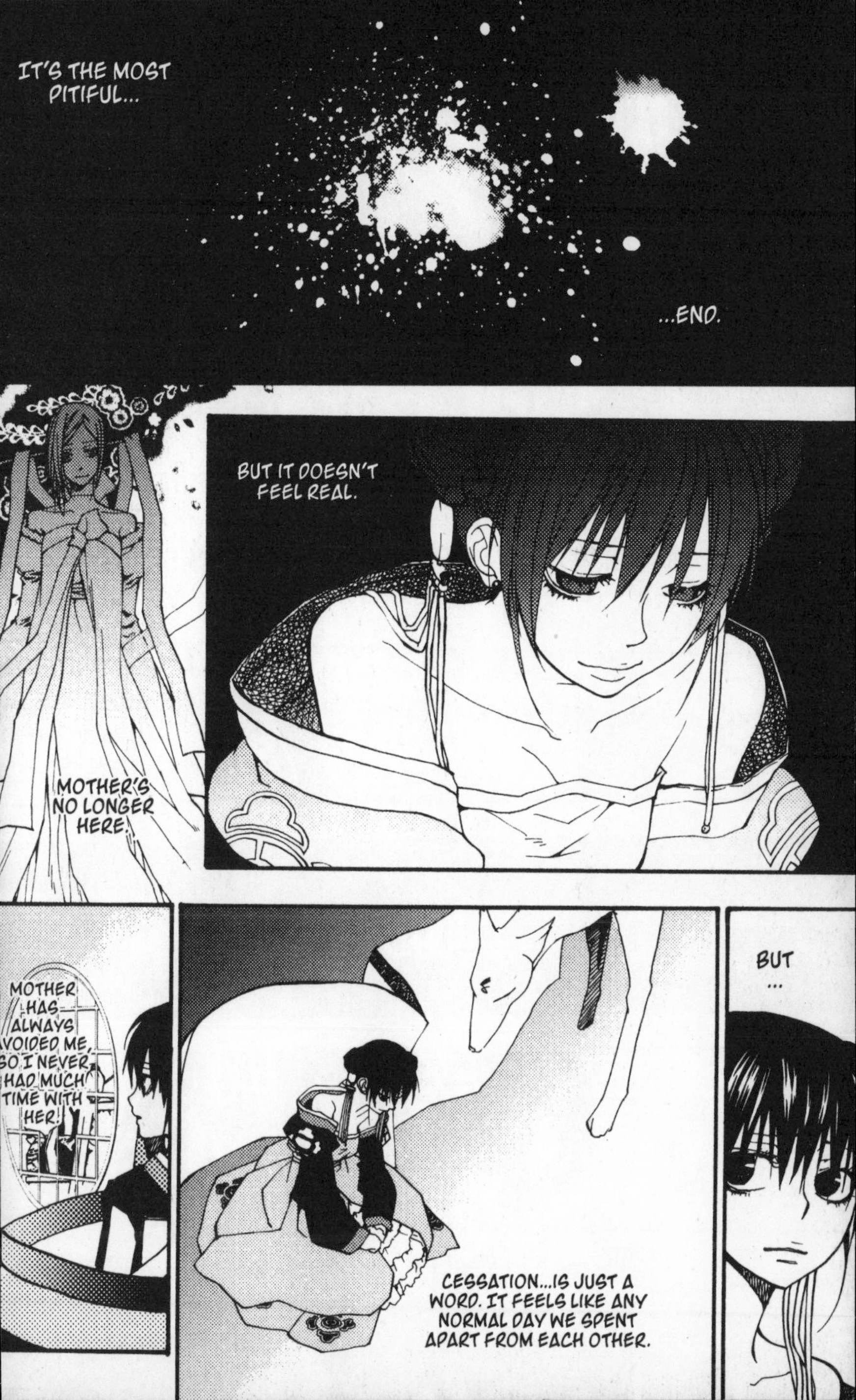
IT'S THE MOST PITIFUL...
...END.
MOTHER'S NO LONGER HERE.
BUT IT DOESN'T FEEL REAL.
MOTHER HAS ALWAYS AVOIDED ME, SO I NEVER HAD MUCH TIME WITH HER!
CESSATION...IS JUST A WORD. IT FEELS LIKE ANY NORMAL DAY WE SPENT APART FROM EACH OTHER.
BUT ...

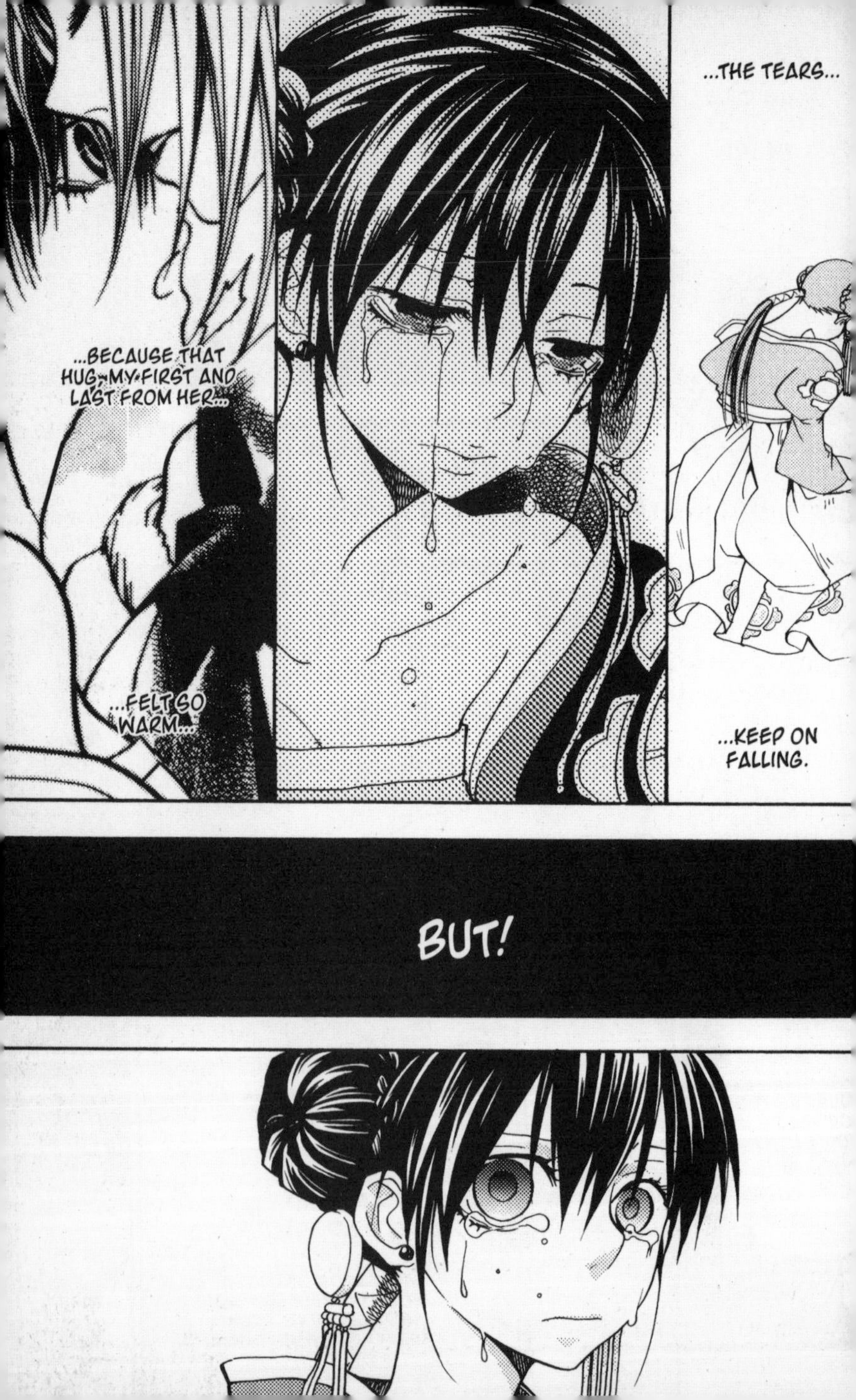
...BECAUSE THAT HUG, MY FIRST AND LAST FROM HER...
...FELT SO WARM...
...THE TEARS...
...KEEP ON FALLING.
BUT!

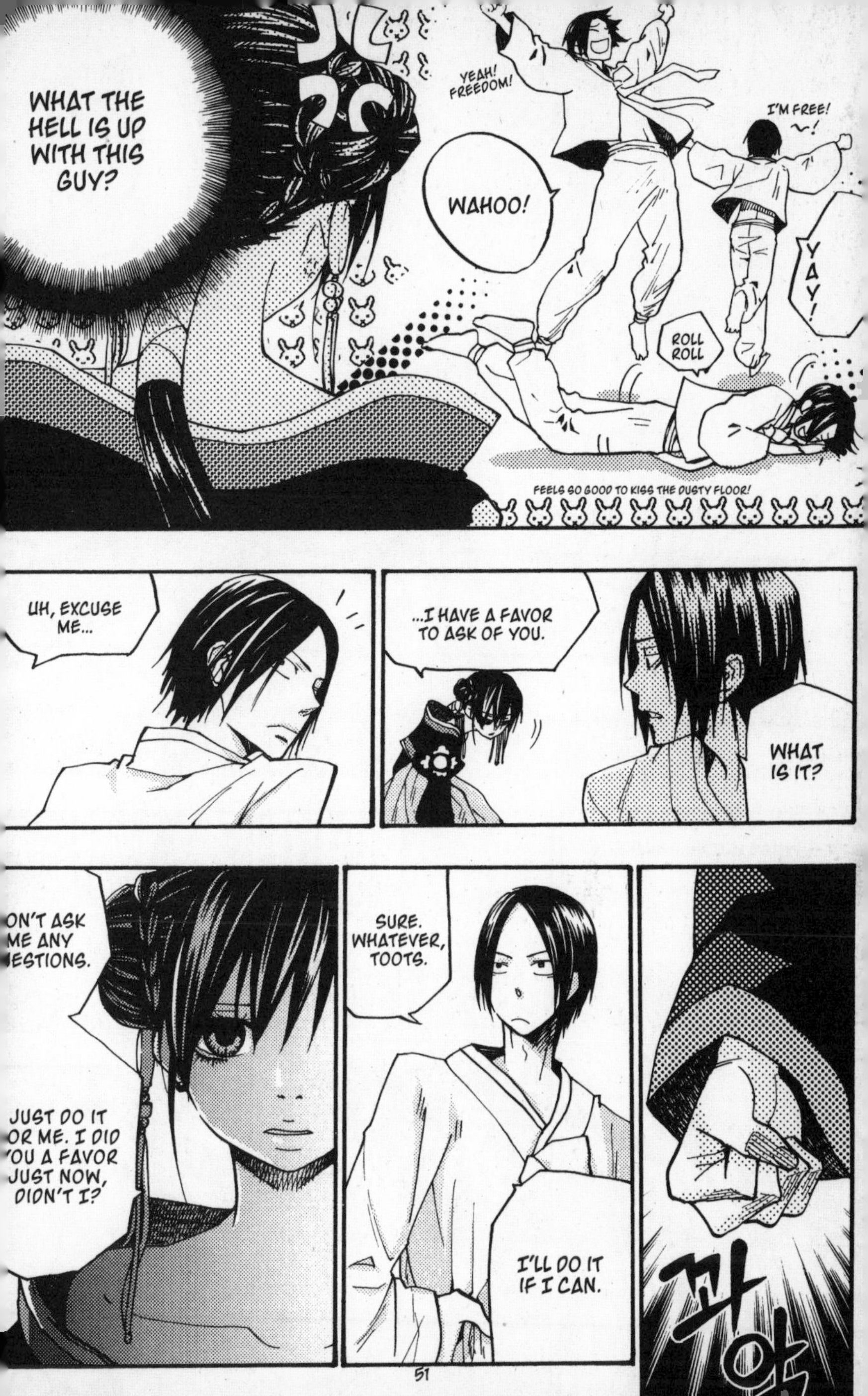
WHAT THE HELL IS UP WITH THIS GUY?
YEAH! FREEDOM!
WAHOO!
I'M FREE! ~!
YAY!
ROLL ROLL
FEELS SO GOOD TO KISS THE DUSTY FLOOR!
UH, EXCUSE ME...
...I HAVE A FAVOR TO ASK OF YOU.
WHAT IS IT?
ON'T ASK ME ANY IESTIONS.
JUST DO IT OR ME. I DID 'OU A FAVOR JUST NOW, DIDN'T I?
SURE. WHATEVER, TOOTS.
I'LL DO IT IF I CAN.

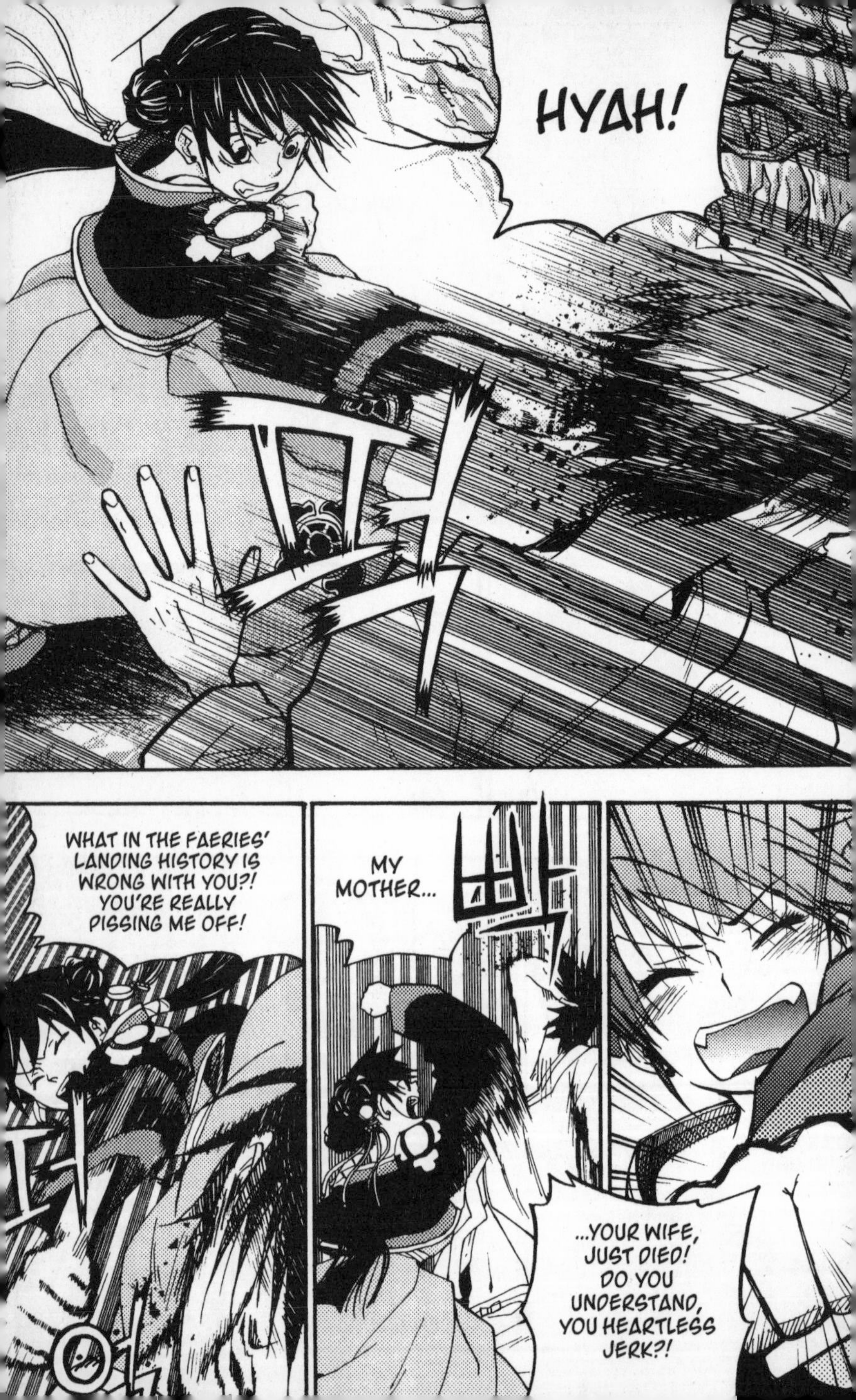
HYAH!
WHAT IN THE FAERIES' LANDING HISTORY IS WRONG WITH YOU?! YOU'RE REALLY PISSING ME OFF!
MY MOTHER...
...YOUR WIFE, JUST DIED! DO YOU UNDERSTAND, YOU HEARTLESS JERK?!

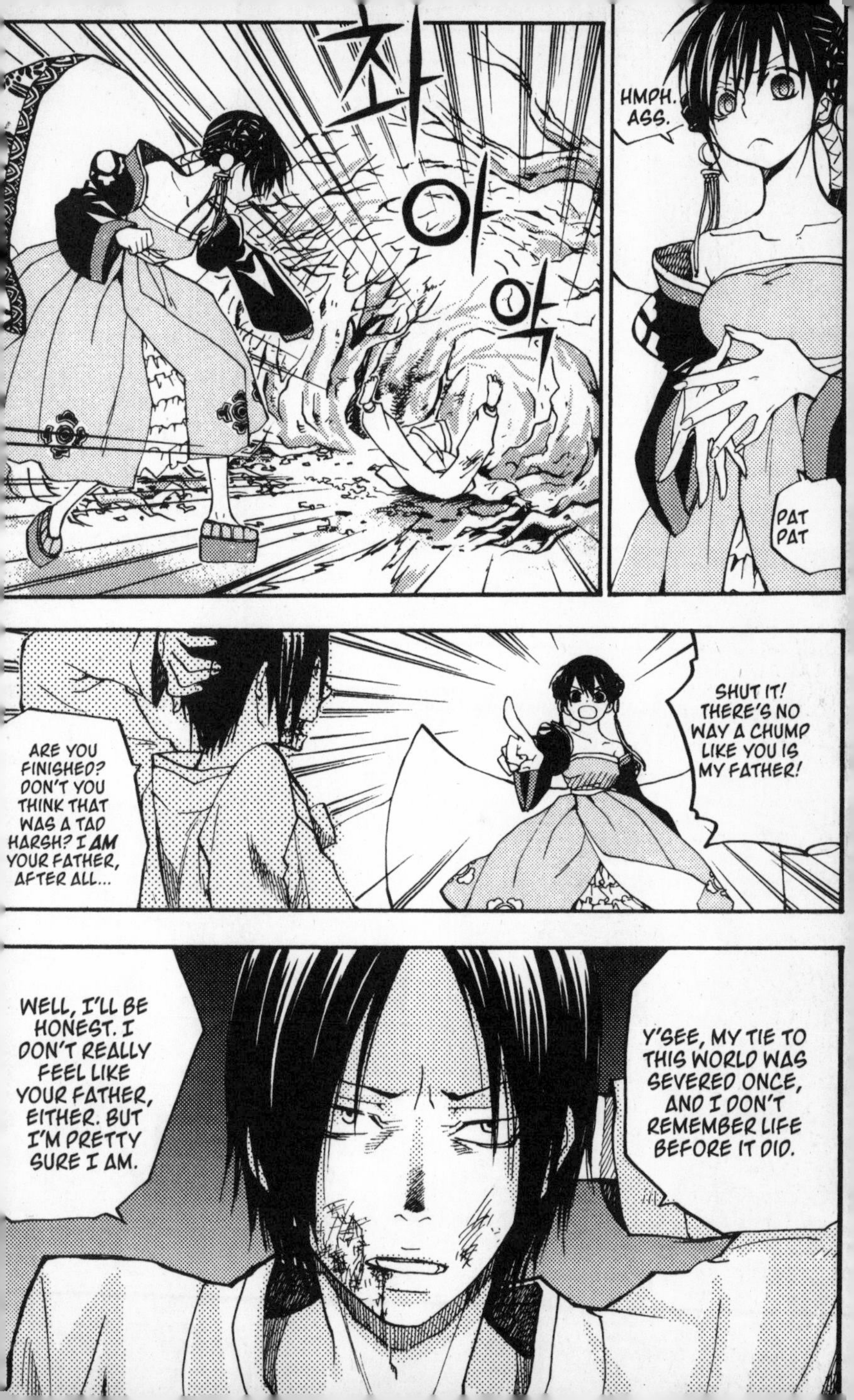
촤아악
HMPH. ASS.
PAT PAT
ARE YOU FINISHED? DON'T YOU THINK THAT WAS A TAD HARSH? I *AM* YOUR FATHER, AFTER ALL...
SHUT IT! THERE'S NO WAY A CHUMP LIKE YOU IS MY FATHER!
WELL, I'LL BE HONEST. I DON'T REALLY FEEL LIKE YOUR FATHER, EITHER. BUT I'M PRETTY SURE I AM.
Y'SEE, MY TIE TO THIS WORLD WAS SEVERED ONCE, AND I DON'T REMEMBER LIFE BEFORE IT DID.

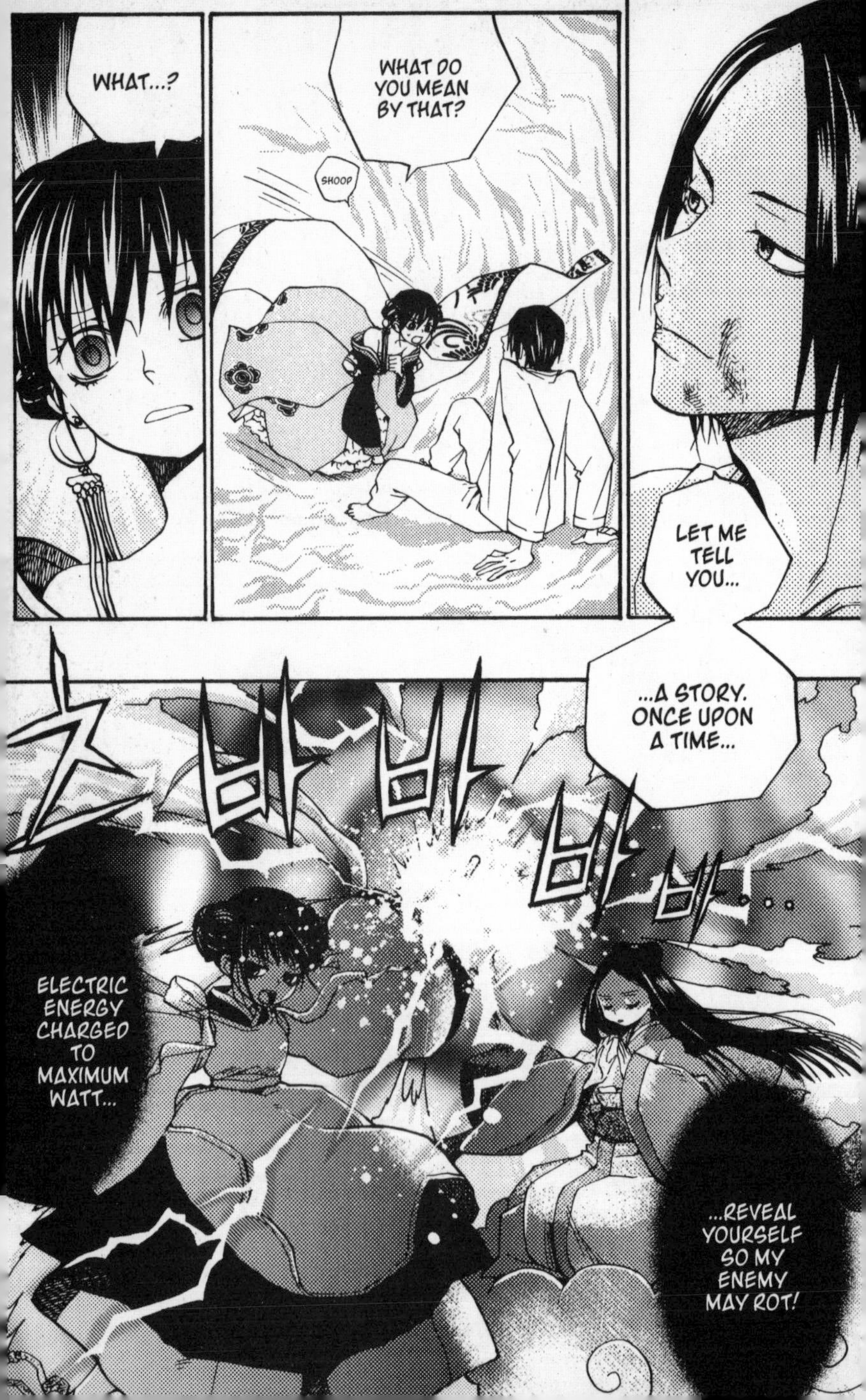
WHAT...?
WHAT DO YOU MEAN BY THAT?
SHOOP
LET ME TELL YOU...
...A STORY. ONCE UPON A TIME...
ELECTRIC ENERGY CHARGED TO MAXIMUM WATT...
...REVEAL YOURSELF SO MY ENEMY MAY ROT!

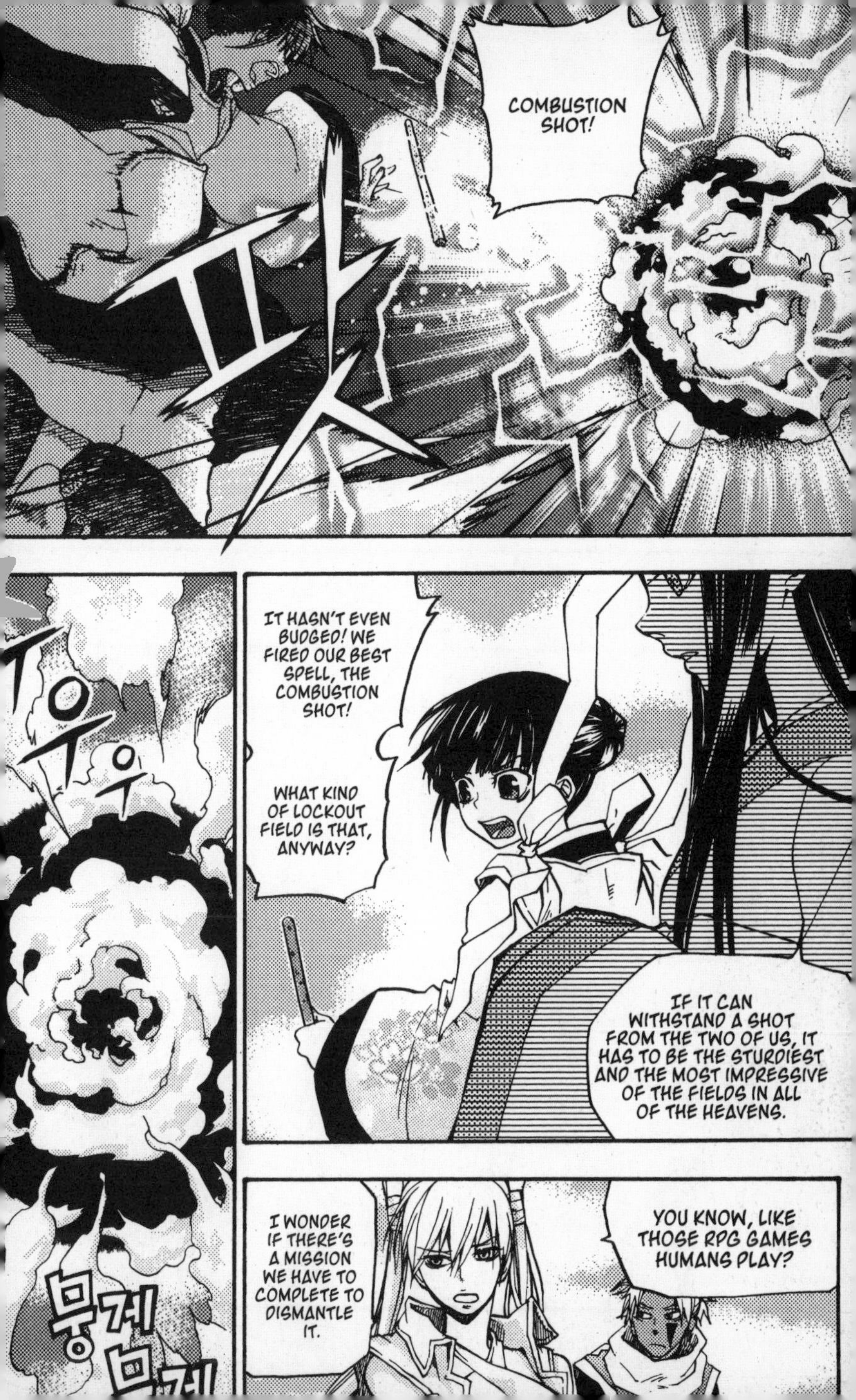
COMBUSTION SHOT!
IT HASN'T EVEN BUDGED! WE FIRED OUR BEST SPELL, THE COMBUSTION SHOT!
WHAT KIND OF LOCKOUT FIELD IS THAT, ANYWAY?
IF IT CAN WITHSTAND A SHOT FROM THE TWO OF US, IT HAS TO BE THE STURDIEST AND THE MOST IMPRESSIVE OF THE FIELDS IN ALL OF THE HEAVENS.
I WONDER IF THERE'S A MISSION WE HAVE TO COMPLETE TO DISMANTLE IT.
YOU KNOW, LIKE THOSE RPG GAMES HUMANS PLAY?

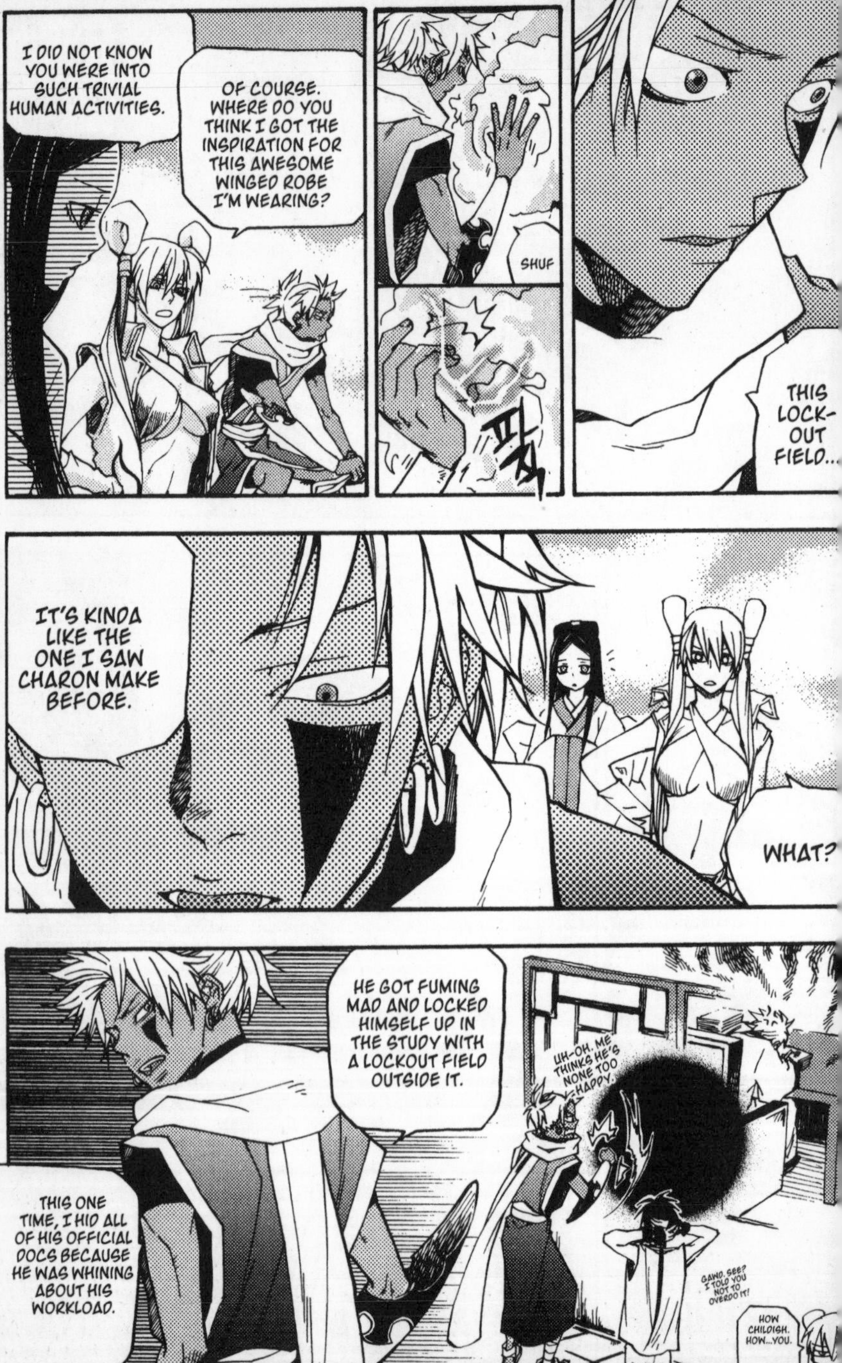
I DID NOT KNOW YOU WERE INTO SUCH TRIVIAL HUMAN ACTIVITIES.
OF COURSE. WHERE DO YOU THINK I GOT THE INSPIRATION FOR THIS AWESOME WINGED ROBE I'M WEARING?
SHUF
THIS LOCK-OUT FIELD...
IT'S KINDA LIKE THE ONE I SAW CHARON MAKE BEFORE.
WHAT?
THIS ONE TIME, I HID ALL OF HIS OFFICIAL DOCS BECAUSE HE WAS WHINING ABOUT HIS WORKLOAD.
HE GOT FUMING MAD AND LOCKED HIMSELF UP IN THE STUDY WITH A LOCKOUT FIELD OUTSIDE IT.
UH-OH. ME THINKS HE'S NONE TOO HAPPY.
GAWD. SEE? I TOLD YOU NOT TO OVERDO IT!
HOW CHILDISH. HOW...YOU.

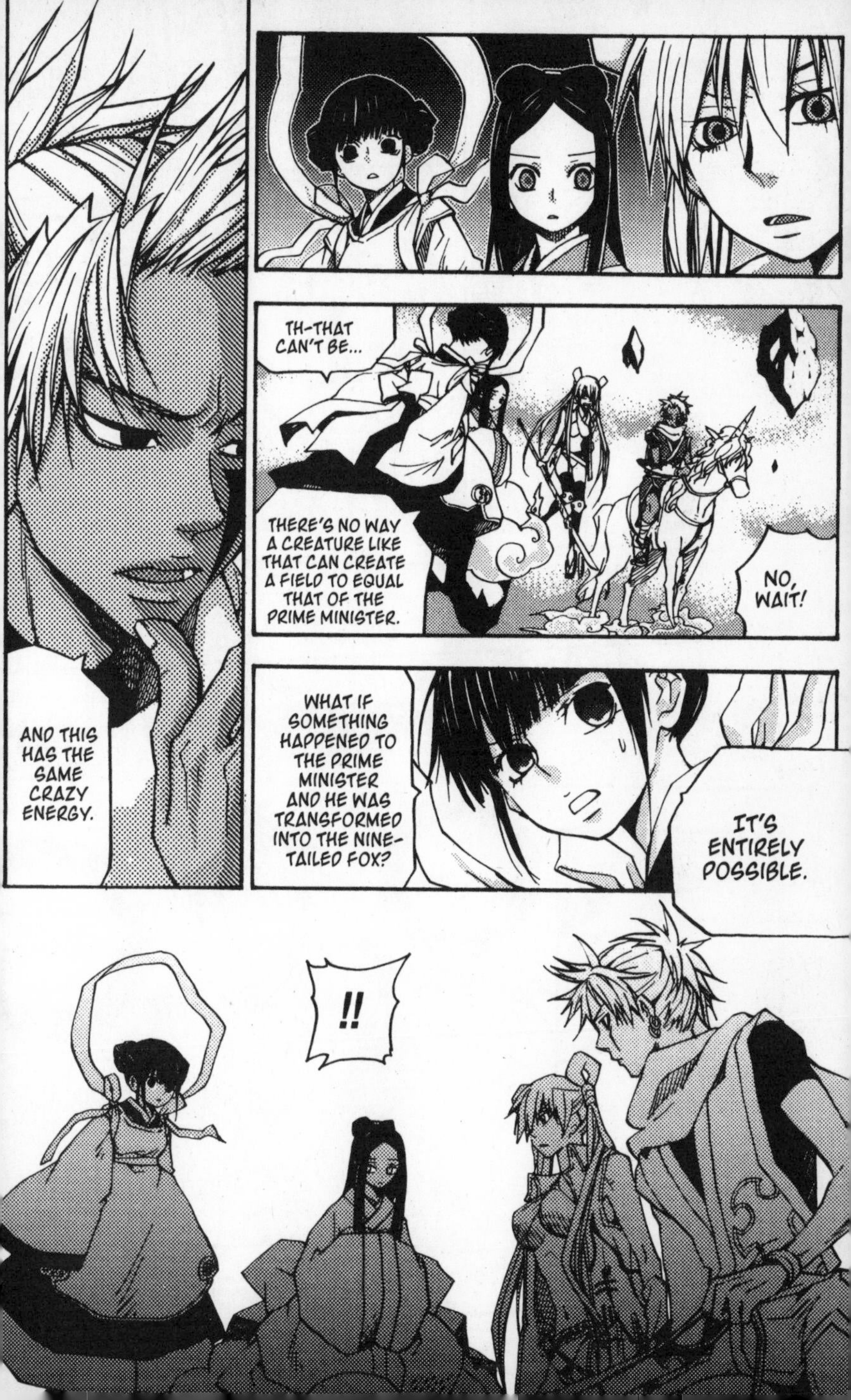
AND THIS HAS THE SAME CRAZY ENERGY.
TH-THAT CAN'T BE...
THERE'S NO WAY A CREATURE LIKE THAT CAN CREATE A FIELD TO EQUAL THAT OF THE PRIME MINISTER.
NO, WAIT!
WHAT IF SOMETHING HAPPENED TO THE PRIME MINISTER AND HE WAS TRANSFORMED INTO THE NINE-TAILED FOX?
IT'S ENTIRELY POSSIBLE.
!!

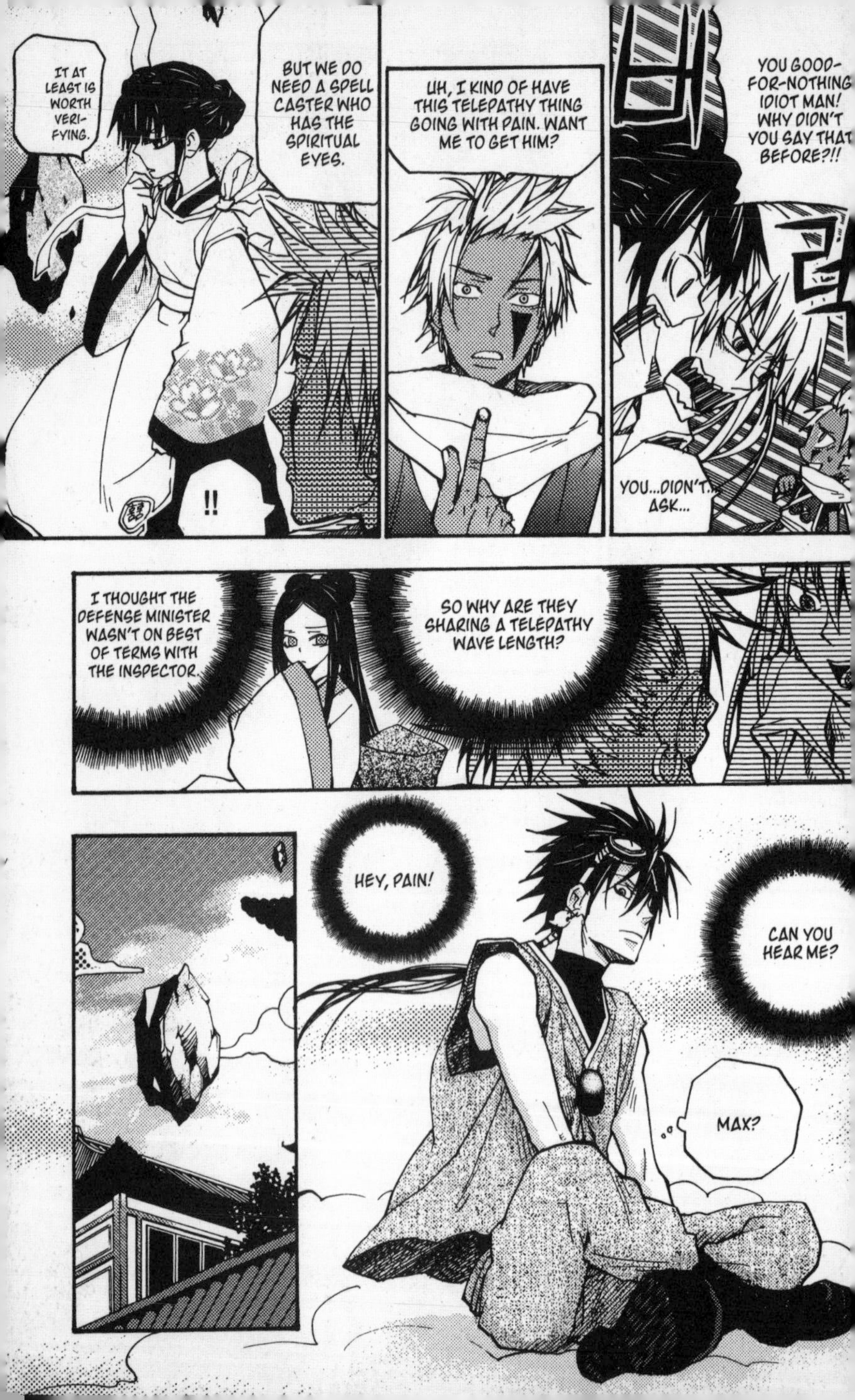
IT AT LEAST IS WORTH VERI-FYING.
BUT WE DO NEED A SPELL CASTER WHO HAS THE SPIRITUAL EYES.
!!
UH, I KIND OF HAVE THIS TELEPATHY THING GOING WITH PAIN. WANT ME TO GET HIM?
YOU GOOD-FOR-NOTHING IDIOT MAN! WHY DIDN'T YOU SAY THAT BEFORE?!!
YOU...DIDN'T... ASK...
I THOUGHT THE DEFENSE MINISTER WASN'T ON BEST OF TERMS WITH THE INSPECTOR.
SO WHY ARE THEY SHARING A TELEPATHY WAVE LENGTH?
HEY, PAIN!
CAN YOU HEAR ME?
MAX?

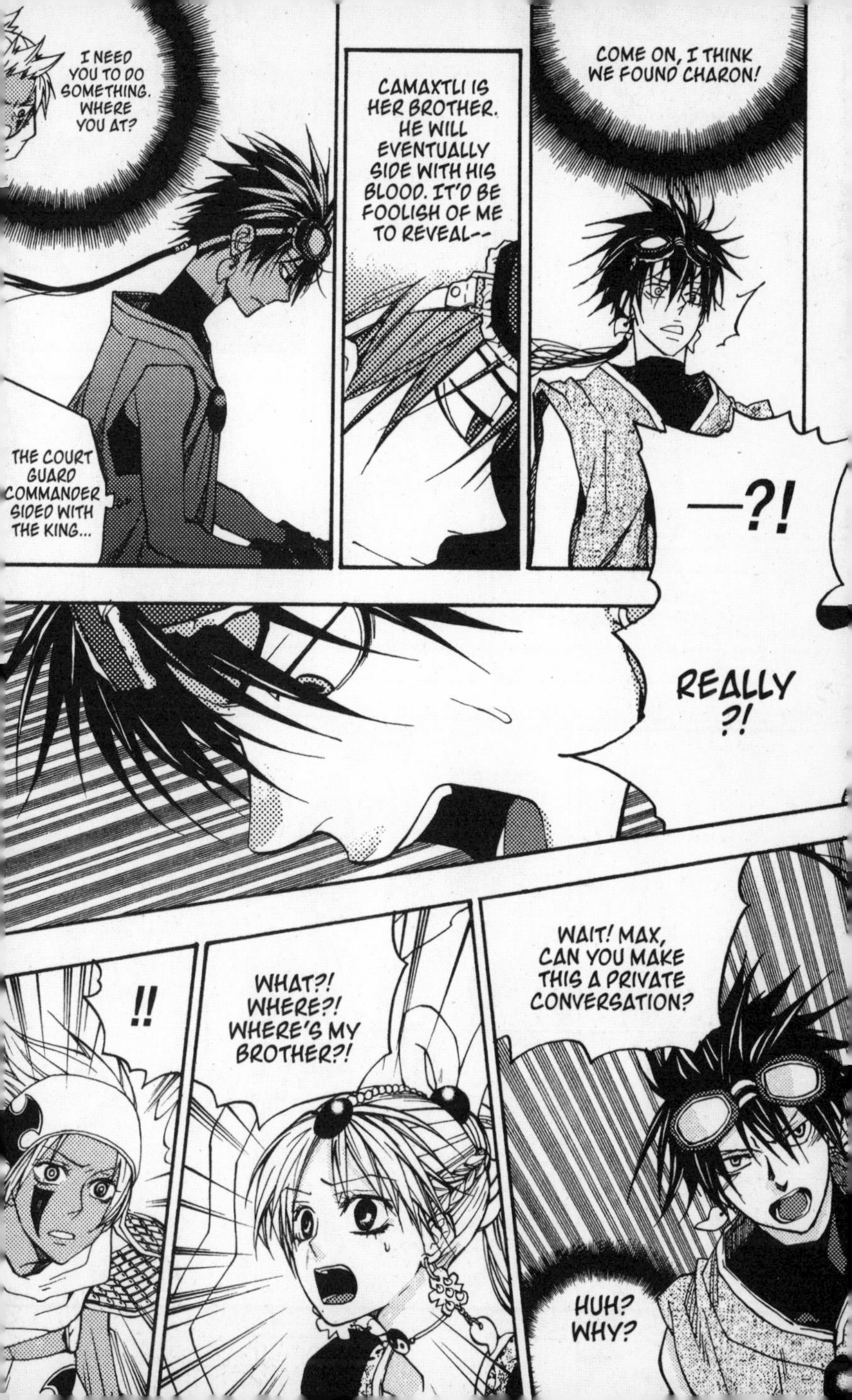
I NEED YOU TO DO SOMETHING. WHERE YOU AT?
THE COURT GUARD COMMANDER SIDED WITH THE KING...
CAMAXTLI IS HER BROTHER. HE WILL EVENTUALLY SIDE WITH HIS BLOOD. IT'D BE FOOLISH OF ME TO REVEAL--
COME ON, I THINK WE FOUND CHARON!
—?!
REALLY ?!
!!
WHAT?! WHERE?! WHERE'S MY BROTHER?!
WAIT! MAX, CAN YOU MAKE THIS A PRIVATE CONVERSATION?
HUH? WHY?

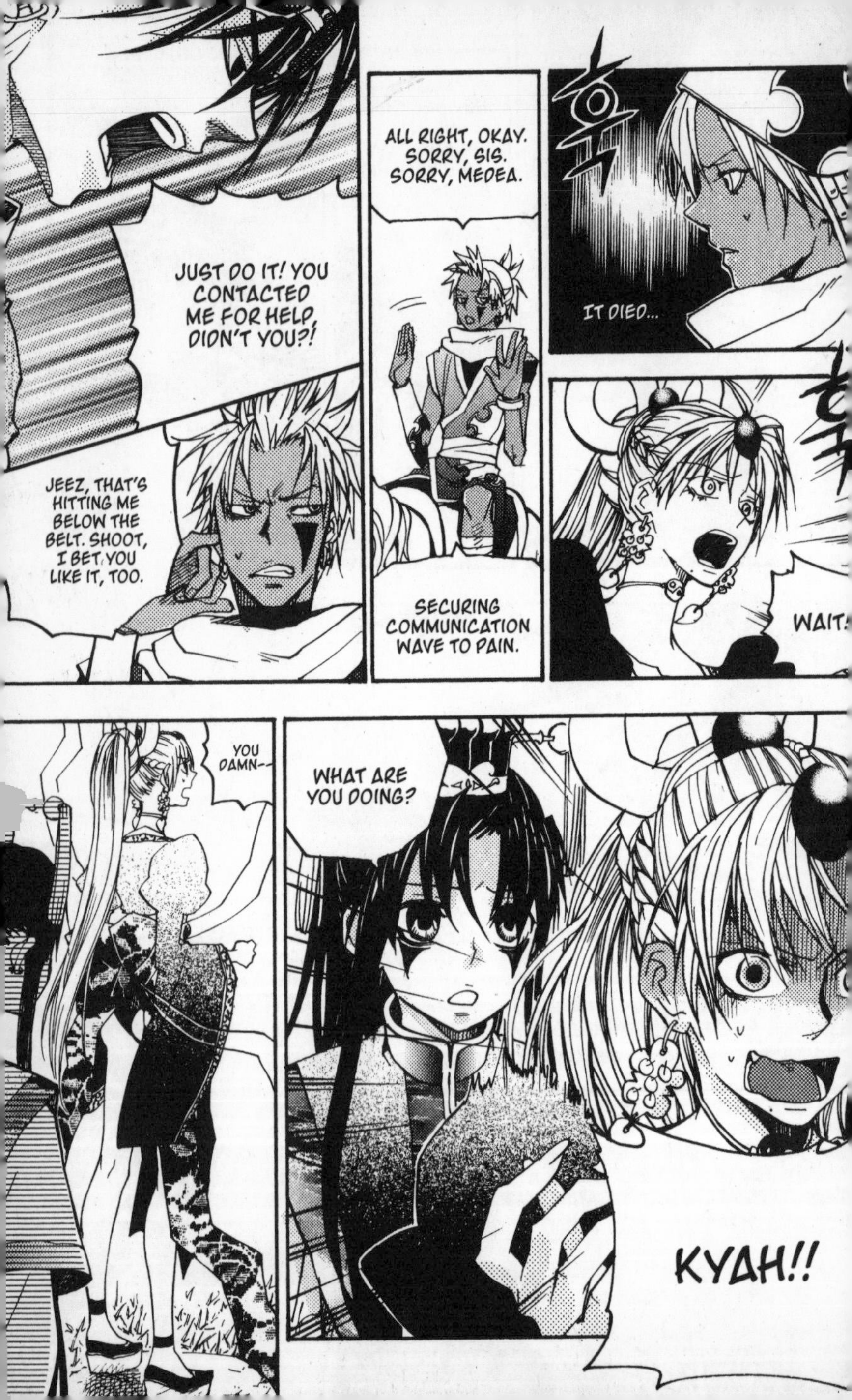
JUST DO IT! YOU CONTACTED ME FOR HELP, DIDN'T YOU?!
JEEZ, THAT'S HITTING ME BELOW THE BELT. SHOOT, I BET YOU LIKE IT, TOO.
ALL RIGHT, OKAY. SORRY, SIS. SORRY, MEDEA.
SECURING COMMUNICATION WAVE TO PAIN.
IT DIED...
WAIT!
YOU DAMN--
WHAT ARE YOU DOING?
KYAH!!

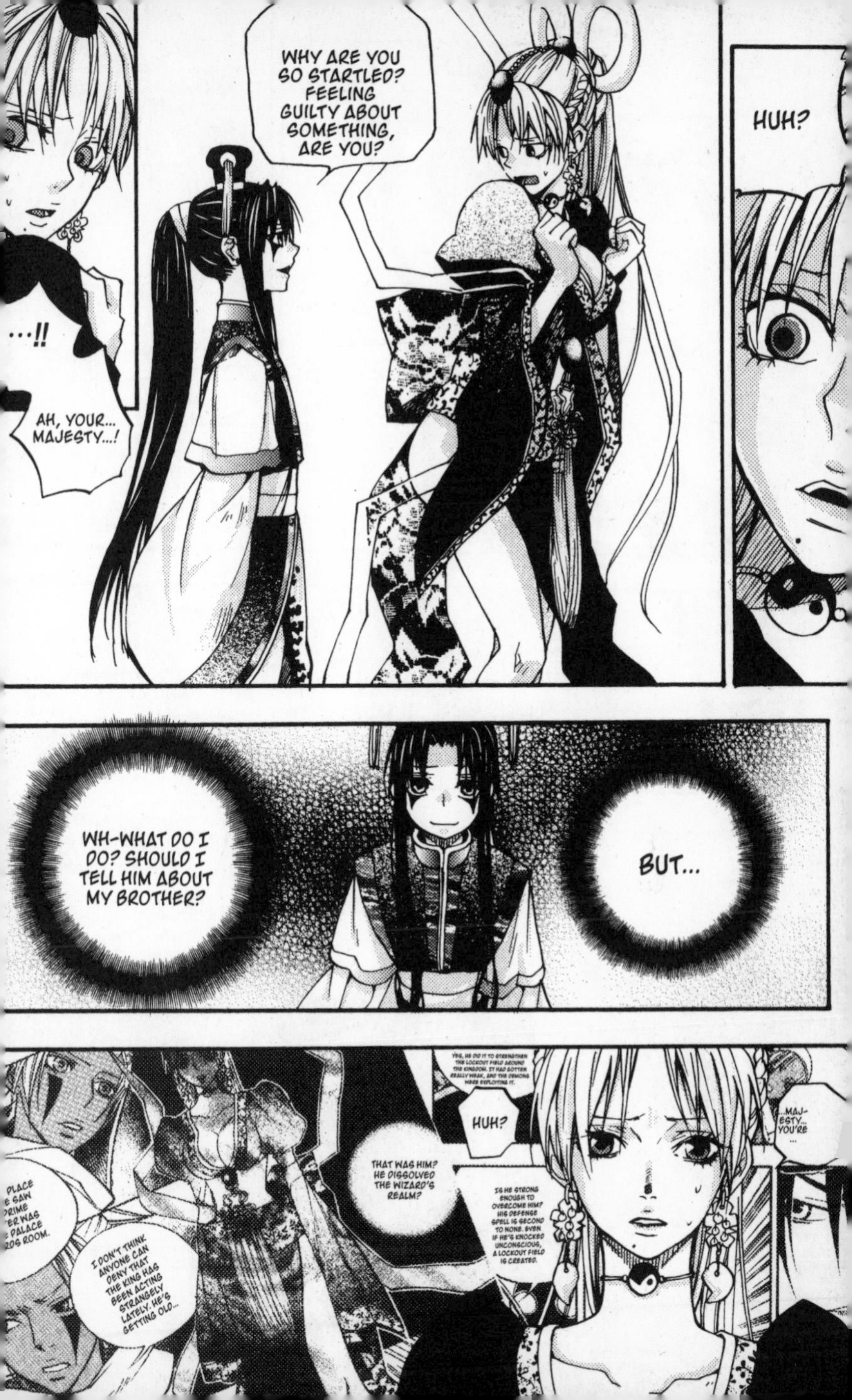
...!!
AH, YOUR... MAJESTY...!
WHY ARE YOU SO STARTLED? FEELING GUILTY ABOUT SOMETHING, ARE YOU?
HUH?
WH-WHAT DO I DO? SHOULD I TELL HIM ABOUT MY BROTHER?
BUT...
I DON'T THINK ANYONE CAN DENY THAT THE KING HAS BEEN ACTING STRANGELY LATELY. HE'S GETTING OLD...
THAT WAS HIM? HE DISSOLVED THE WIZARD'S REALM?
YES, HE DID IT TO STRENGTHEN THE LOCKOUT FIELD AROUND THE KINGDOM. IT HAD GOTTEN REALLY WEAK, AND THE DEMONS WERE EXPLOITING IT.
HUH?
IS HE STRONG ENOUGH TO OVERCOME HIM? HIS DEFENSE SPELL IS SECOND TO NONE. EVEN IF HE'S KNOCKED UNCONSCIOUS, A LOCKOUT FIELD IS CREATED.
...MAJ-ESTY... YOU'RE ...

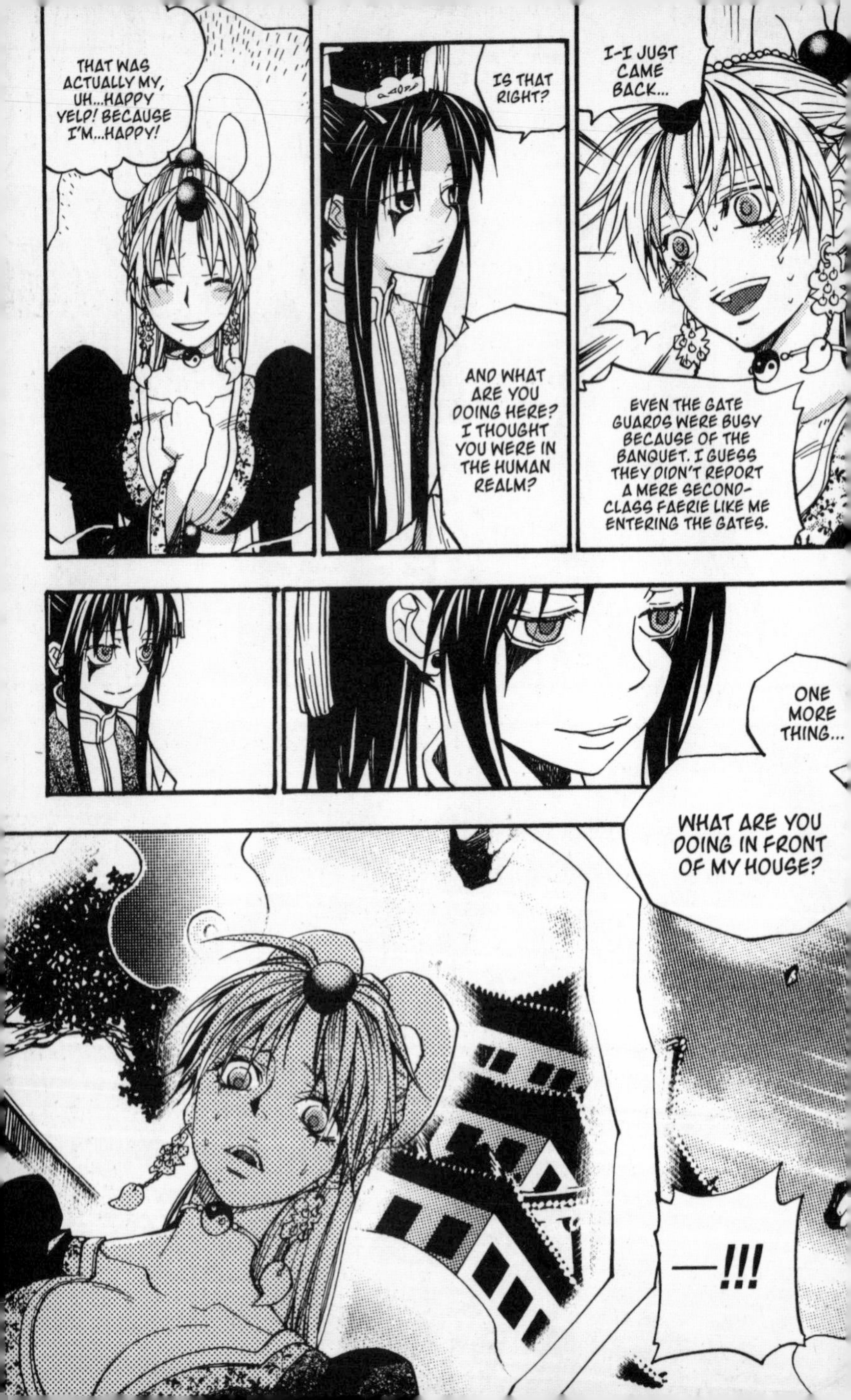
THAT WAS ACTUALLY MY, UH...HAPPY YELP! BECAUSE I'M...HAPPY!
IS THAT RIGHT?
AND WHAT ARE YOU DOING HERE? I THOUGHT YOU WERE IN THE HUMAN REALM?
I-I JUST CAME BACK...
EVEN THE GATE GUARDS WERE BUSY BECAUSE OF THE BANQUET. I GUESS THEY DIDN'T REPORT A MERE SECOND-CLASS FAERIE LIKE ME ENTERING THE GATES.
ONE MORE THING...
WHAT ARE YOU DOING IN FRONT OF MY HOUSE?
—!!!

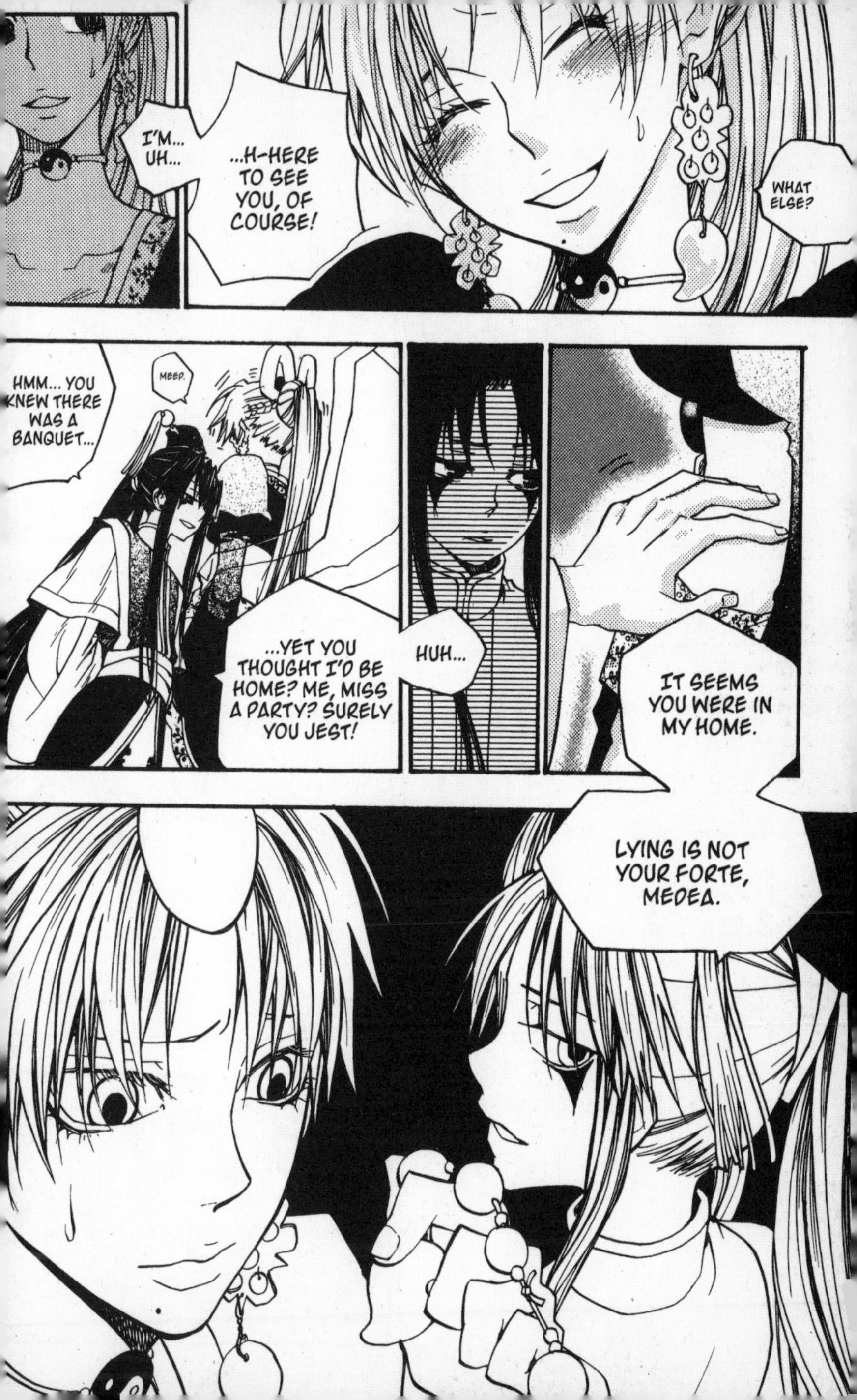
I'M... UH...
...H-HERE TO SEE YOU, OF COURSE!
WHAT ELSE?
HMM... YOU KNEW THERE WAS A BANQUET...
MEEP.
...YET YOU THOUGHT I'D BE HOME? ME, MISS A PARTY? SURELY YOU JEST!
HUH...
IT SEEMS YOU WERE IN MY HOME.
LYING IS NOT YOUR FORTE, MEDEA.

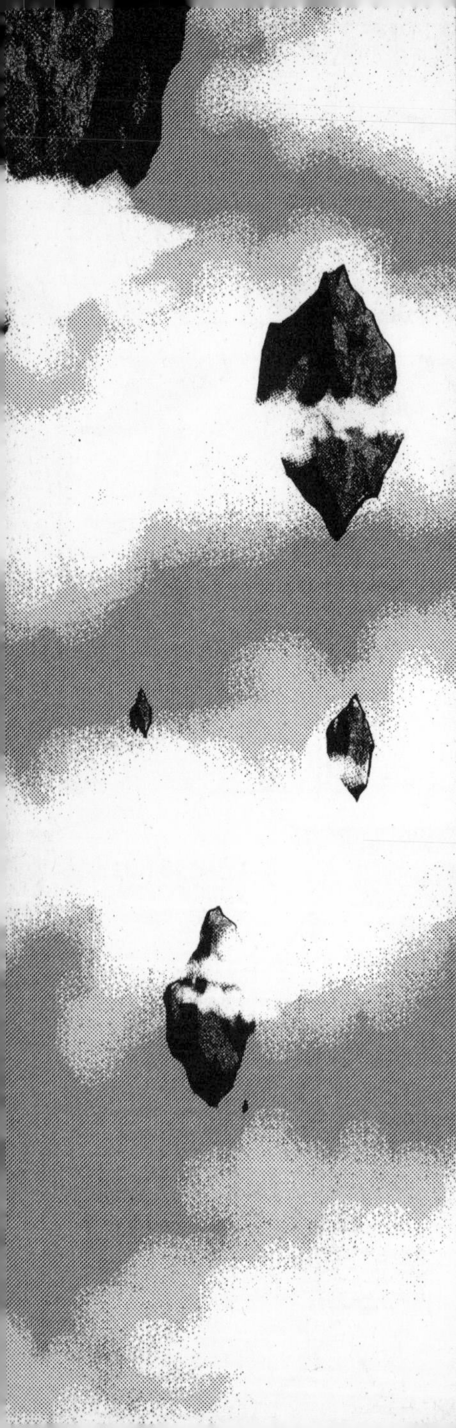

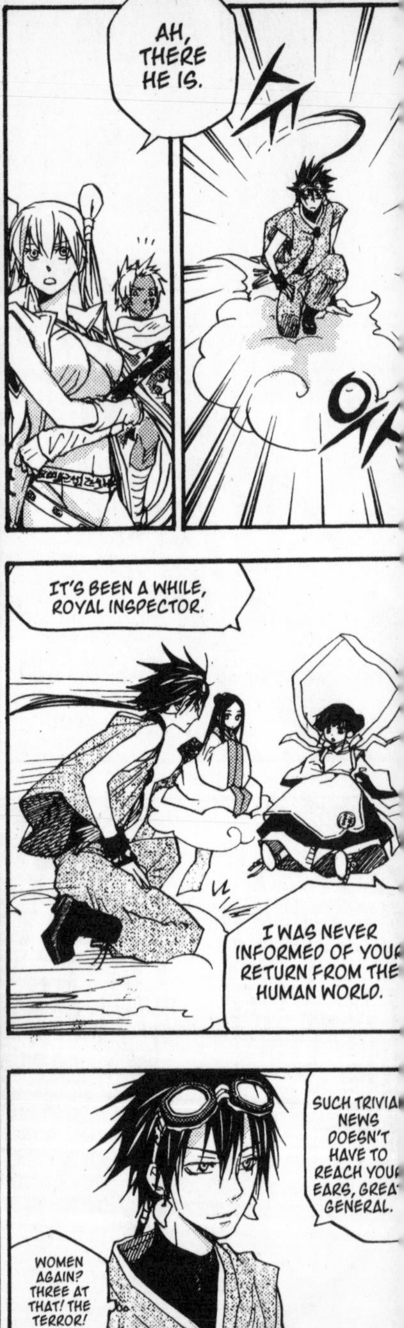
AH, THERE HE IS.
IT'S BEEN A WHILE, ROYAL INSPECTOR.
I WAS NEVER INFORMED OF YOUR RETURN FROM THE HUMAN WORLD.
SUCH TRIVIAL NEWS DOESN'T HAVE TO REACH YOUR EARS, GREAT GENERAL.
WOMEN AGAIN? THREE AT THAT! THE TERROR!

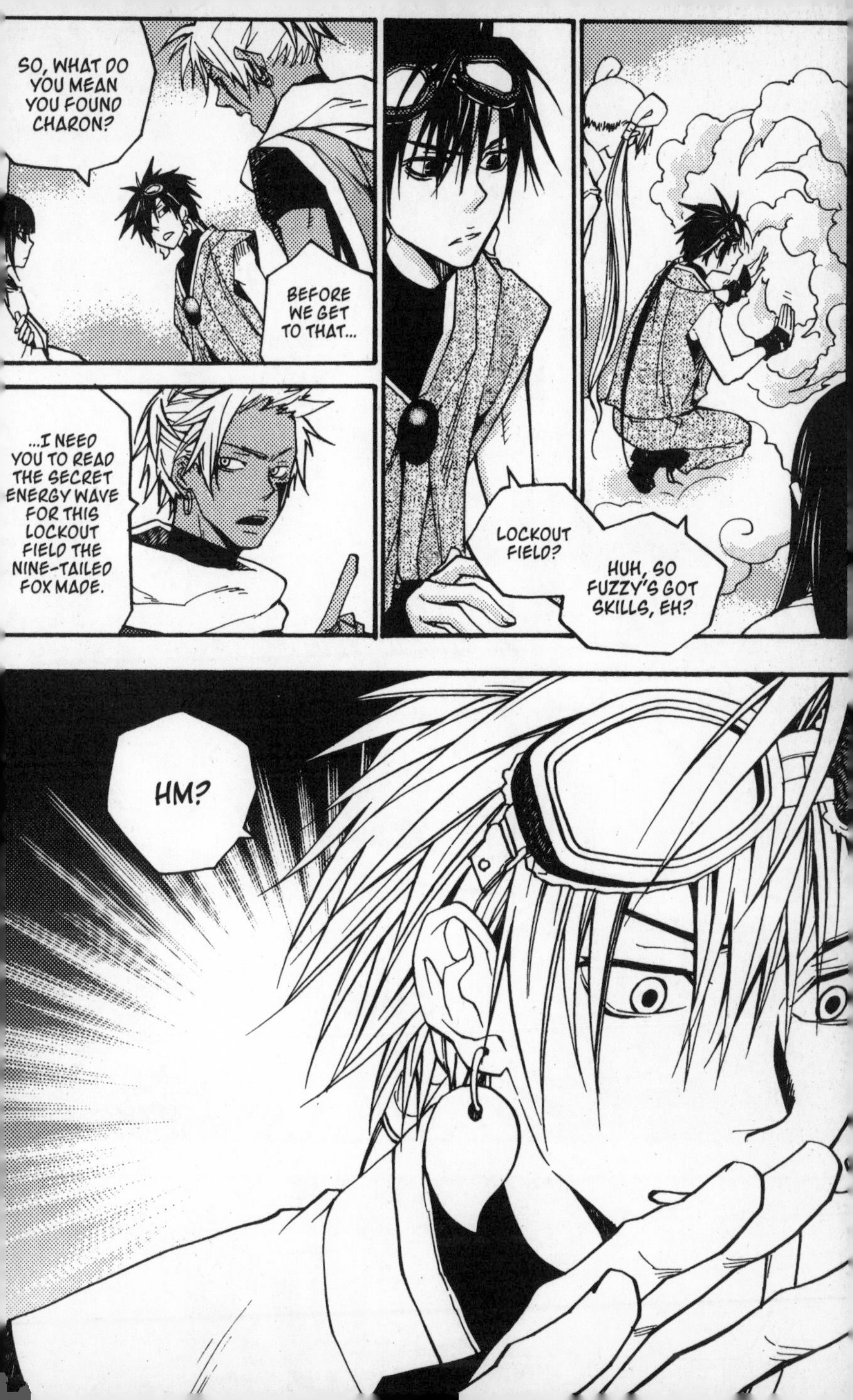
SO, WHAT DO YOU MEAN YOU FOUND CHARON?
BEFORE WE GET TO THAT...
...I NEED YOU TO READ THE SECRET ENERGY WAVE FOR THIS LOCKOUT FIELD THE NINE-TAILED FOX MADE.
LOCKOUT FIELD?
HUH, SO FUZZY'S GOT SKILLS, EH?
HM?

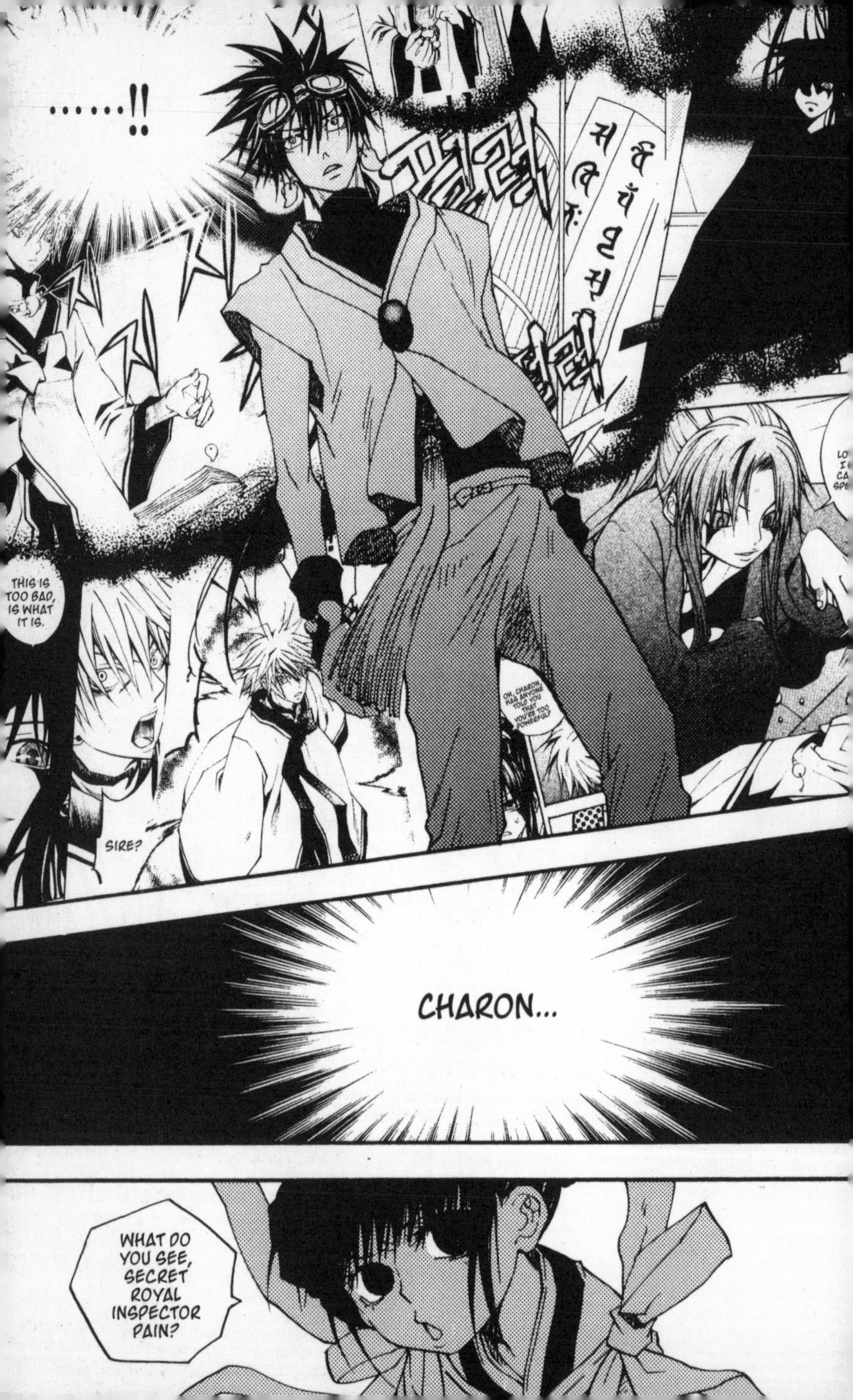
......!!
THIS IS TOO BAD, IS WHAT IT IS.
OH, CHARON, HAS ANYONE TOLD YOU THAT YOU'RE TOO POWERFUL?
SIRE?
CHARON...
WHAT DO YOU SEE, SECRET ROYAL INSPECTOR PAIN?

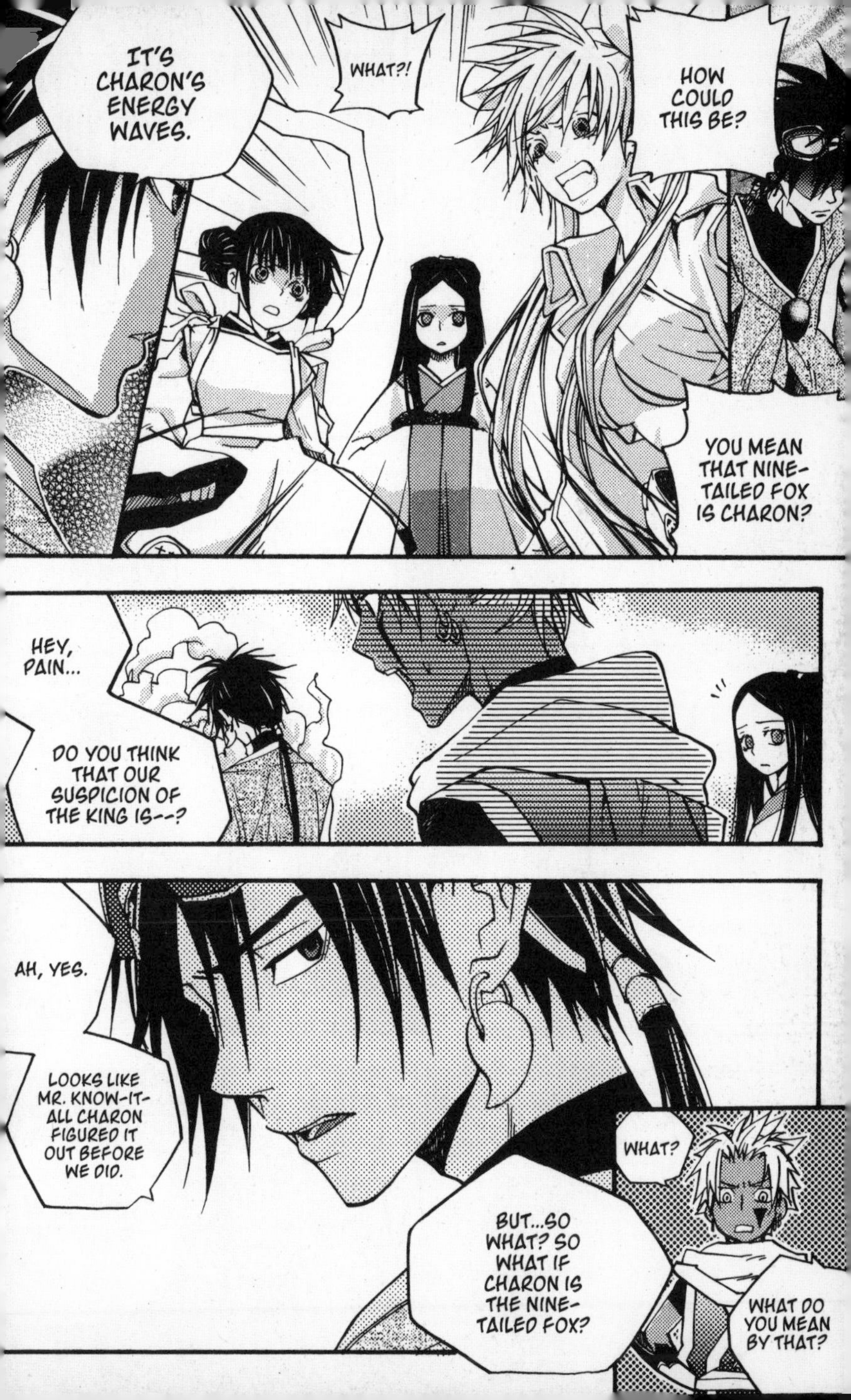
IT'S CHARON'S ENERGY WAVES.
WHAT?!
HOW COULD THIS BE?
YOU MEAN THAT NINE-TAILED FOX IS CHARON?
HEY, PAIN...
DO YOU THINK THAT OUR SUSPICION OF THE KING IS--?
AH, YES.
LOOKS LIKE MR. KNOW-IT-ALL CHARON FIGURED IT OUT BEFORE WE DID.
WHAT?
BUT...SO WHAT? SO WHAT IF CHARON IS THE NINE-TAILED FOX?
WHAT DO YOU MEAN BY THAT?

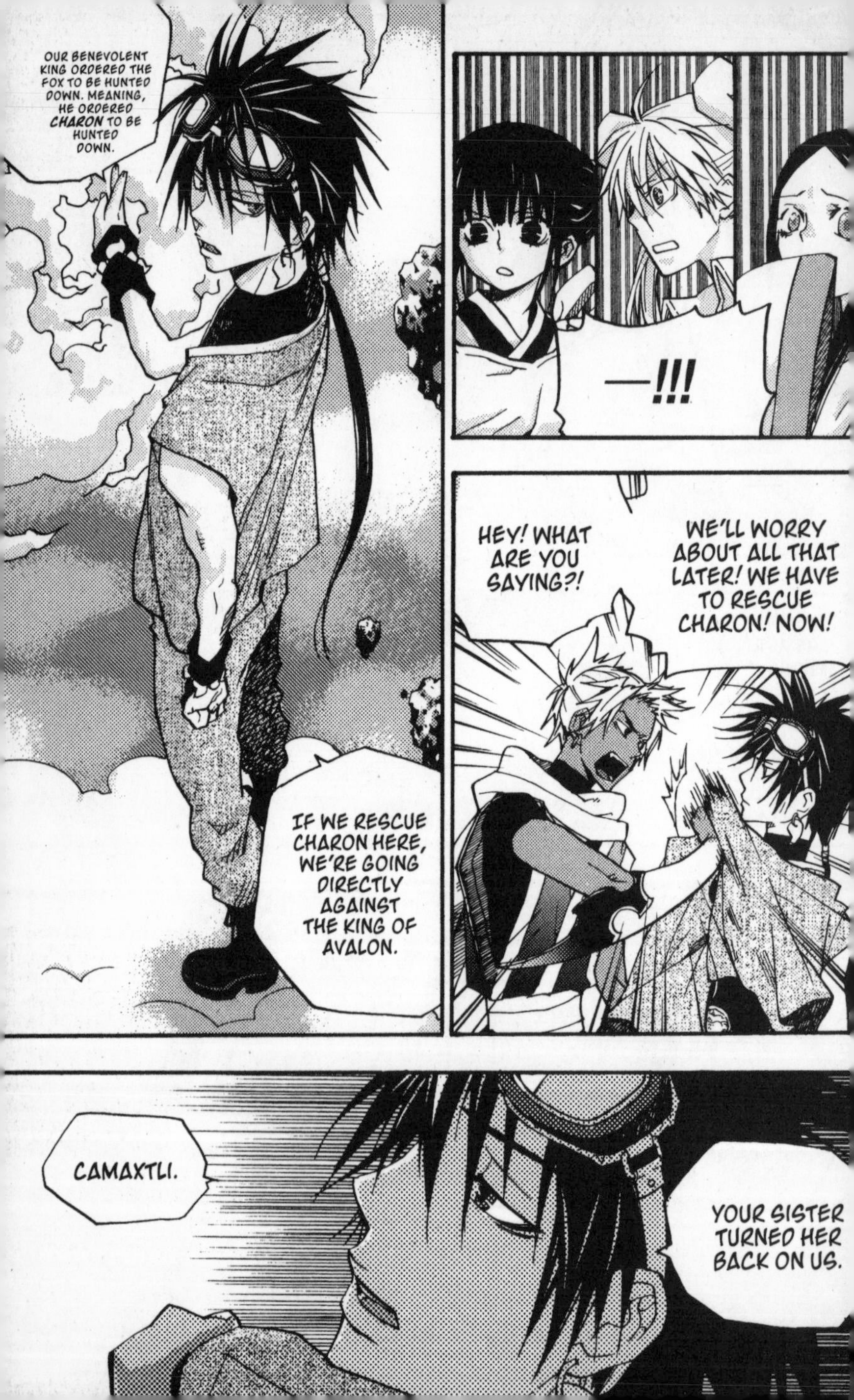
OUR BENEVOLENT KING ORDERED THE FOX TO BE HUNTED DOWN. MEANING, HE ORDERED CHARON TO BE HUNTED DOWN.
IF WE RESCUE CHARON HERE, WE'RE GOING DIRECTLY AGAINST THE KING OF AVALON.
—!!!
HEY! WHAT ARE YOU SAYING?!
WE'LL WORRY ABOUT ALL THAT LATER! WE HAVE TO RESCUE CHARON! NOW!
CAMAXTLI.
YOUR SISTER TURNED HER BACK ON US.

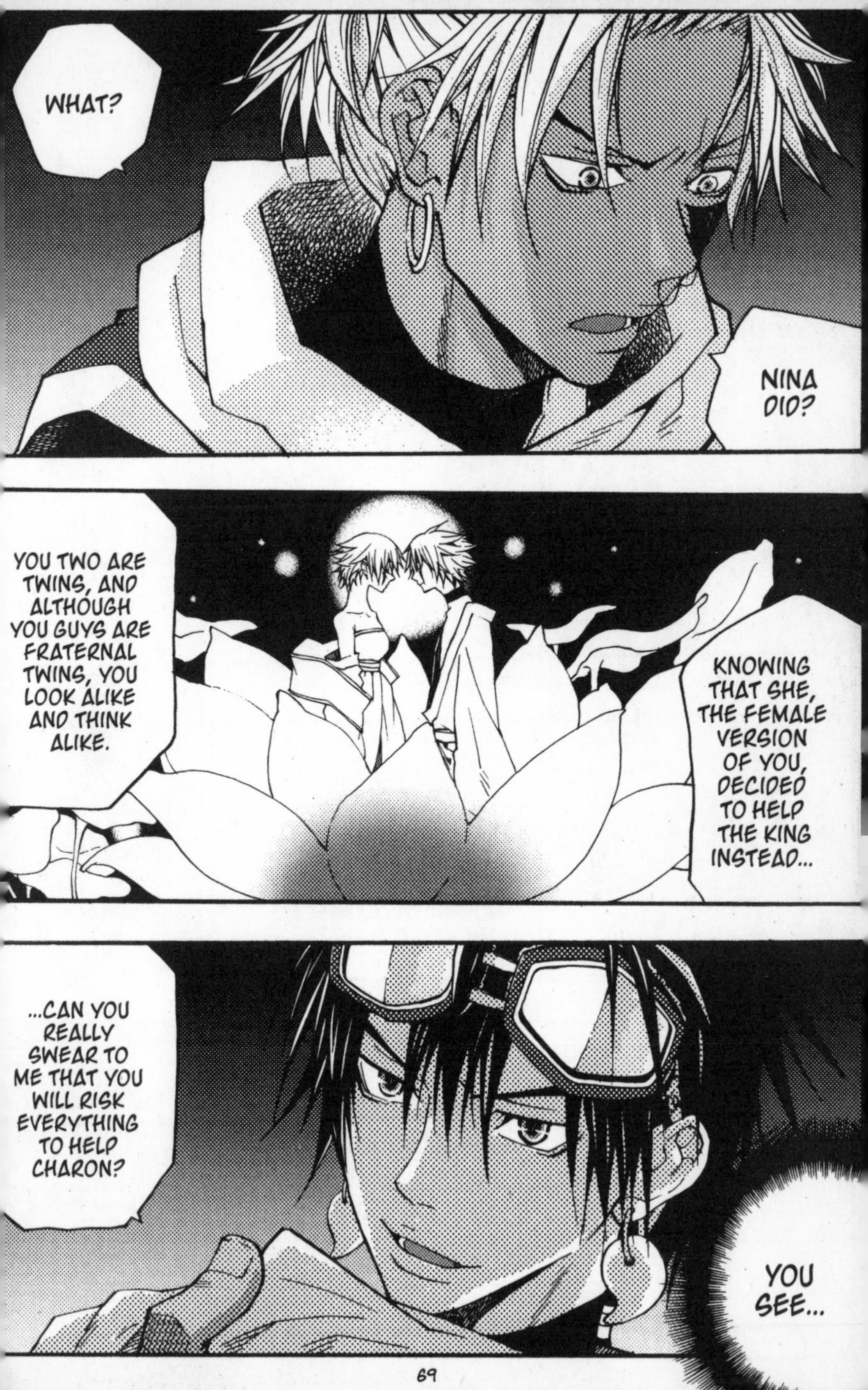
WHAT?
NINA DID?
YOU TWO ARE TWINS, AND ALTHOUGH YOU GUYS ARE FRATERNAL TWINS, YOU LOOK ALIKE AND THINK ALIKE.
KNOWING THAT SHE, THE FEMALE VERSION OF YOU, DECIDED TO HELP THE KING INSTEAD...
...CAN YOU REALLY SWEAR TO ME THAT YOU WILL RISK EVERYTHING TO HELP CHARON?
YOU SEE...

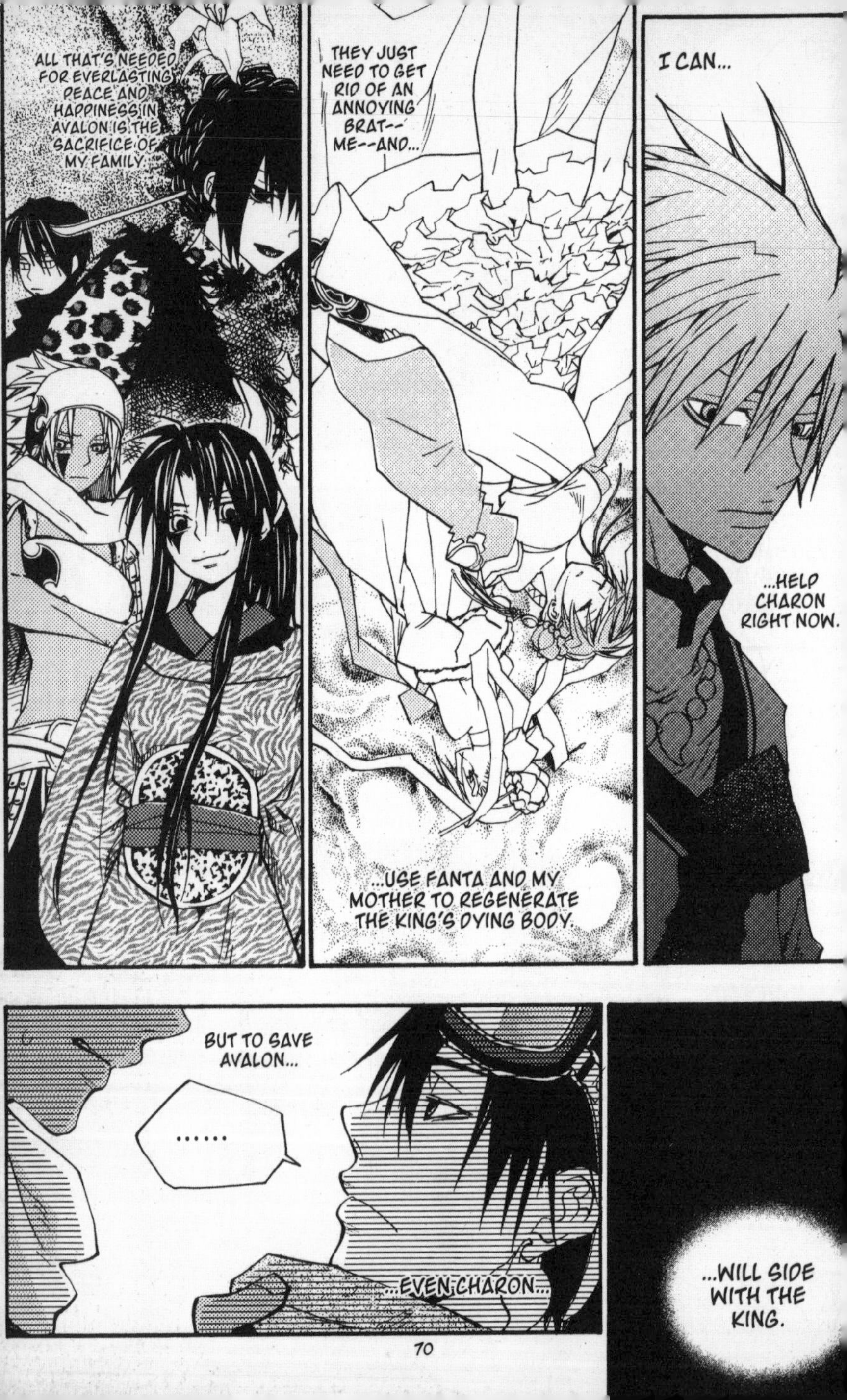

ALL THAT'S NEEDED FOR EVERLASTING PEACE AND HAPPINESS IN AVALON IS THE SACRIFICE OF MY FAMILY.
THEY JUST NEED TO GET RID OF AN ANNOYING BRAT-- ME--AND...
...USE FANTA AND MY MOTHER TO REGENERATE THE KING'S DYING BODY.
I CAN...
...HELP CHARON RIGHT NOW.
BUT TO SAVE AVALON...
......
...EVEN CHARON...
...WILL SIDE WITH THE KING.

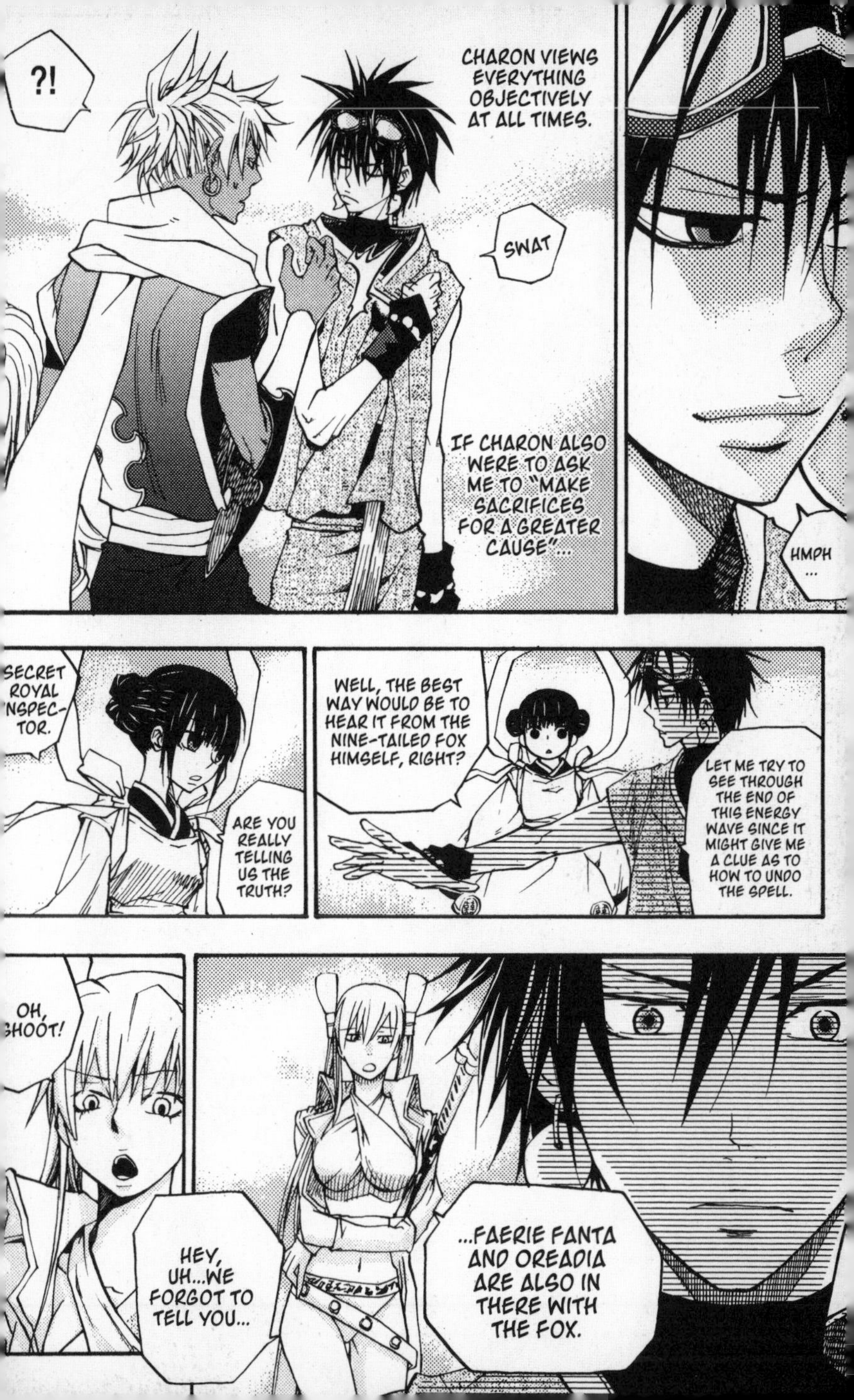

?!
CHARON VIEWS EVERYTHING OBJECTIVELY AT ALL TIMES.
SWAT
IF CHARON ALSO WERE TO ASK ME TO "MAKE SACRIFICES FOR A GREATER CAUSE"...
HMPH ...
SECRET ROYAL NSPEC- TOR.
ARE YOU REALLY TELLING US THE TRUTH?
WELL, THE BEST WAY WOULD BE TO HEAR IT FROM THE NINE-TAILED FOX HIMSELF, RIGHT?
LET ME TRY TO SEE THROUGH THE END OF THIS ENERGY WAVE SINCE IT MIGHT GIVE ME A CLUE AS TO HOW TO UNDO THE SPELL.
OH, SHOOT!
HEY, UH...WE FORGOT TO TELL YOU...
...FAERIE FANTA AND OREADIA ARE ALSO IN THERE WITH THE FOX.

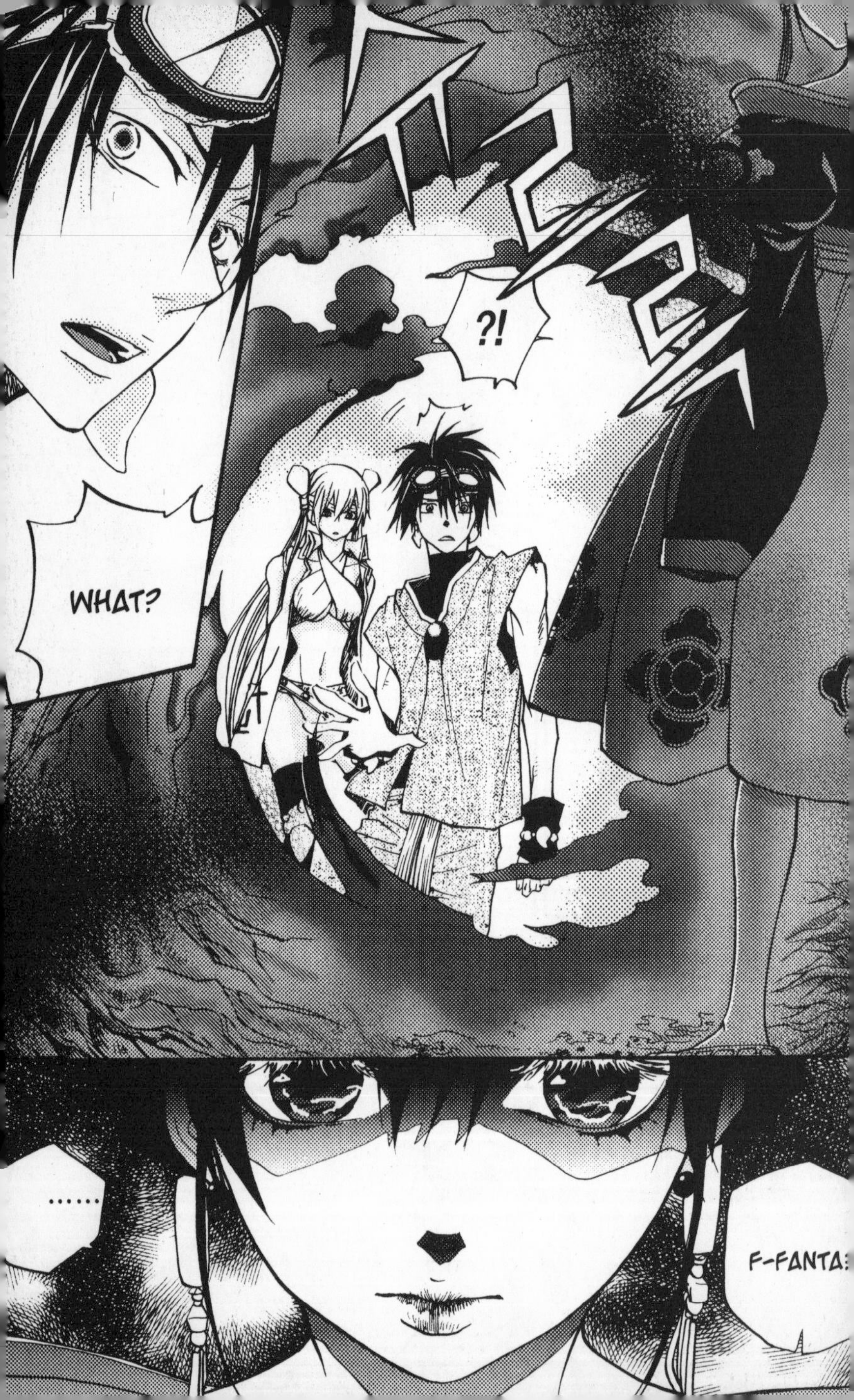
WHAT?
?!
......
F-FANTA

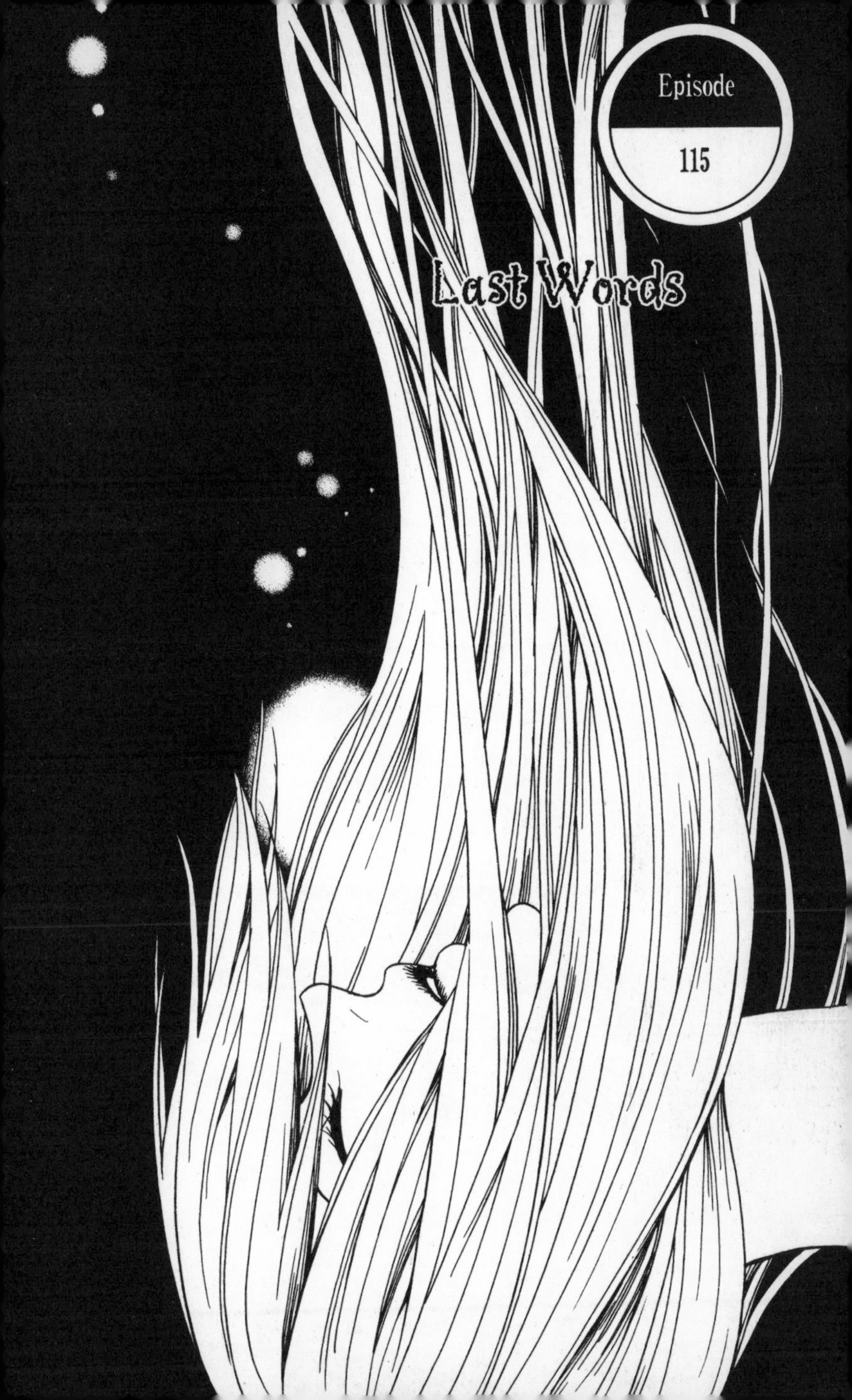
Episode
115
Last Words

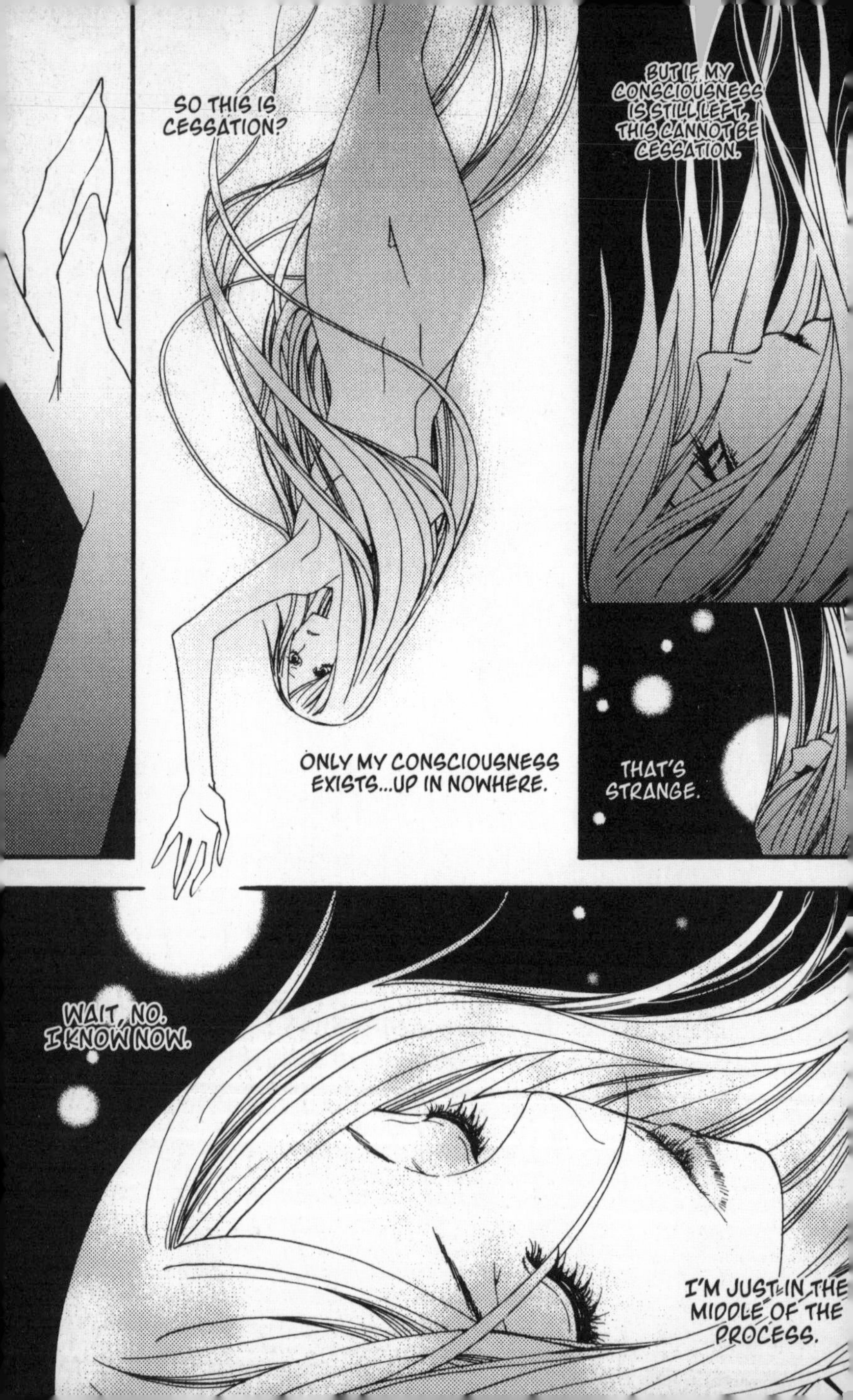
SO THIS IS CESSATION?
ONLY MY CONSCIOUSNESS EXISTS...UP IN NOWHERE.
BUT IF MY CONSCIOUSNESS IS STILL LEFT, THIS CANNOT BE CESSATION.
THAT'S STRANGE.
WAIT, NO. I KNOW NOW.
I'M JUST IN THE MIDDLE OF THE PROCESS.

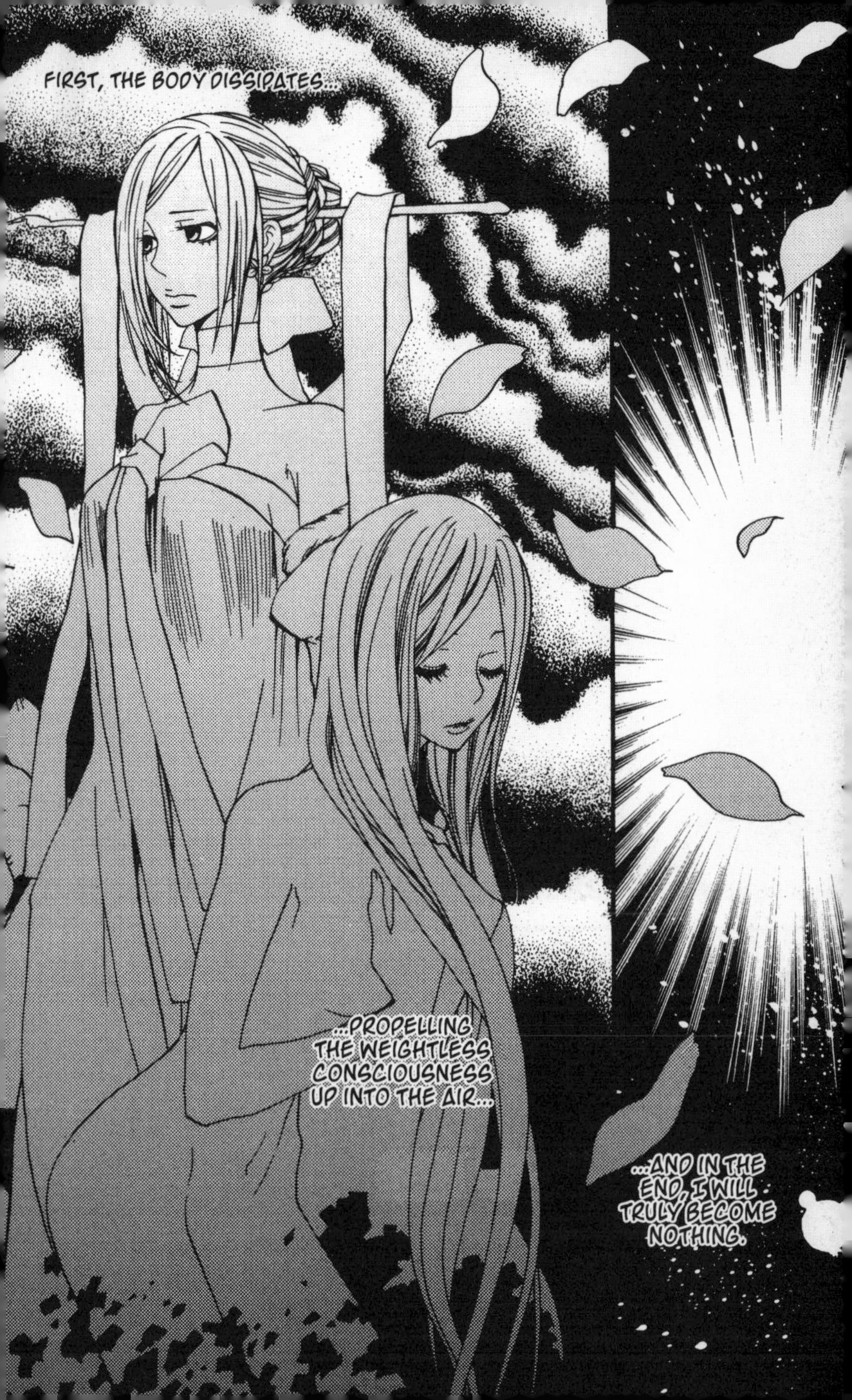
FIRST, THE BODY DISSIPATES...
...PROPELLING THE WEIGHTLESS CONSCIOUSNESS UP INTO THE AIR...
...AND IN THE END, I WILL TRULY BECOME NOTHING.

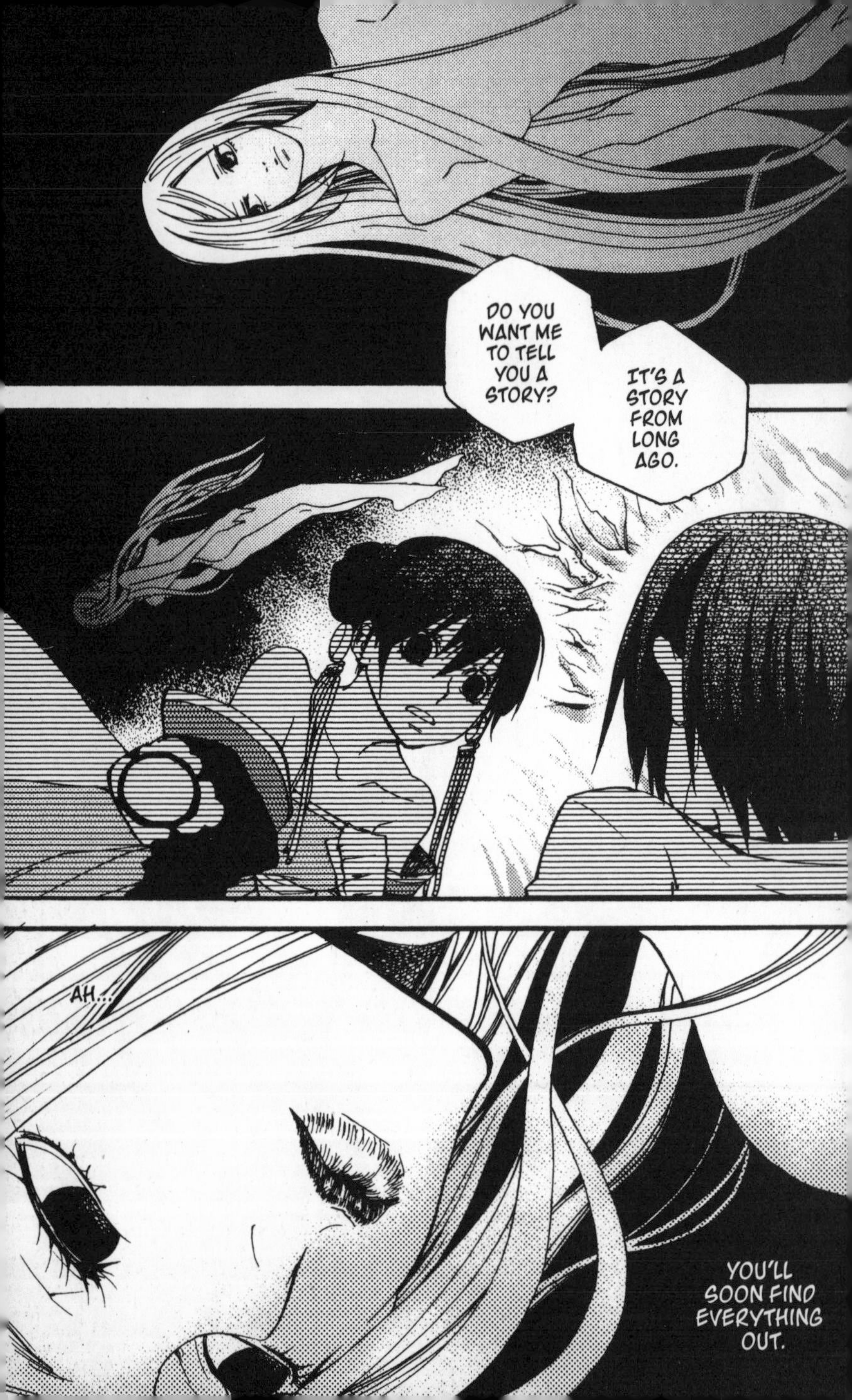
DO YOU WANT ME TO TELL YOU A STORY?
IT'S A STORY FROM LONG AGO.
AH...
YOU'LL SOON FIND EVERYTHING OUT.

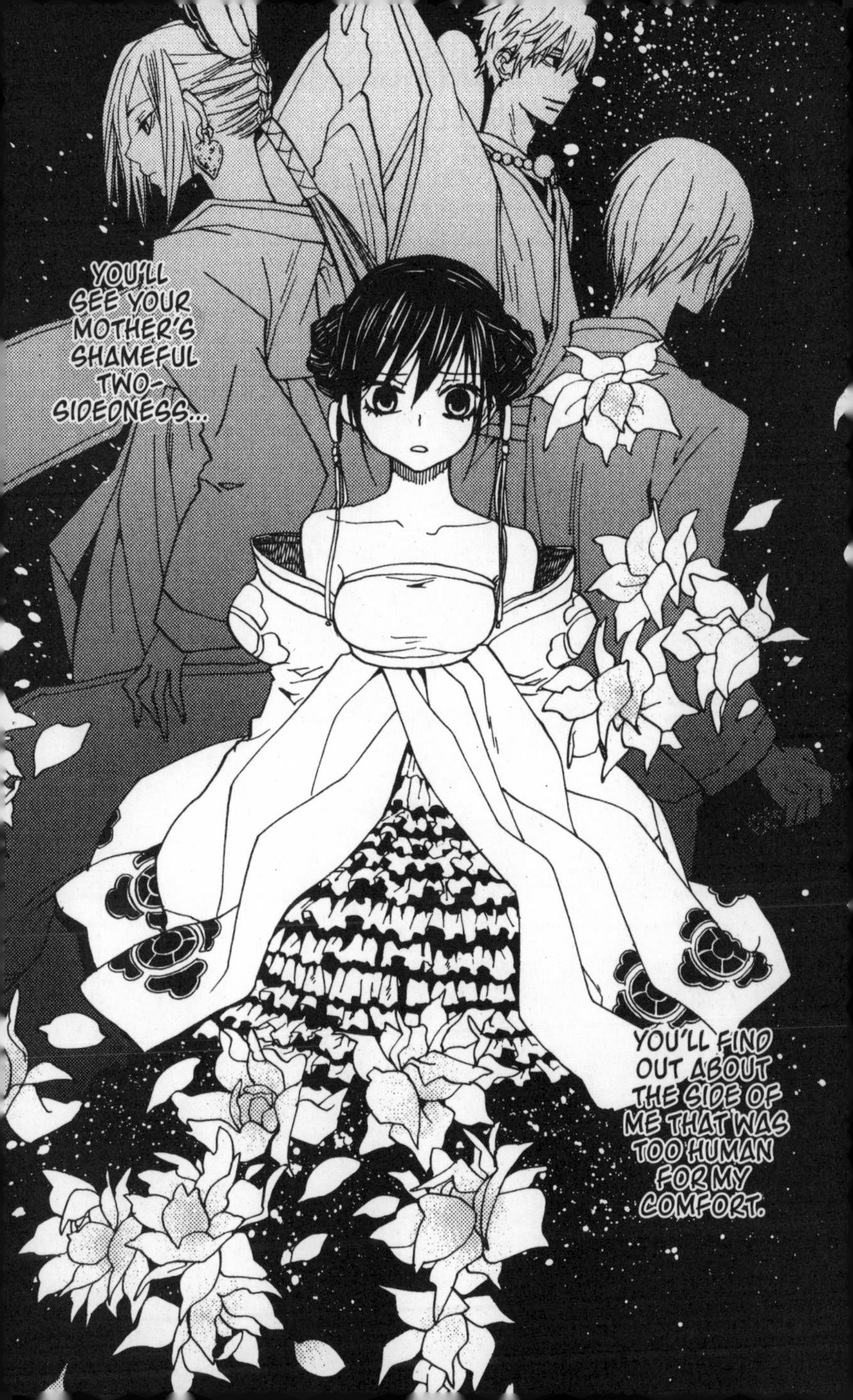
YOU'LL SEE YOUR MOTHER'S SHAMEFUL TWO-SIDEDNESS...
YOU'LL FIND OUT ABOUT THE SIDE OF ME THAT WAS TOO HUMAN FOR MY COMFORT.

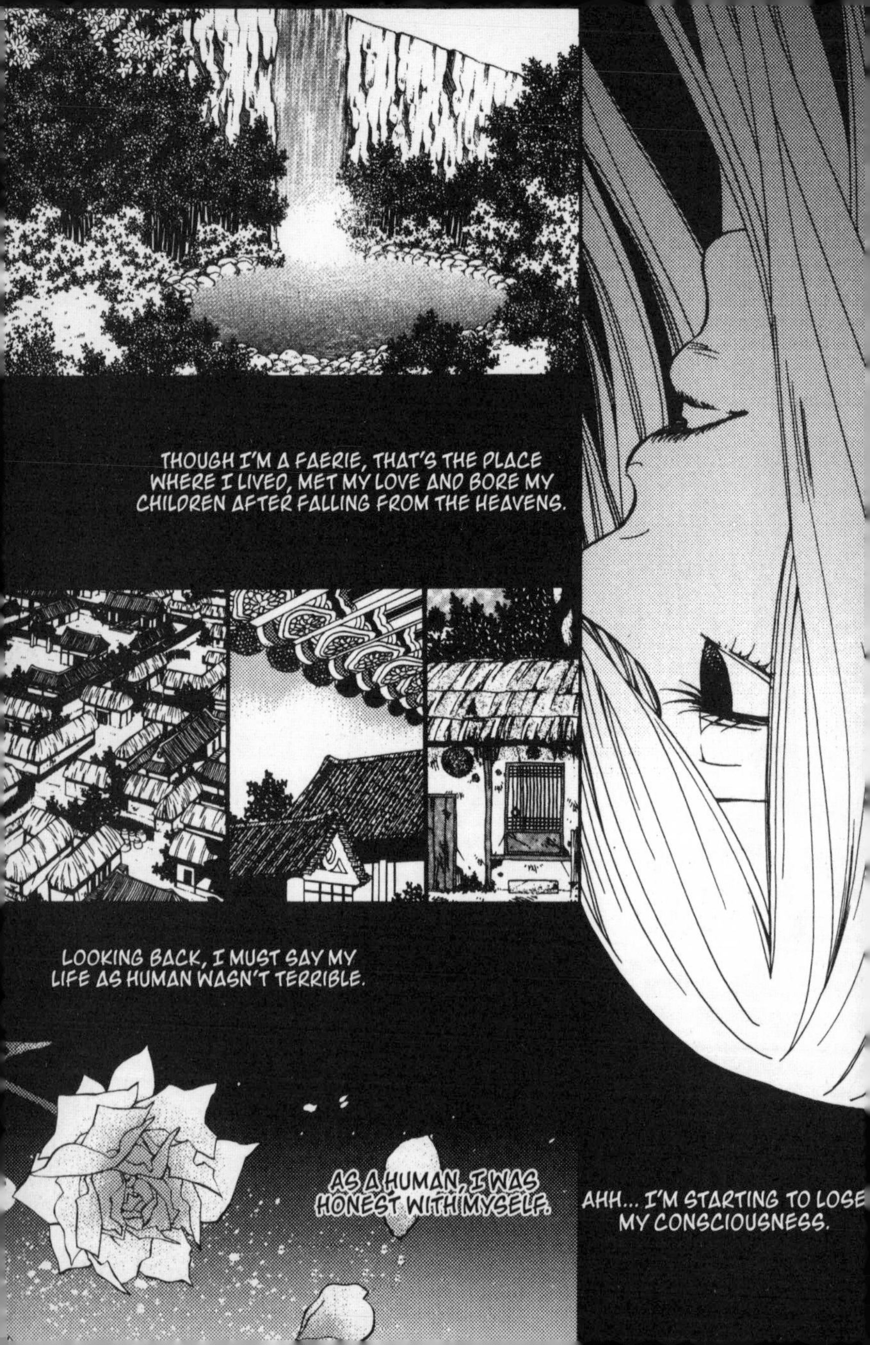
THOUGH I'M A FAERIE, THAT'S THE PLACE WHERE I LIVED, MET MY LOVE AND BORE MY CHILDREN AFTER FALLING FROM THE HEAVENS.
LOOKING BACK, I MUST SAY MY LIFE AS HUMAN WASN'T TERRIBLE.
AS A HUMAN, I WAS HONEST WITH MYSELF.
AHH... I'M STARTING TO LOSE MY CONSCIOUSNESS.

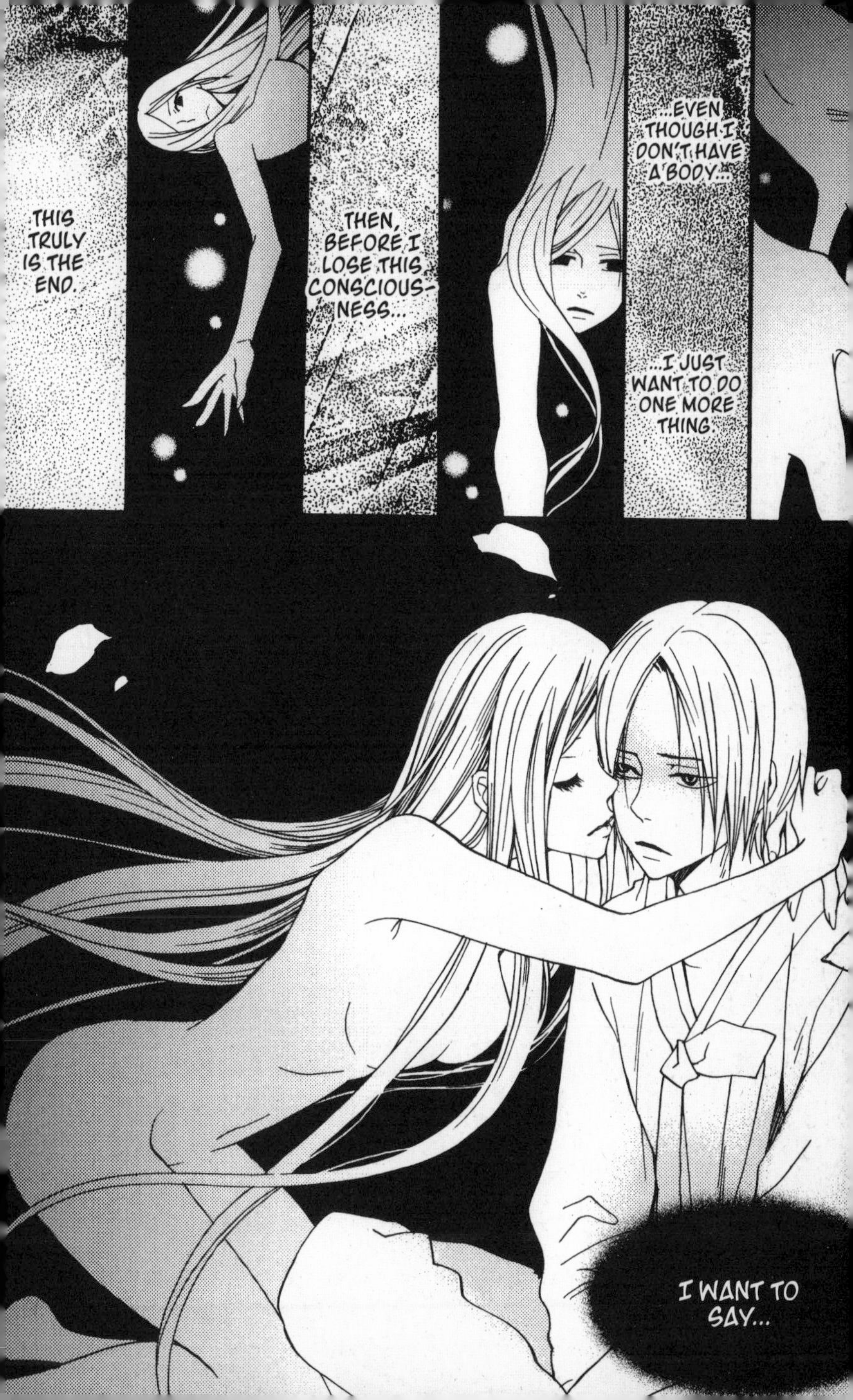
THIS TRULY IS THE END.
THEN, BEFORE I LOSE THIS CONSCIOUSNESS...
...EVEN THOUGH I DON'T HAVE A BODY...
...I JUST WANT TO DO ONE MORE THING.
I WANT TO SAY...

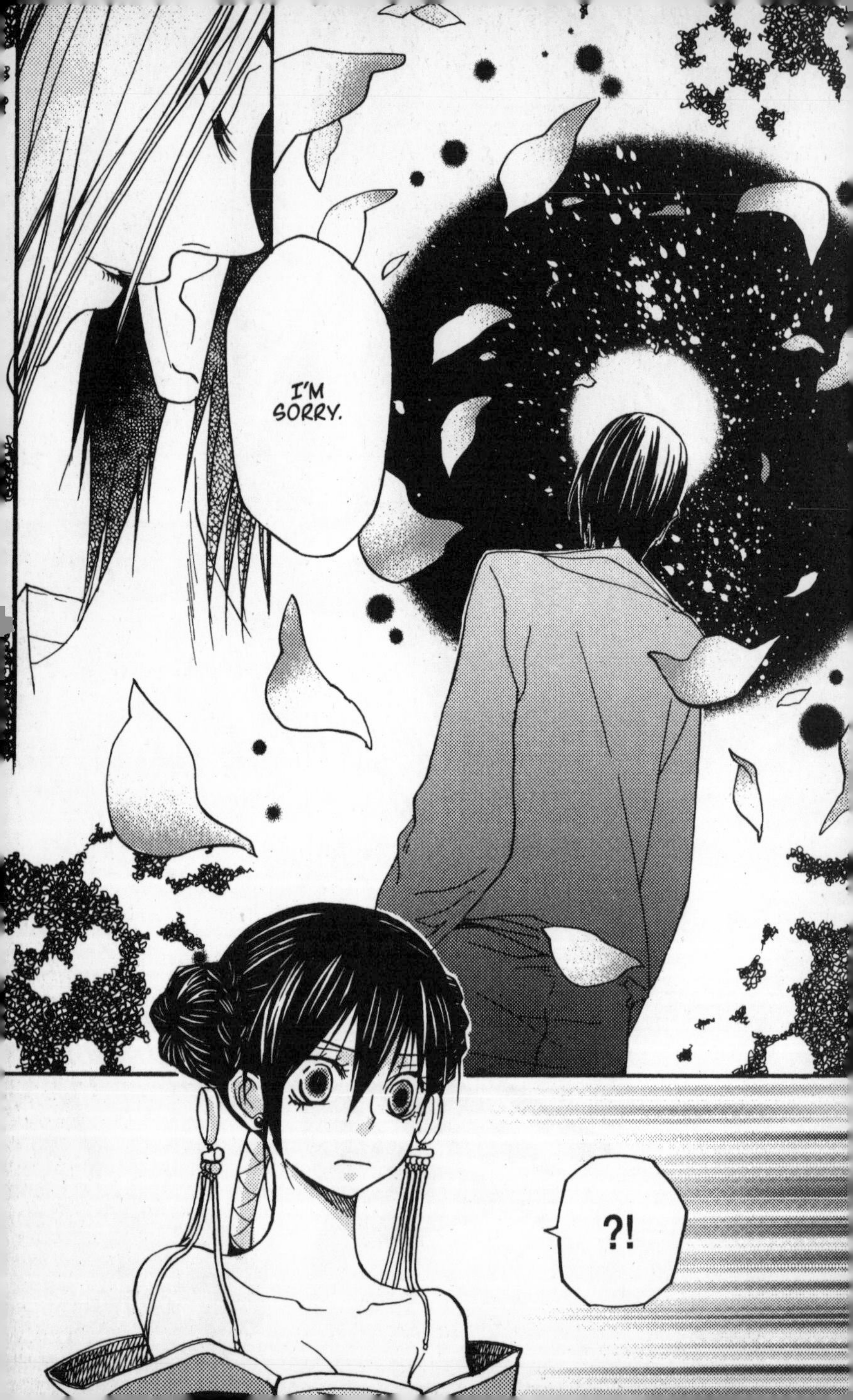
I'M SORRY.
?!

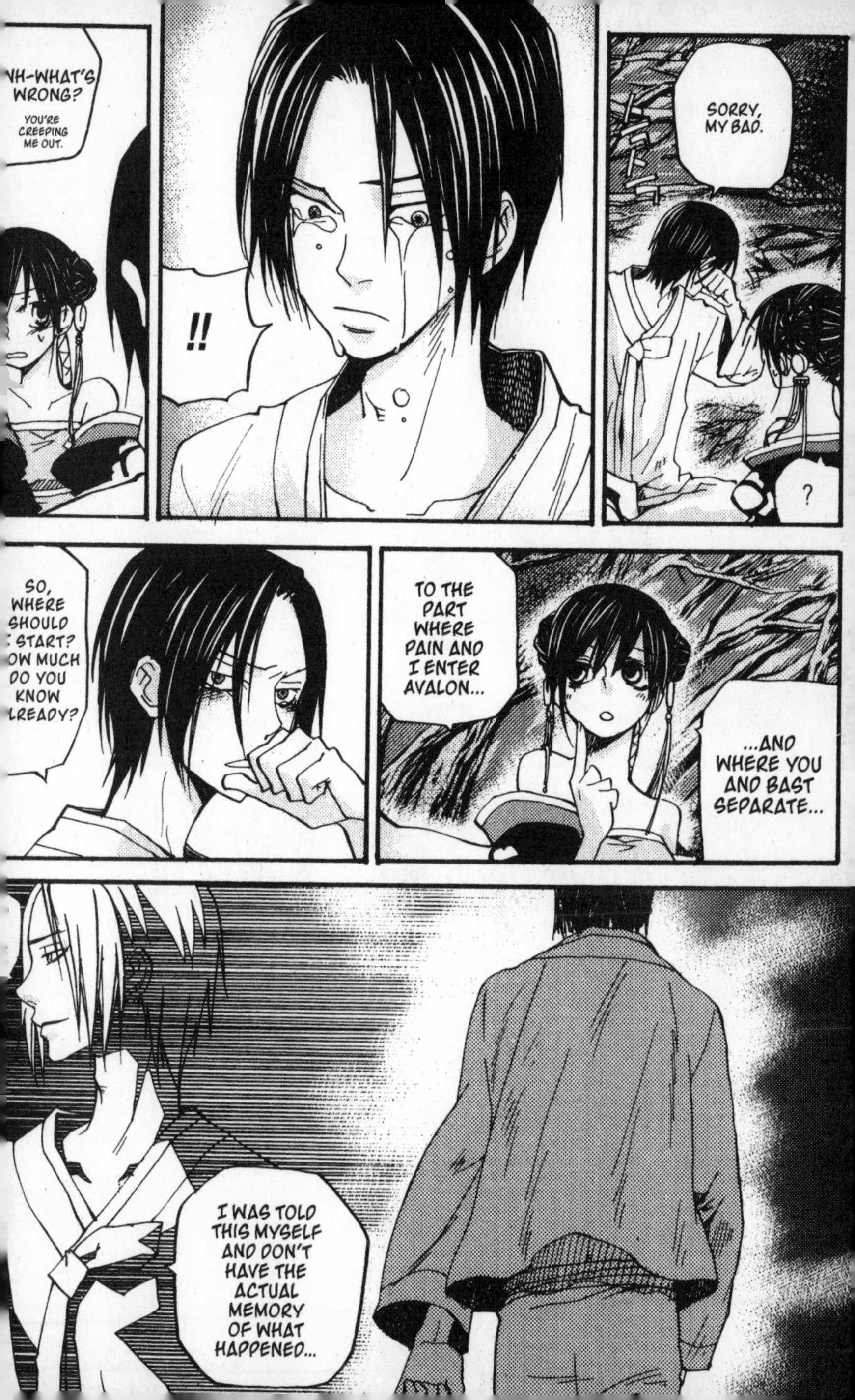

WH-WHAT'S WRONG?
YOU'RE CREEPING ME OUT.
!!
SORRY, MY BAD.
?
SO, WHERE SHOULD I START? HOW MUCH DO YOU KNOW ALREADY?
TO THE PART WHERE PAIN AND I ENTER AVALON...
...AND WHERE YOU AND BAST SEPARATE...
I WAS TOLD THIS MYSELF AND DON'T HAVE THE ACTUAL MEMORY OF WHAT HAPPENED...

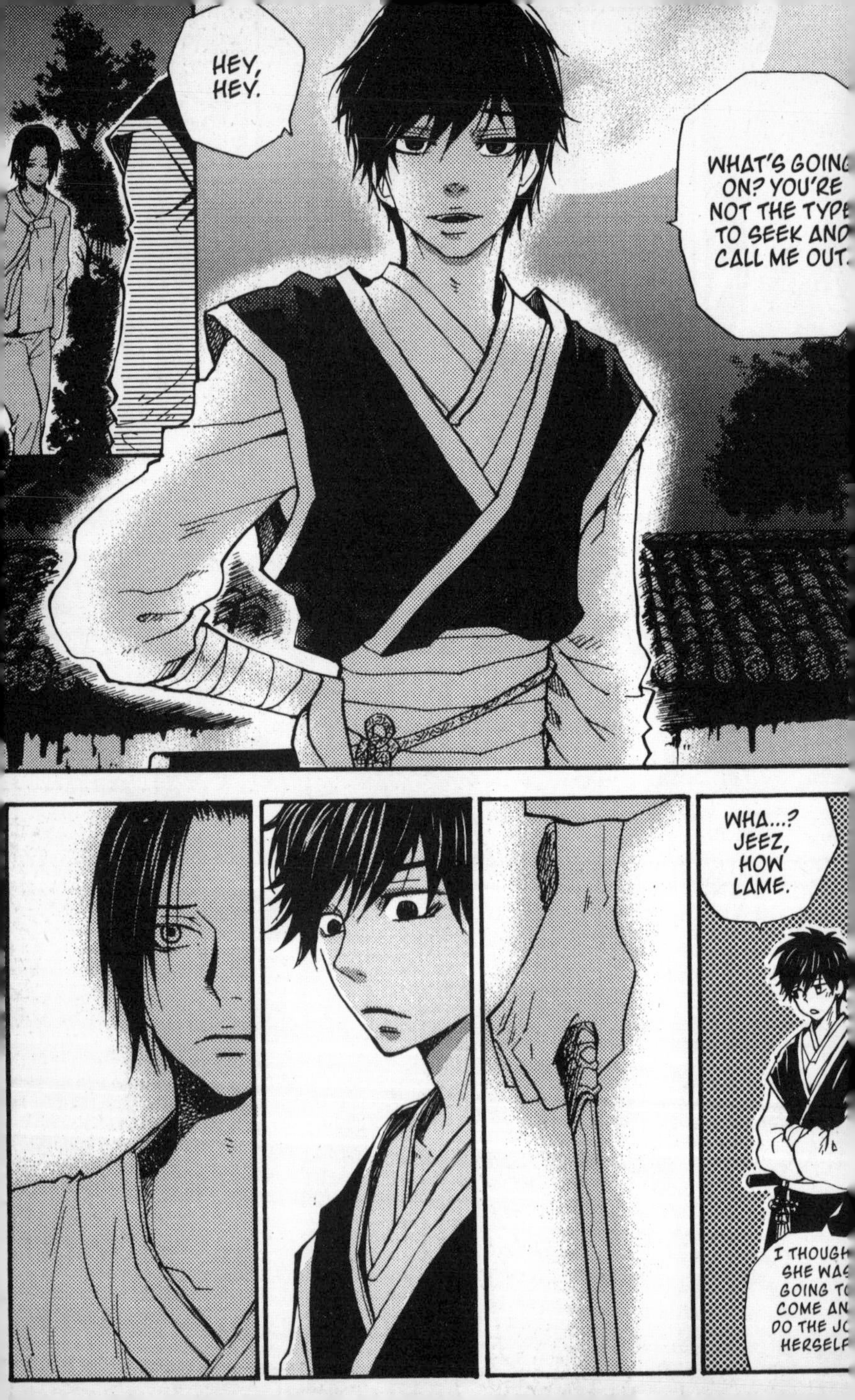
HEY, HEY.
WHAT'S GOIN ON? YOU'RE NOT THE TYPE TO SEEK AND CALL ME OUT.
WHA...? JEEZ, HOW LAME.
I THOUGH SHE WAS GOING TO COME AN DO THE JO HERSELF

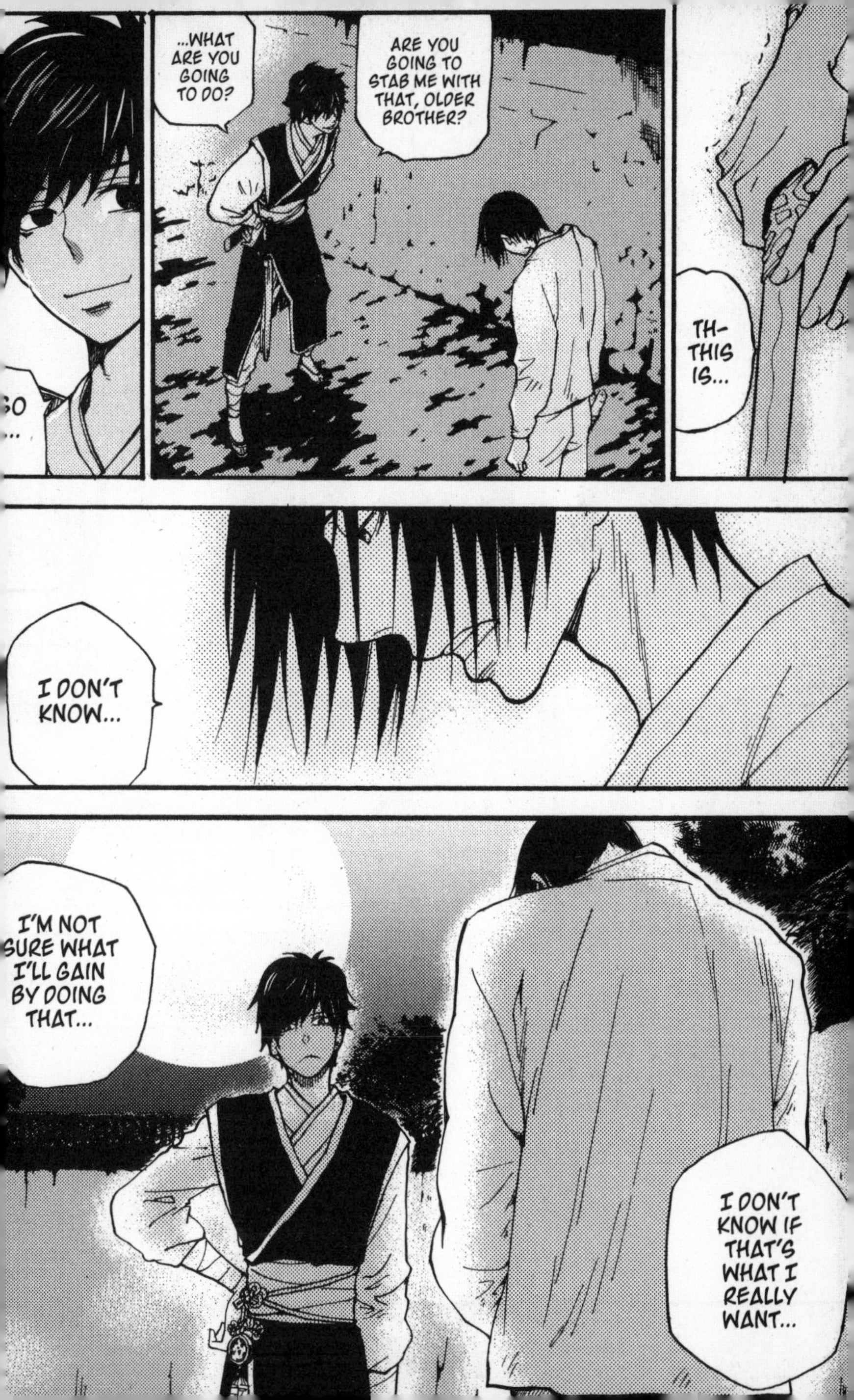
...WHAT ARE YOU GOING TO DO?
ARE YOU GOING TO STAB ME WITH THAT, OLDER BROTHER?
TH-THIS IS...
I DON'T KNOW...
I'M NOT SURE WHAT I'LL GAIN BY DOING THAT...
I DON'T KNOW IF THAT'S WHAT I REALLY WANT...

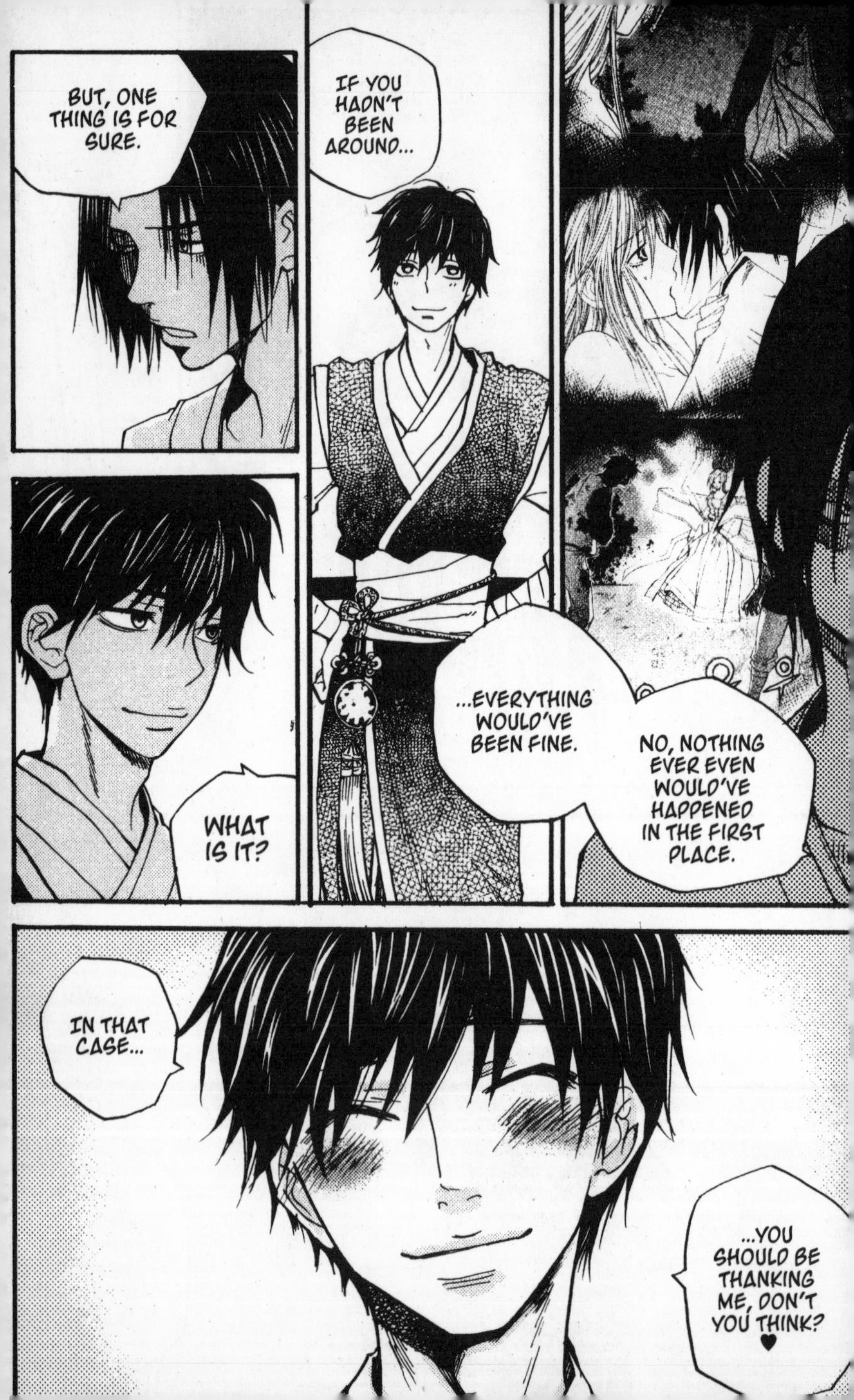
BUT, ONE THING IS FOR SURE.
WHAT IS IT?
IF YOU HADN'T BEEN AROUND...
...EVERYTHING WOULD'VE BEEN FINE.
NO, NOTHING EVER EVEN WOULD'VE HAPPENED IN THE FIRST PLACE.
IN THAT CASE...
...YOU SHOULD BE THANKING ME, DON'T YOU THINK? ♥

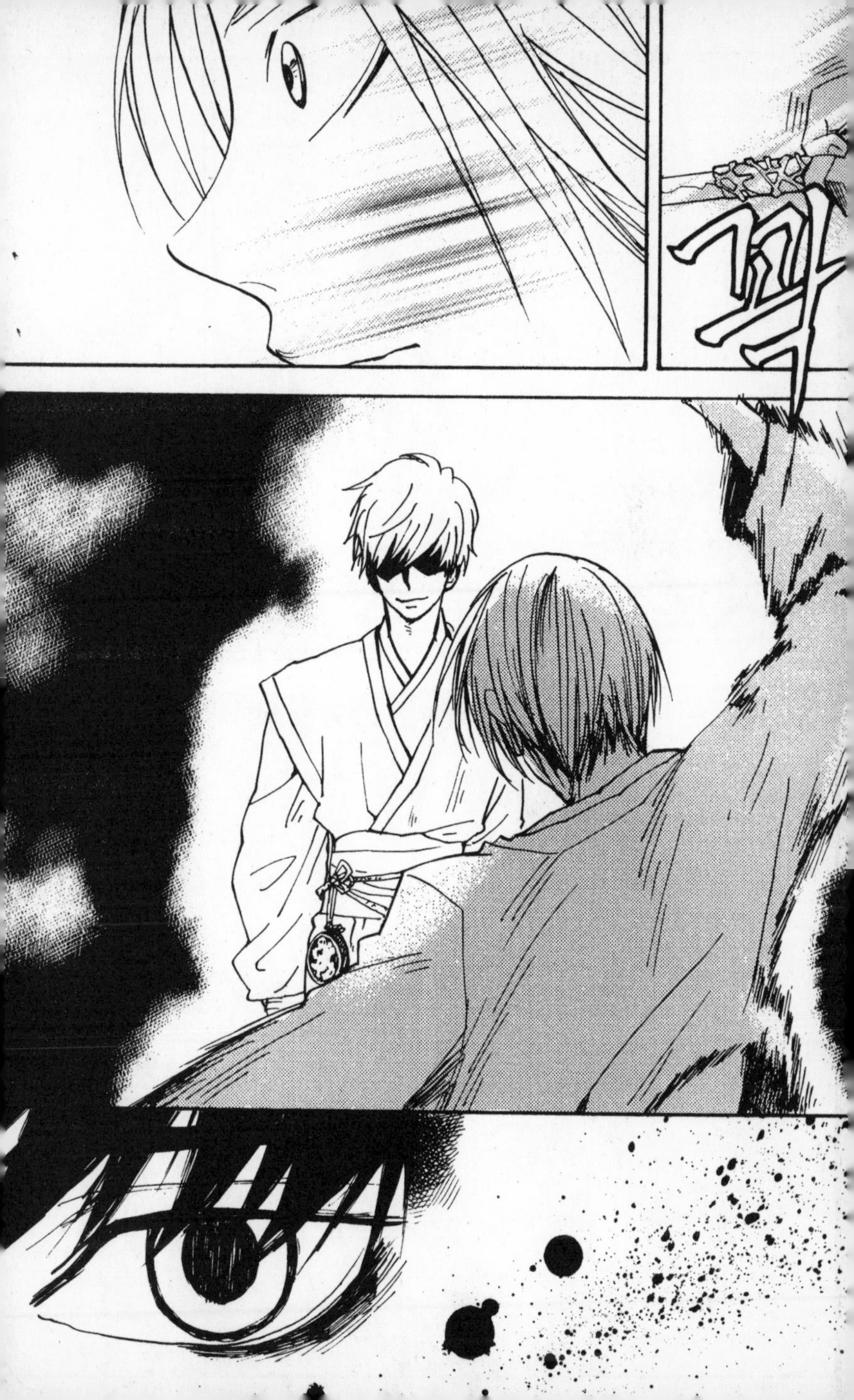
꽉

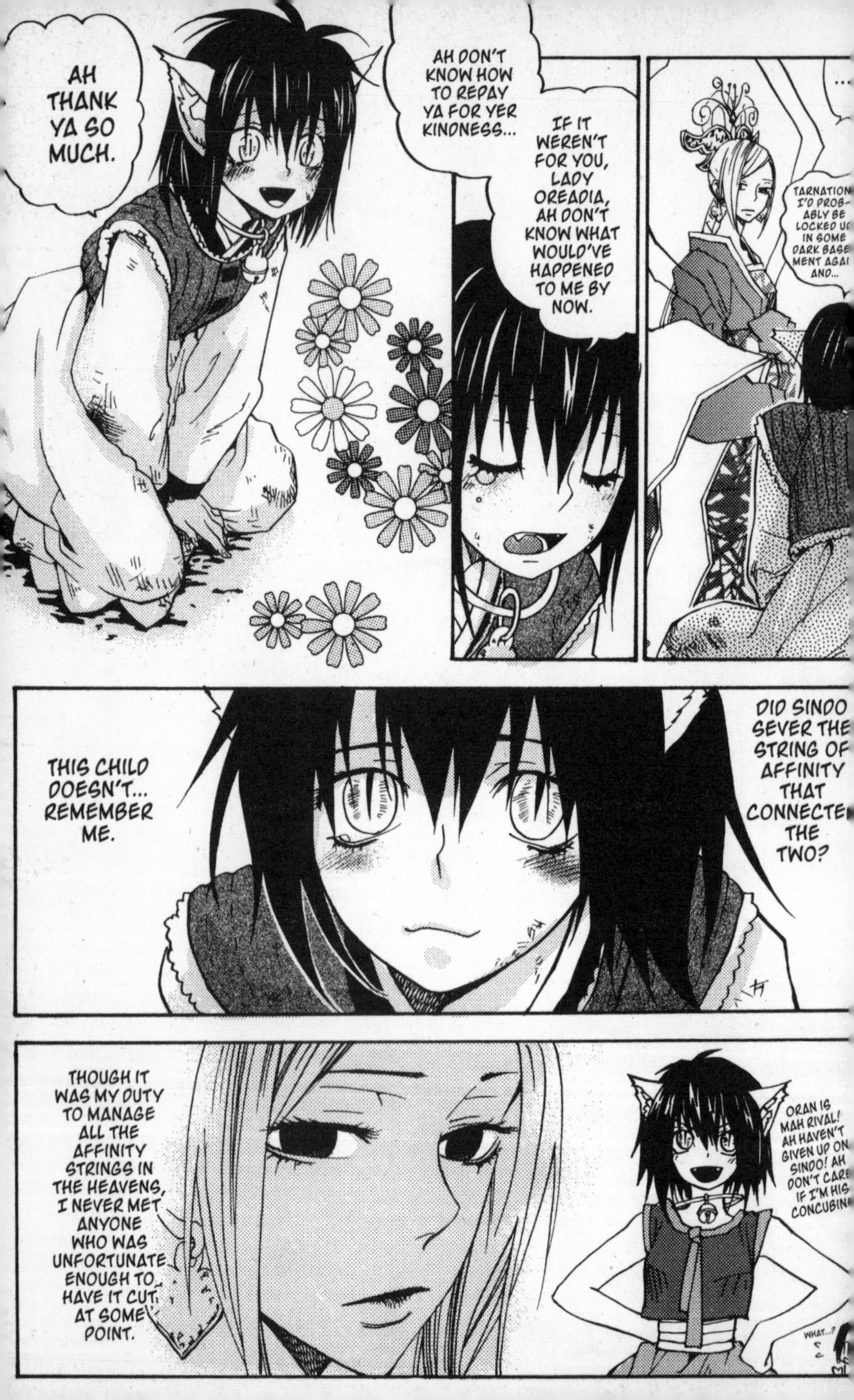
AH THANK YA SO MUCH.
AH DON'T KNOW HOW TO REPAY YA FOR YER KINDNESS...
IF IT WEREN'T FOR YOU, LADY OREADIA, AH DON'T KNOW WHAT WOULD'VE HAPPENED TO ME BY NOW.
...
TARNATION I'D PROBABLY BE LOCKED U IN SOME DARK BASE MENT AGAI AND...
THIS CHILD DOESN'T... REMEMBER ME.
DID SINDO SEVER THE STRING OF AFFINITY THAT CONNECTE THE TWO?
THOUGH IT WAS MY DUTY TO MANAGE ALL THE AFFINITY STRINGS IN THE HEAVENS, I NEVER MET ANYONE WHO WAS UNFORTUNATE ENOUGH TO HAVE IT CUT AT SOME POINT.
ORAN IS MAH RIVAL! AH HAVEN'T GIVEN UP ON SINDO! AH DON'T CARE IF I'M HIS CONCUBIN
WHAT...?

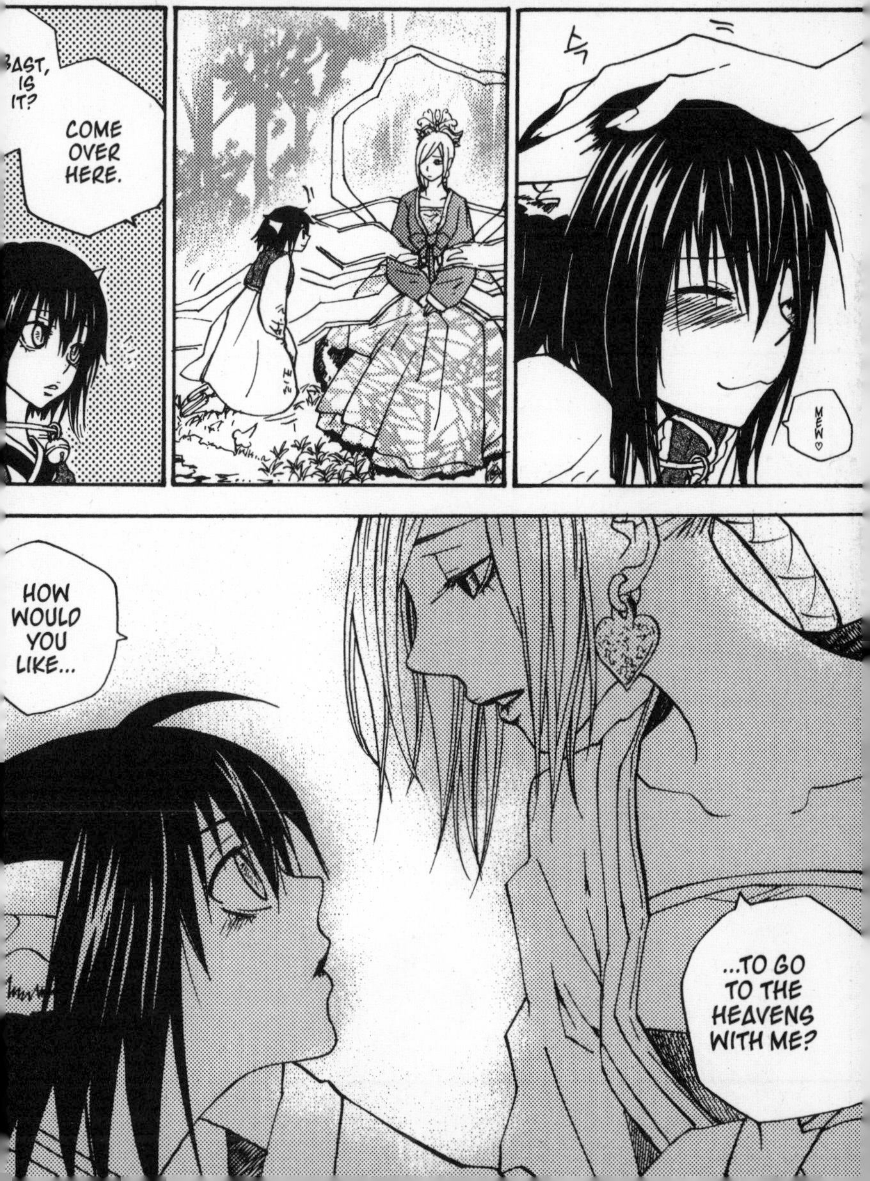
BAST, IS IT?
COME OVER HERE.
MEW♡
HOW WOULD YOU LIKE...
...TO GO TO THE HEAVENS WITH ME?

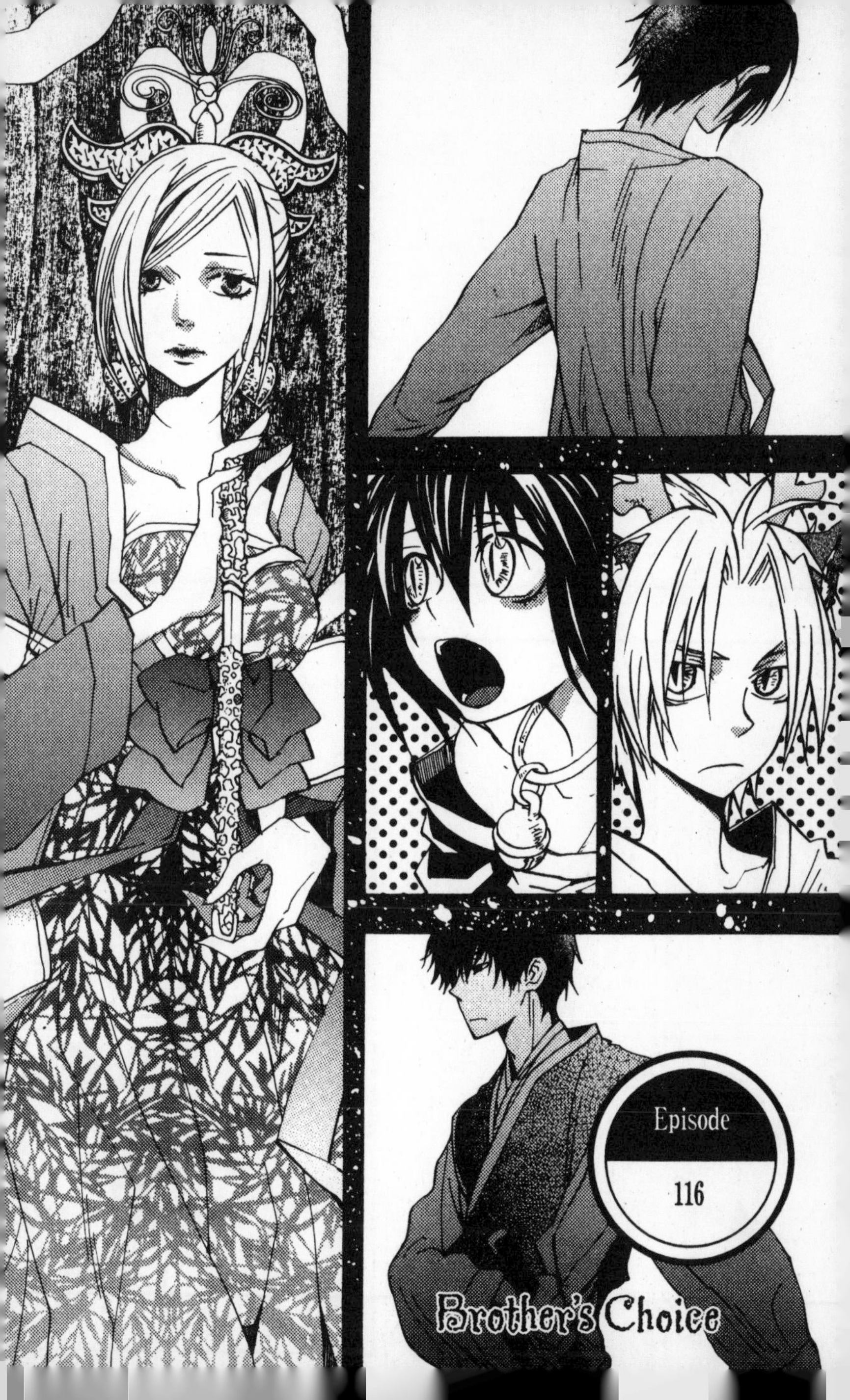
Episode
116
Brother's Choice

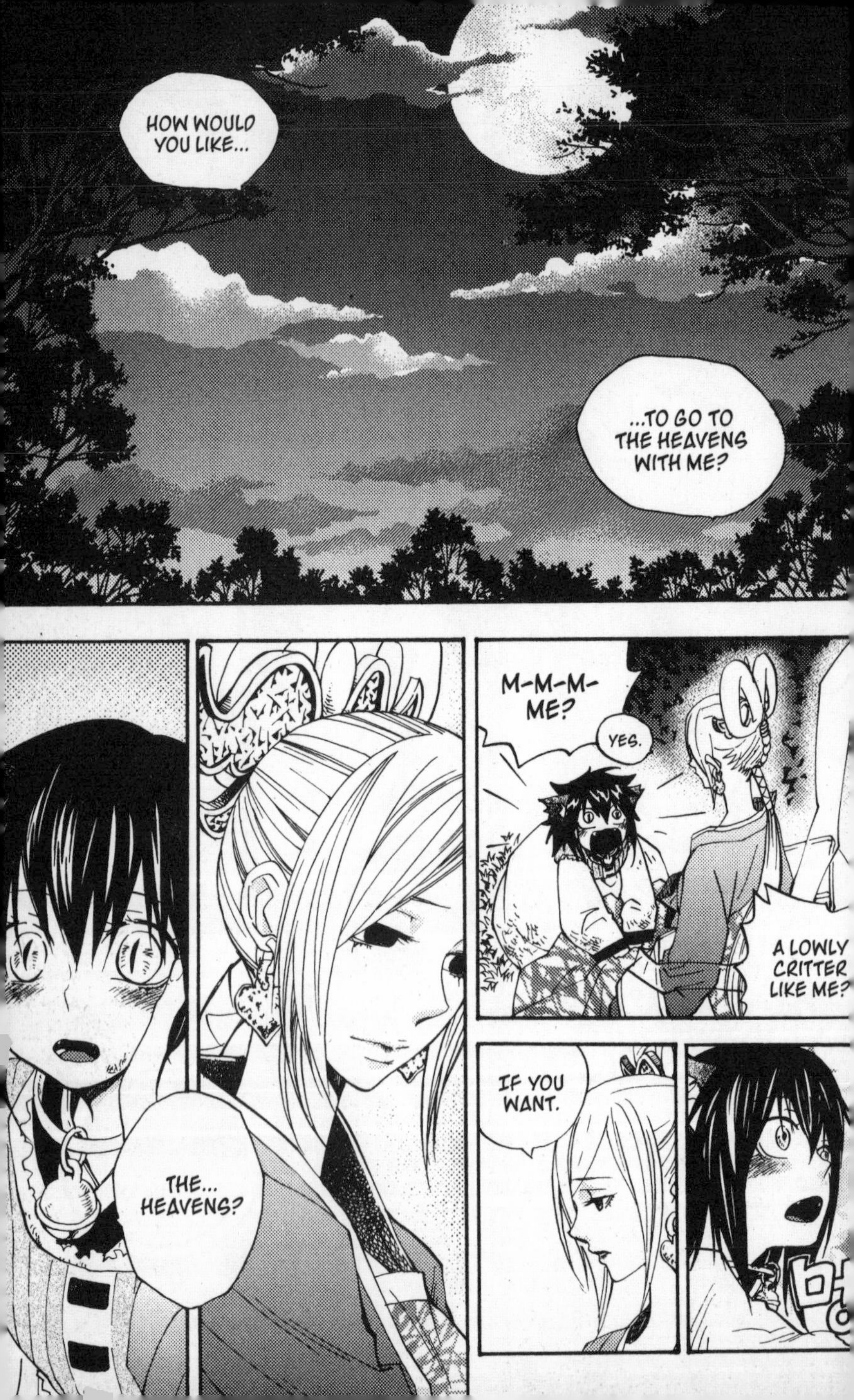
HOW WOULD YOU LIKE...
...TO GO TO THE HEAVENS WITH ME?
THE... HEAVENS?
M-M-M-ME?
YES.
A LOWLY CRITTER LIKE ME?
IF YOU WANT.

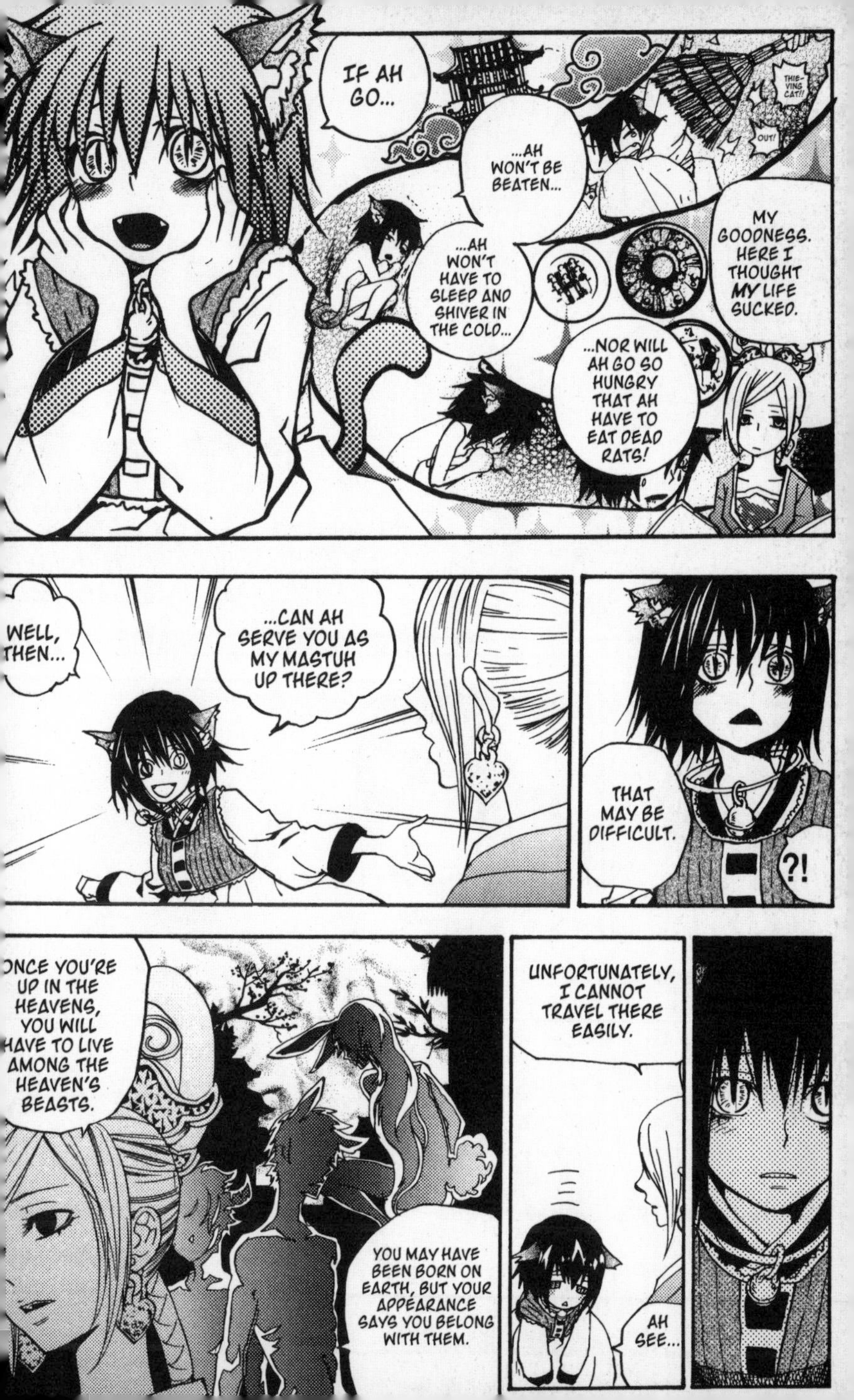
IF AH GO...
...AH WON'T BE BEATEN...
THIE-VING CAT!!
OUT!
...AH WON'T HAVE TO SLEEP AND SHIVER IN THE COLD...
MY GOODNESS. HERE I THOUGHT MY LIFE SUCKED.
...NOR WILL AH GO SO HUNGRY THAT AH HAVE TO EAT DEAD RATS!
WELL, THEN...
...CAN AH SERVE YOU AS MY MASTUH UP THERE?
THAT MAY BE DIFFICULT.
?!
ONCE YOU'RE UP IN THE HEAVENS, YOU WILL HAVE TO LIVE AMONG THE HEAVEN'S BEASTS.
YOU MAY HAVE BEEN BORN ON EARTH, BUT YOUR APPEARANCE SAYS YOU BELONG WITH THEM.
UNFORTUNATELY, I CANNOT TRAVEL THERE EASILY.
AH SEE...

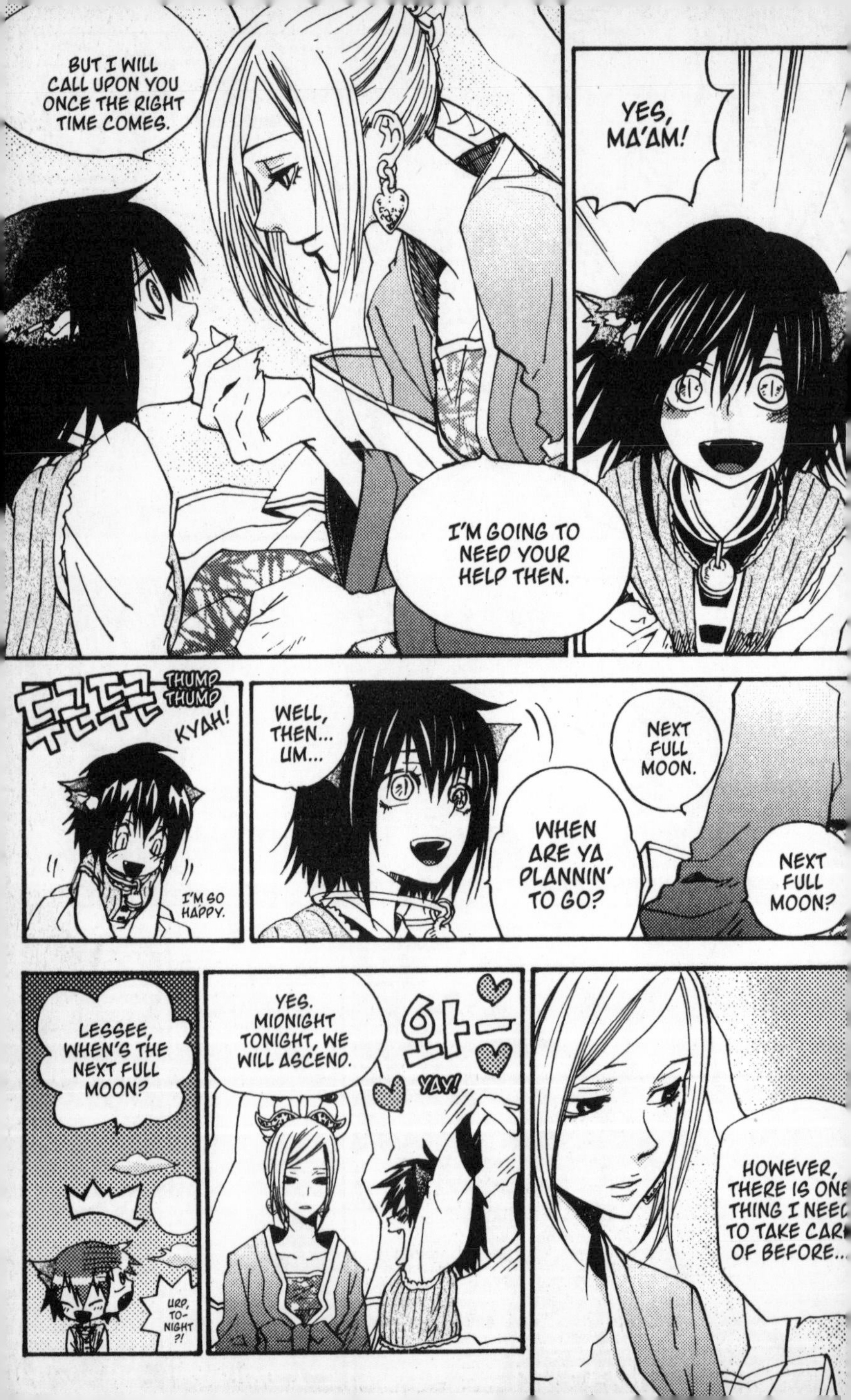

BUT I WILL CALL UPON YOU ONCE THE RIGHT TIME COMES.
I'M GOING TO NEED YOUR HELP THEN.
YES, MA'AM!
두근두근
THUMP THUMP
KYAH!
I'M SO HAPPY.
WELL, THEN... UM...
WHEN ARE YA PLANNIN' TO GO?
NEXT FULL MOON.
NEXT FULL MOON?
LESSEE, WHEN'S THE NEXT FULL MOON?
URP, TO-NIGHT?!
YES. MIDNIGHT TONIGHT, WE WILL ASCEND.
와-
YAY!
HOWEVER, THERE IS ONE THING I NEED TO TAKE CAR OF BEFORE...

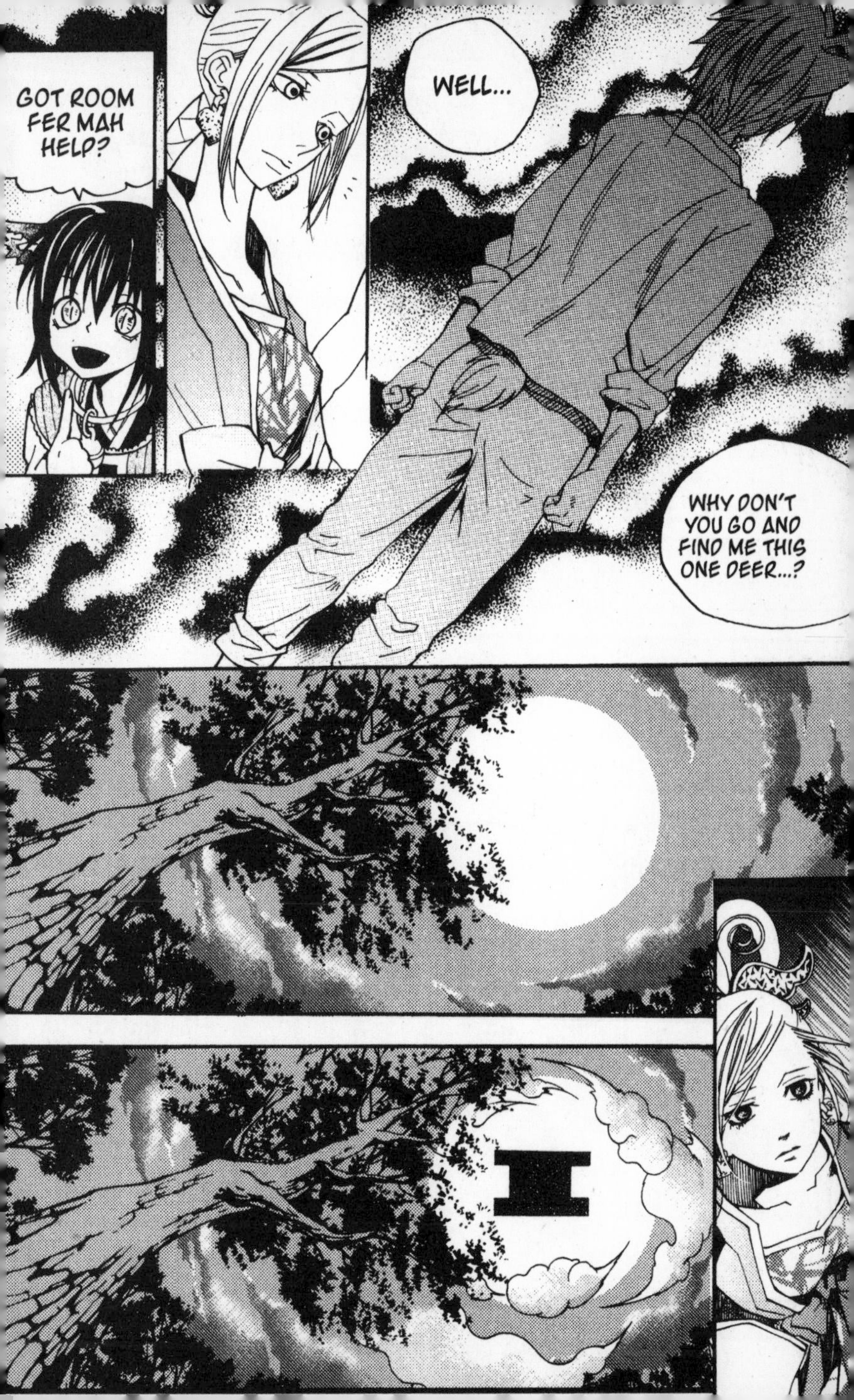
GOT ROOM FER MAH HELP?
WELL...
WHY DON'T YOU GO AND FIND ME THIS ONE DEER...?

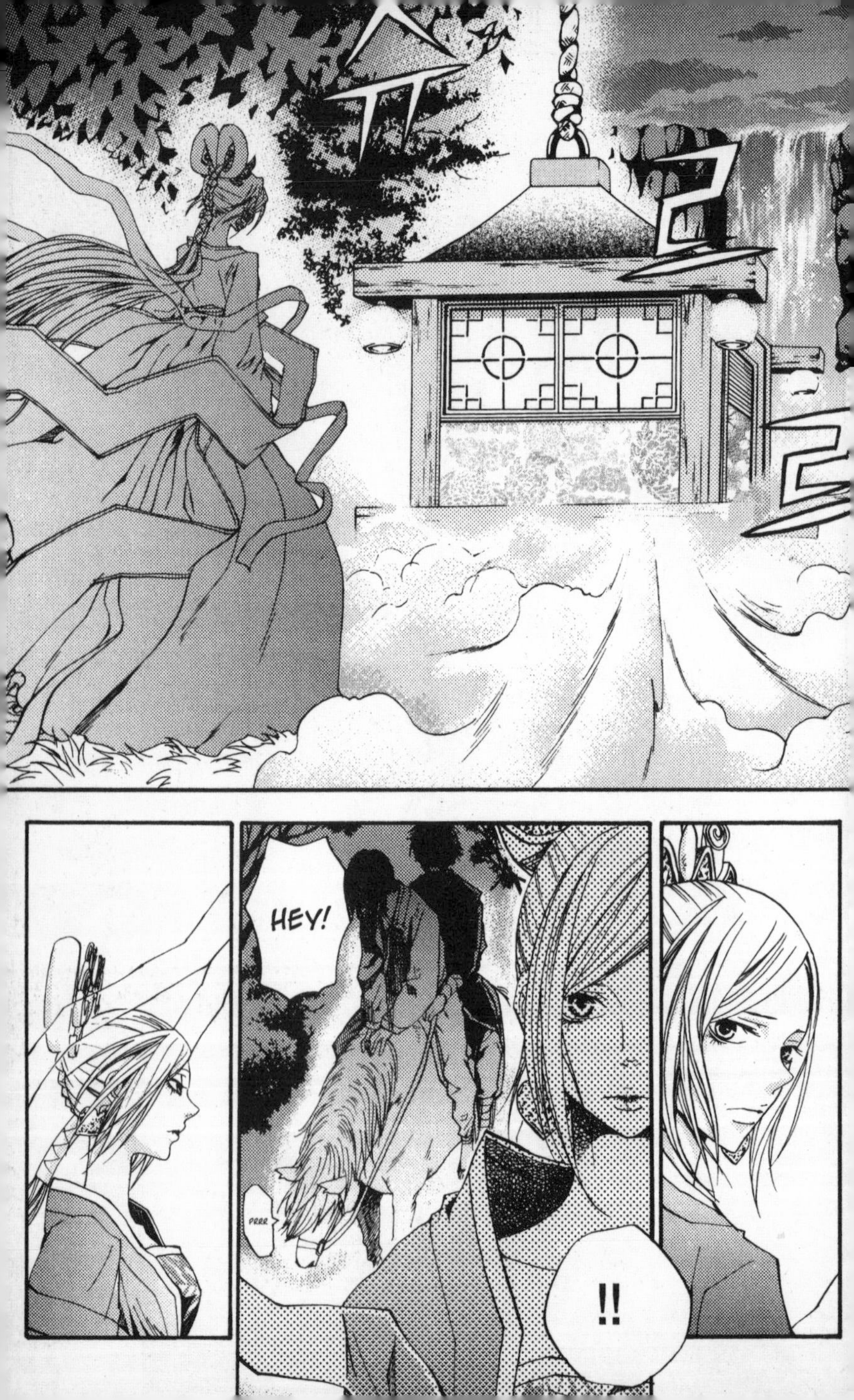
HEY!
PRRR
!!

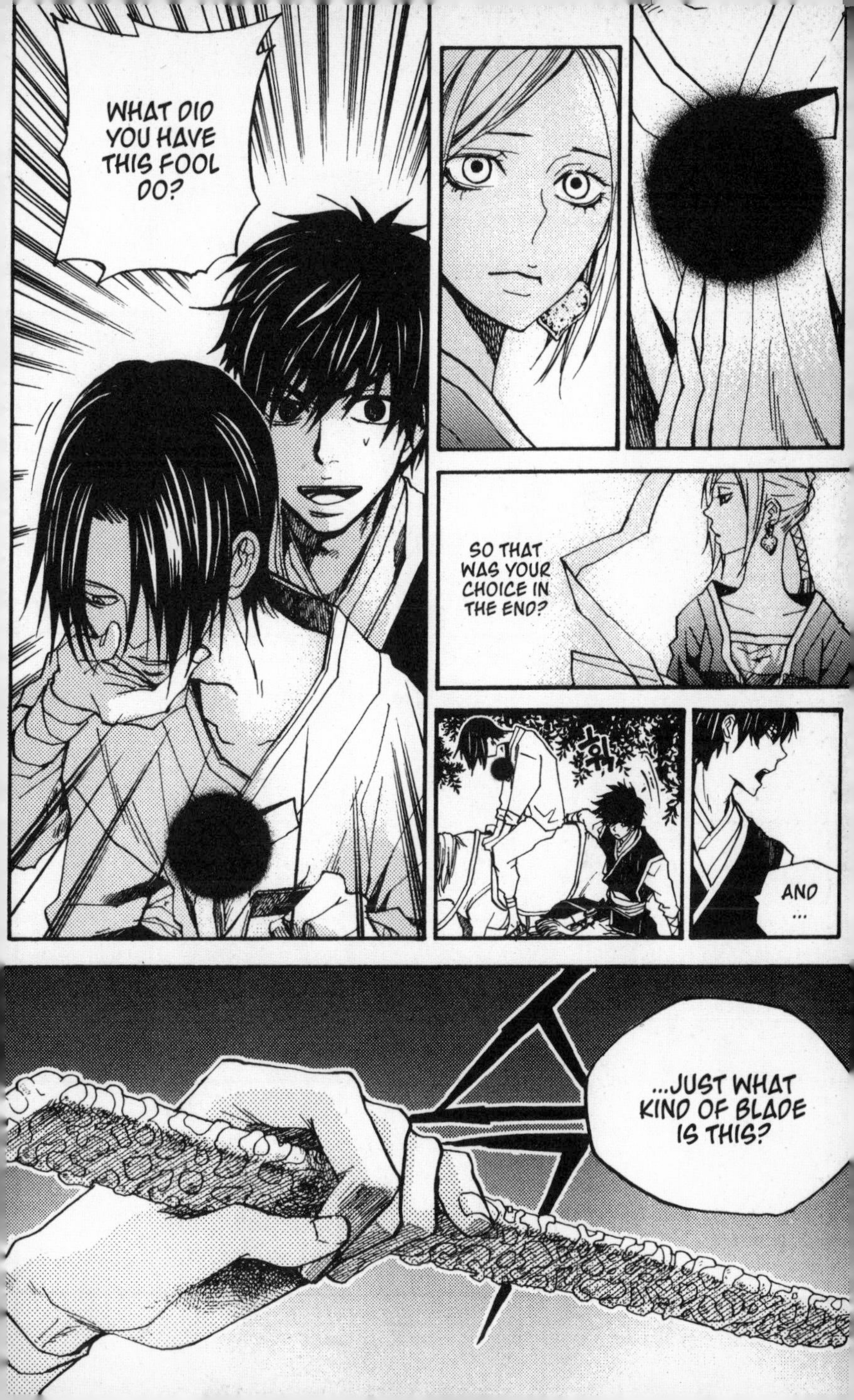
WHAT DID YOU HAVE THIS FOOL DO?
SO THAT WAS YOUR CHOICE IN THE END?
AND ...
...JUST WHAT KIND OF BLADE IS THIS?

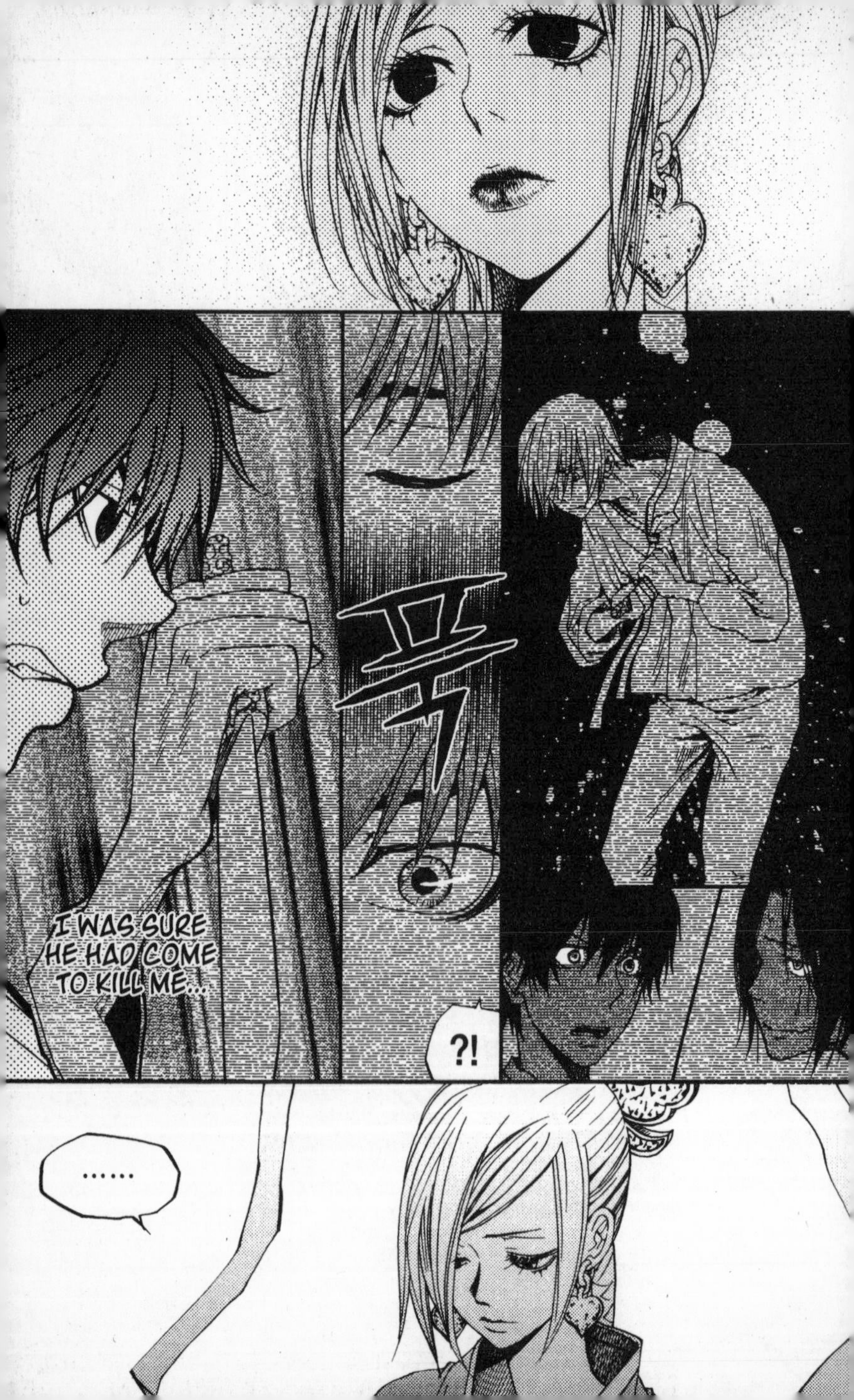
I WAS SURE HE HAD COME TO KILL ME...
푹
?!
......

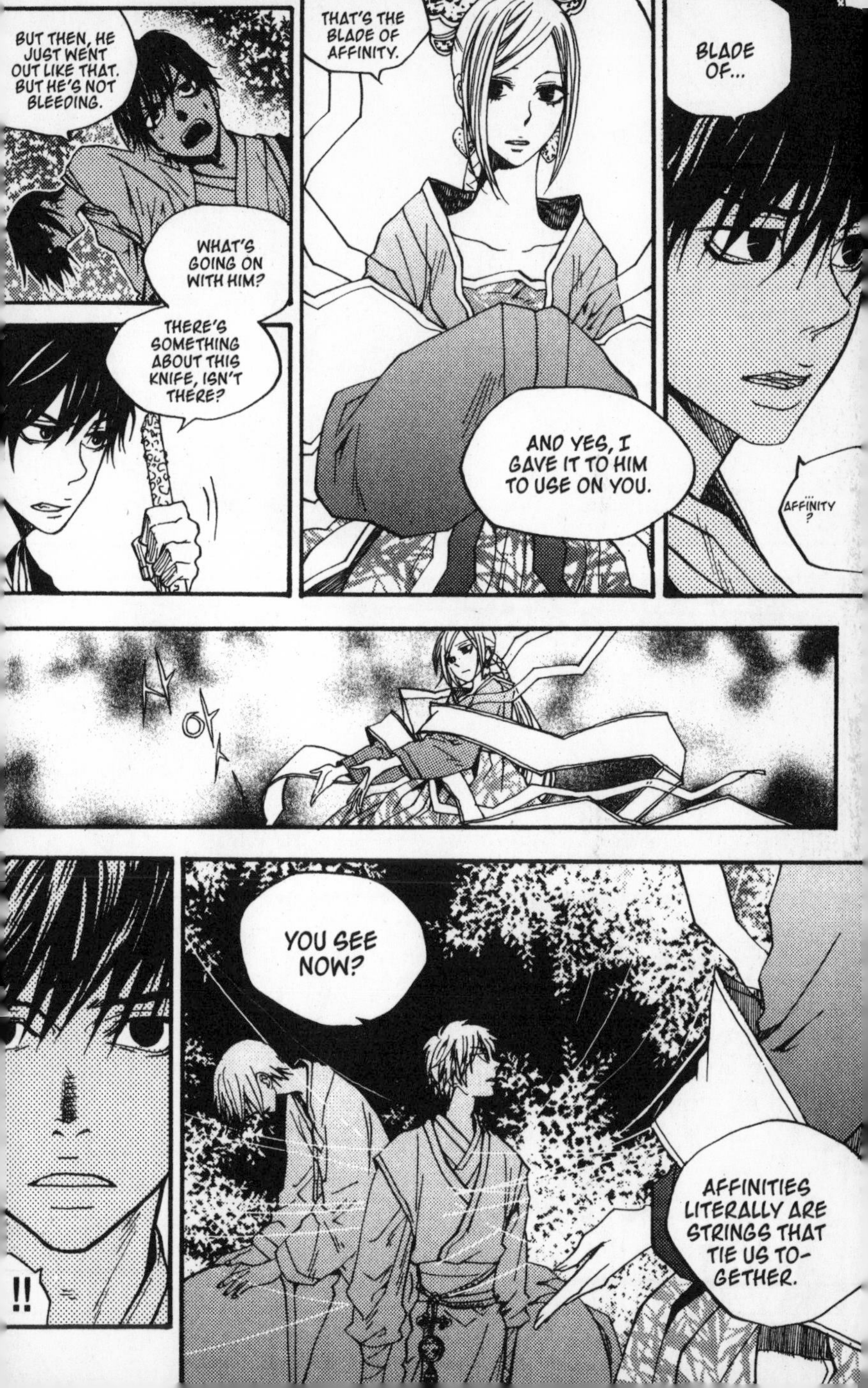
BUT THEN, HE JUST WENT OUT LIKE THAT. BUT HE'S NOT BLEEDING.
WHAT'S GOING ON WITH HIM?
THERE'S SOMETHING ABOUT THIS KNIFE, ISN'T THERE?
THAT'S THE BLADE OF AFFINITY.
AND YES, I GAVE IT TO HIM TO USE ON YOU.
BLADE OF...
...AFFINITY?
!!
YOU SEE NOW?
AFFINITIES LITERALLY ARE STRINGS THAT TIE US TO-GETHER.

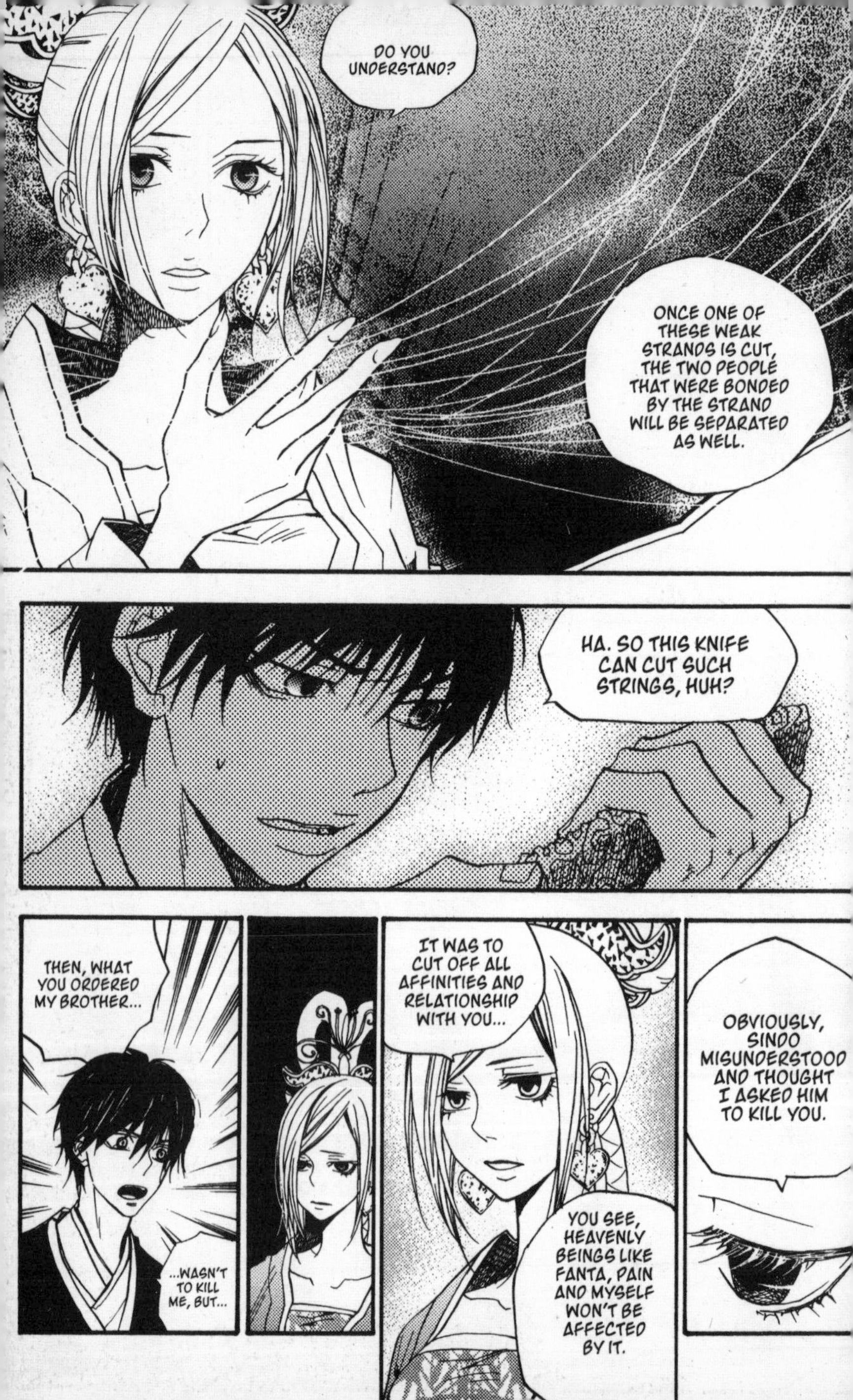
DO YOU UNDERSTAND?
ONCE ONE OF THESE WEAK STRANDS IS CUT, THE TWO PEOPLE THAT WERE BONDED BY THE STRAND WILL BE SEPARATED AS WELL.
HA. SO THIS KNIFE CAN CUT SUCH STRINGS, HUH?
THEN, WHAT YOU ORDERED MY BROTHER...
...WASN'T TO KILL ME, BUT...
IT WAS TO CUT OFF ALL AFFINITIES AND RELATIONSHIP WITH YOU...
YOU SEE, HEAVENLY BEINGS LIKE FANTA, PAIN AND MYSELF WON'T BE AFFECTED BY IT.
OBVIOUSLY, SINDO MISUNDERSTOOD AND THOUGHT I ASKED HIM TO KILL YOU.

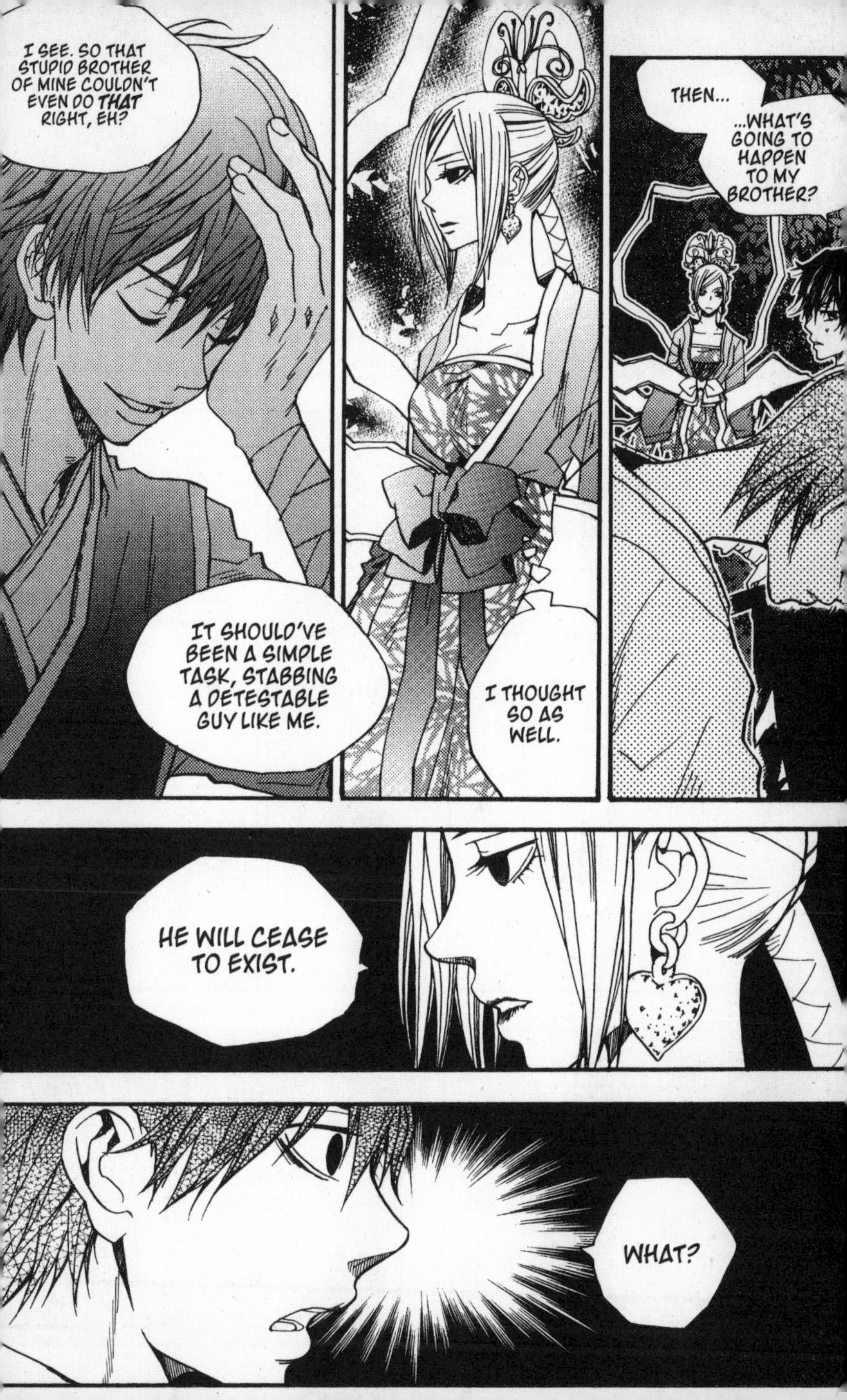
I SEE. SO THAT STUPID BROTHER OF MINE COULDN'T EVEN DO **THAT** RIGHT, EH?
IT SHOULD'VE BEEN A SIMPLE TASK, STABBING A DETESTABLE GUY LIKE ME.
I THOUGHT SO AS WELL.
THEN...
...WHAT'S GOING TO HAPPEN TO MY BROTHER?
HE WILL CEASE TO EXIST.
WHAT?

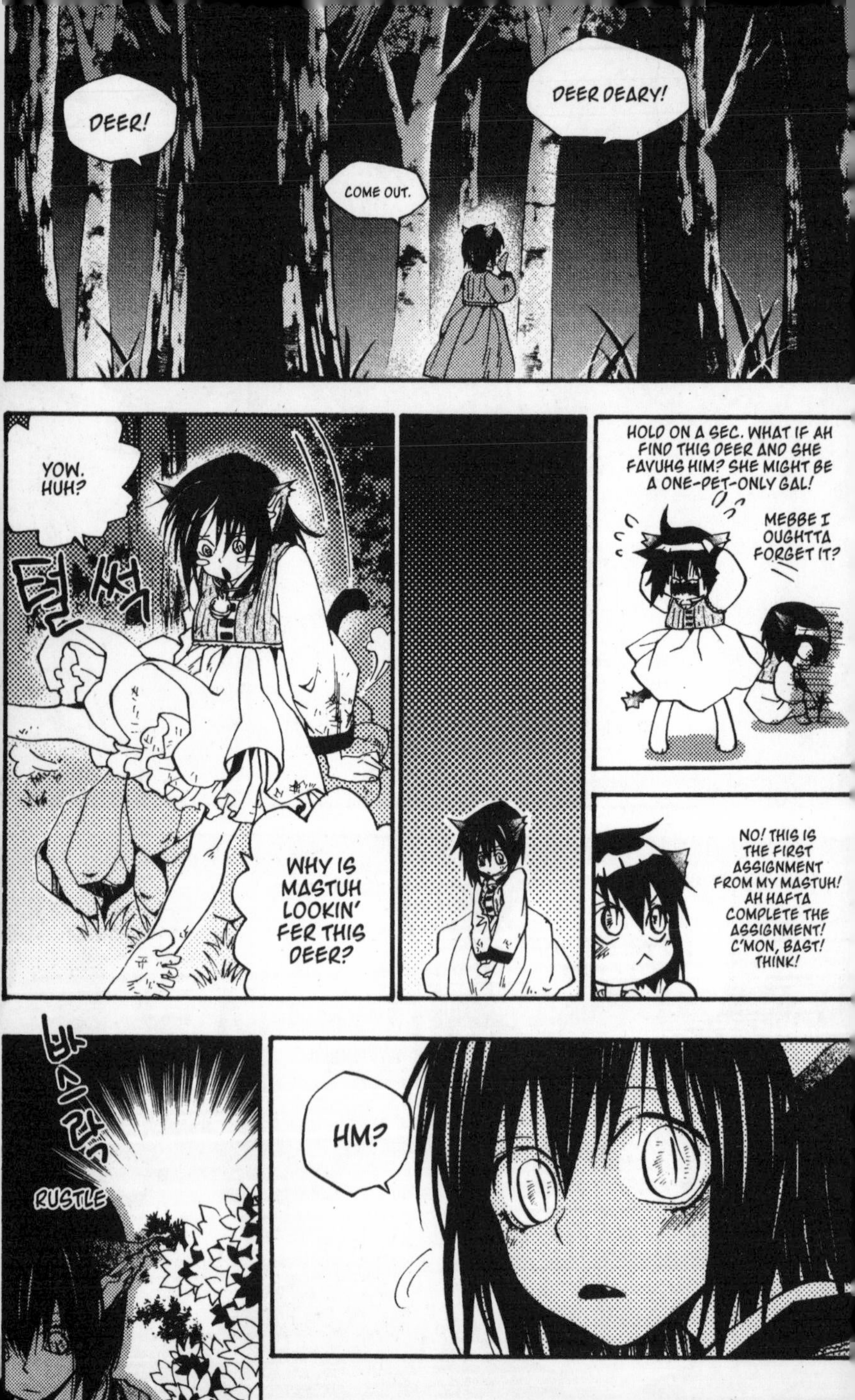
DEER!
COME OUT.
DEER DEARY!
YOW. HUH?
털썩
WHY IS MASTUH LOOKIN' FER THIS DEER?
HOLD ON A SEC. WHAT IF AH FIND THIS DEER AND SHE FAVUHS HIM? SHE MIGHT BE A ONE-PET-ONLY GAL!
MEBBE I OUGHTTA FORGET IT?
NO! THIS IS THE FIRST ASSIGNMENT FROM MY MASTUH! AH HAFTA COMPLETE THE ASSIGNMENT! C'MON, BAST! THINK!
바스락
RUSTLE
HM?

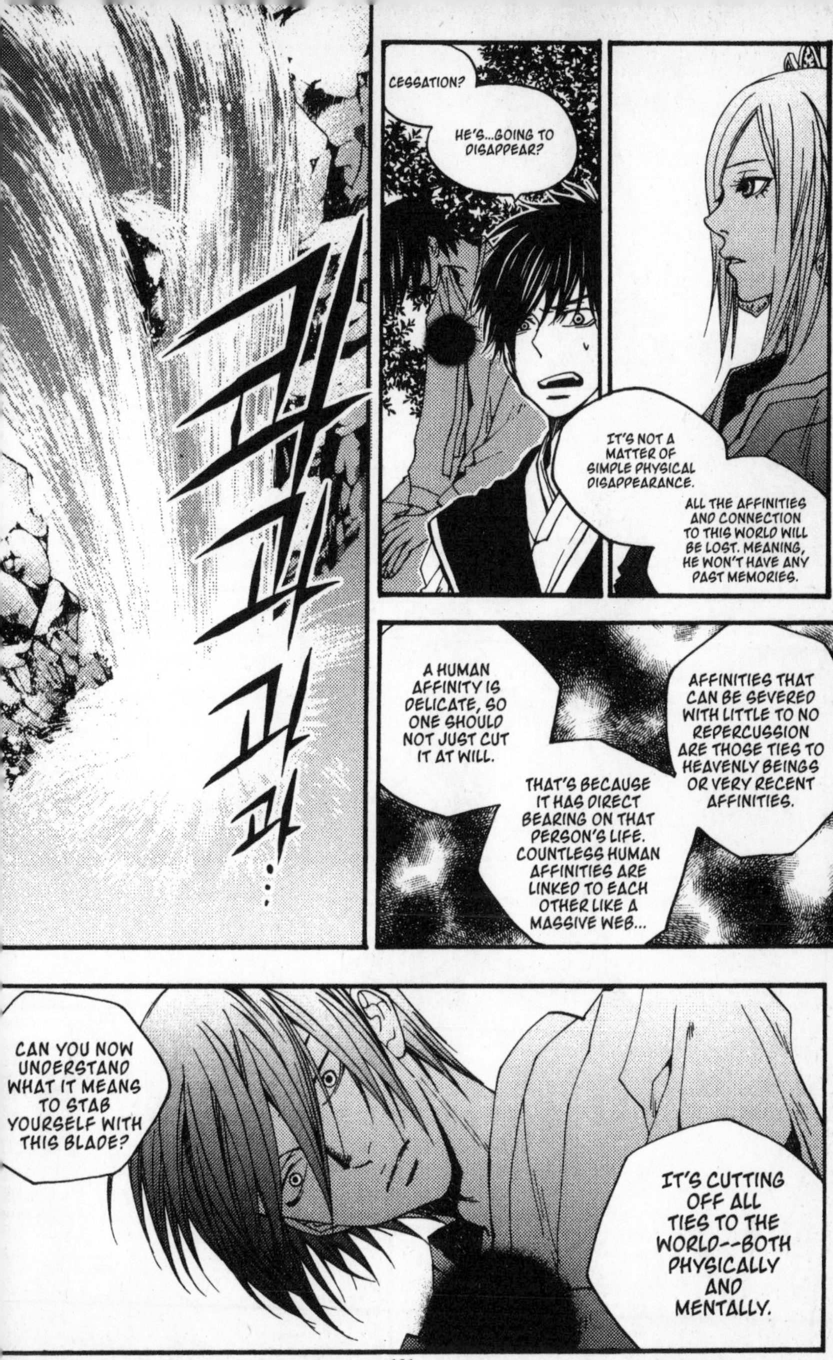
콰콰과과...
CESSATION?
HE'S...GOING TO DISAPPEAR?
IT'S NOT A MATTER OF SIMPLE PHYSICAL DISAPPEARANCE.
ALL THE AFFINITIES AND CONNECTION TO THIS WORLD WILL BE LOST. MEANING, HE WON'T HAVE ANY PAST MEMORIES.
A HUMAN AFFINITY IS DELICATE, SO ONE SHOULD NOT JUST CUT IT AT WILL.
THAT'S BECAUSE IT HAS DIRECT BEARING ON THAT PERSON'S LIFE. COUNTLESS HUMAN AFFINITIES ARE LINKED TO EACH OTHER LIKE A MASSIVE WEB...
AFFINITIES THAT CAN BE SEVERED WITH LITTLE TO NO REPERCUSSION ARE THOSE TIES TO HEAVENLY BEINGS OR VERY RECENT AFFINITIES.
CAN YOU NOW UNDERSTAND WHAT IT MEANS TO STAB YOURSELF WITH THIS BLADE?
IT'S CUTTING OFF ALL TIES TO THE WORLD--BOTH PHYSICALLY AND MENTALLY.

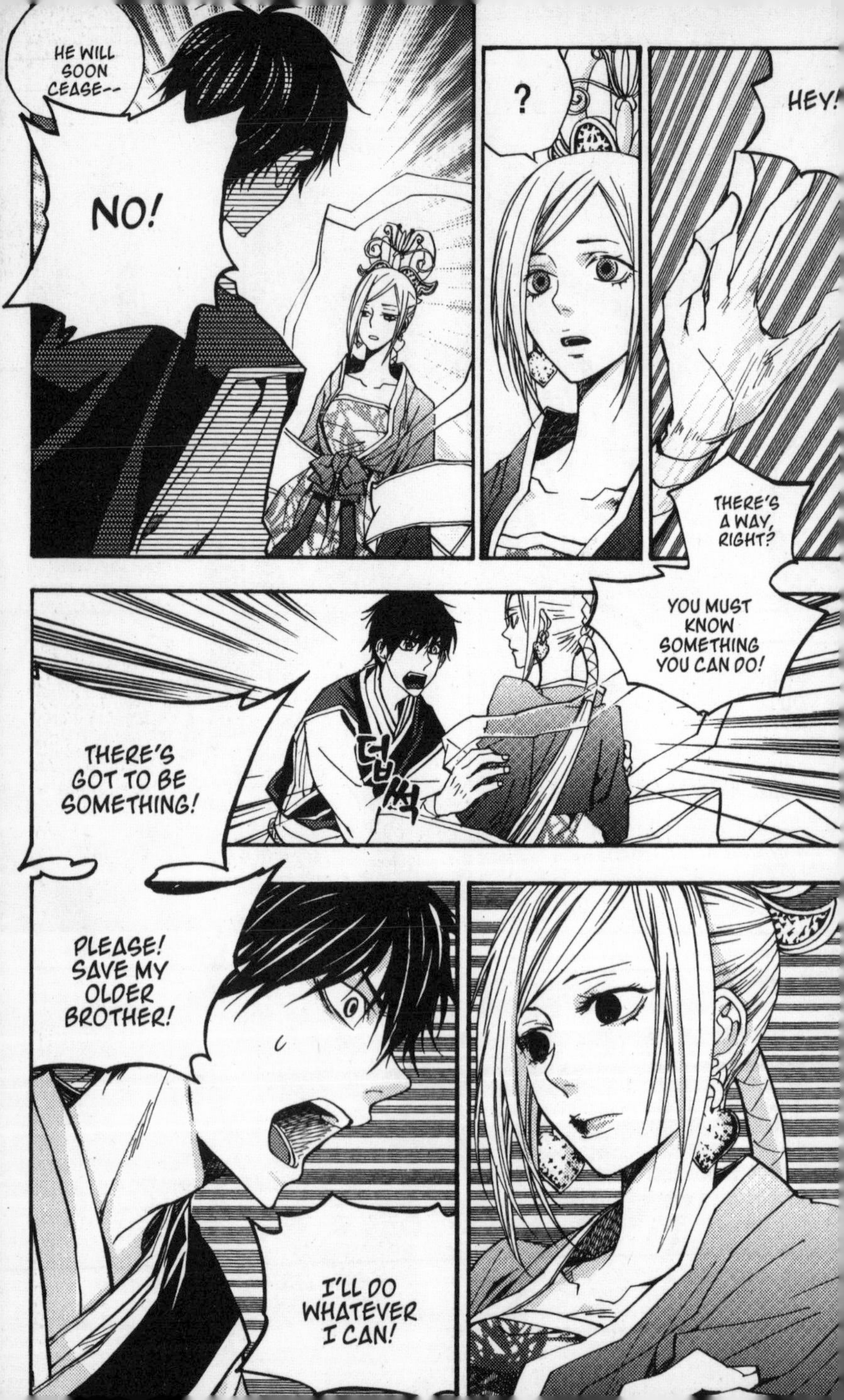
HE WILL SOON CEASE--
NO!
?
HEY!
THERE'S A WAY, RIGHT?
YOU MUST KNOW SOMETHING YOU CAN DO!
덥석
THERE'S GOT TO BE SOMETHING!
PLEASE! SAVE MY OLDER BROTHER!
I'LL DO WHATEVER I CAN!

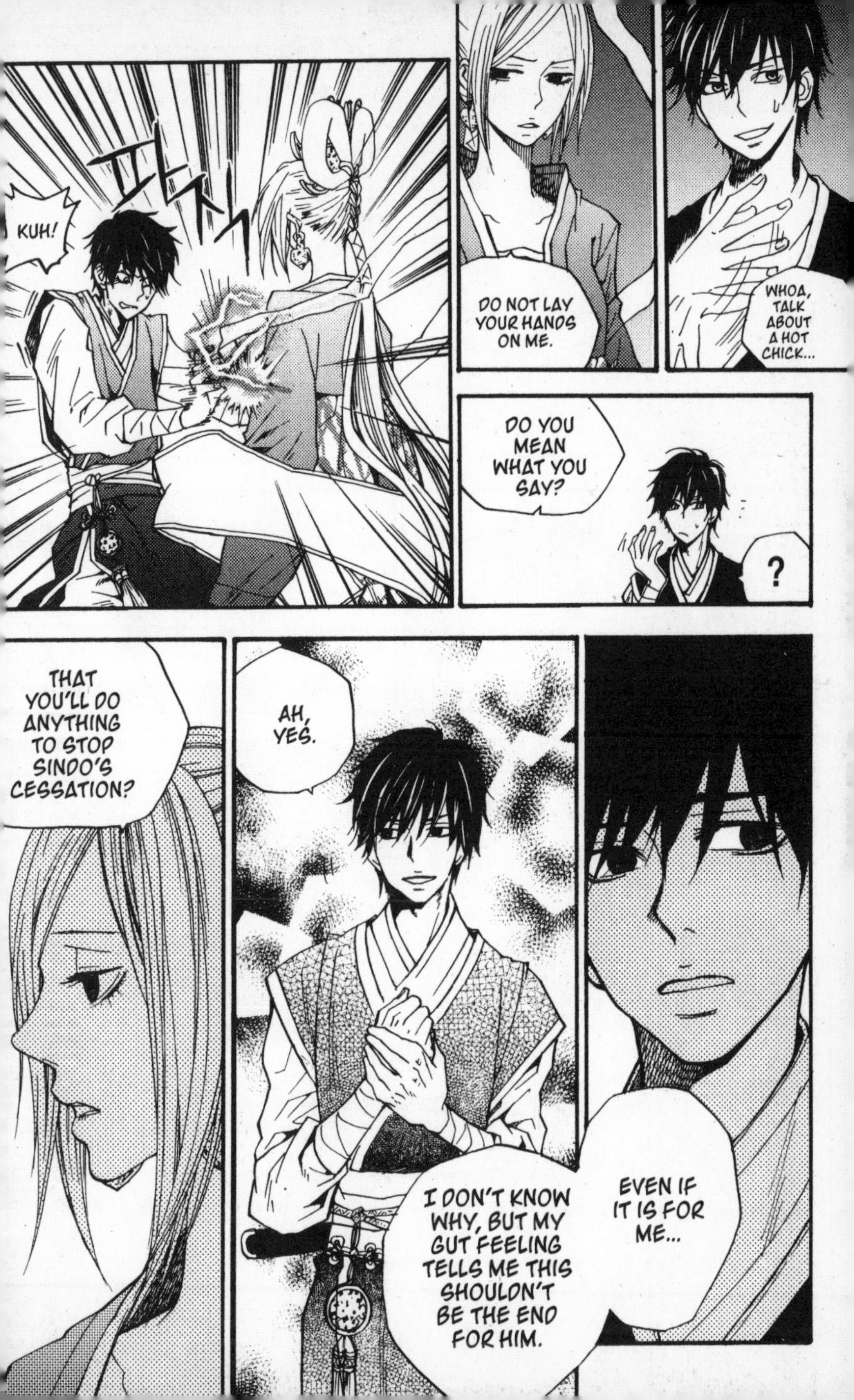
KUH!
DO NOT LAY YOUR HANDS ON ME.
WHOA, TALK ABOUT A HOT CHICK...
DO YOU MEAN WHAT YOU SAY?
?
THAT YOU'LL DO ANYTHING TO STOP SINDO'S CESSATION?
AH, YES.
I DON'T KNOW WHY, BUT MY GUT FEELING TELLS ME THIS SHOULDN'T BE THE END FOR HIM.
EVEN IF IT IS FOR ME...

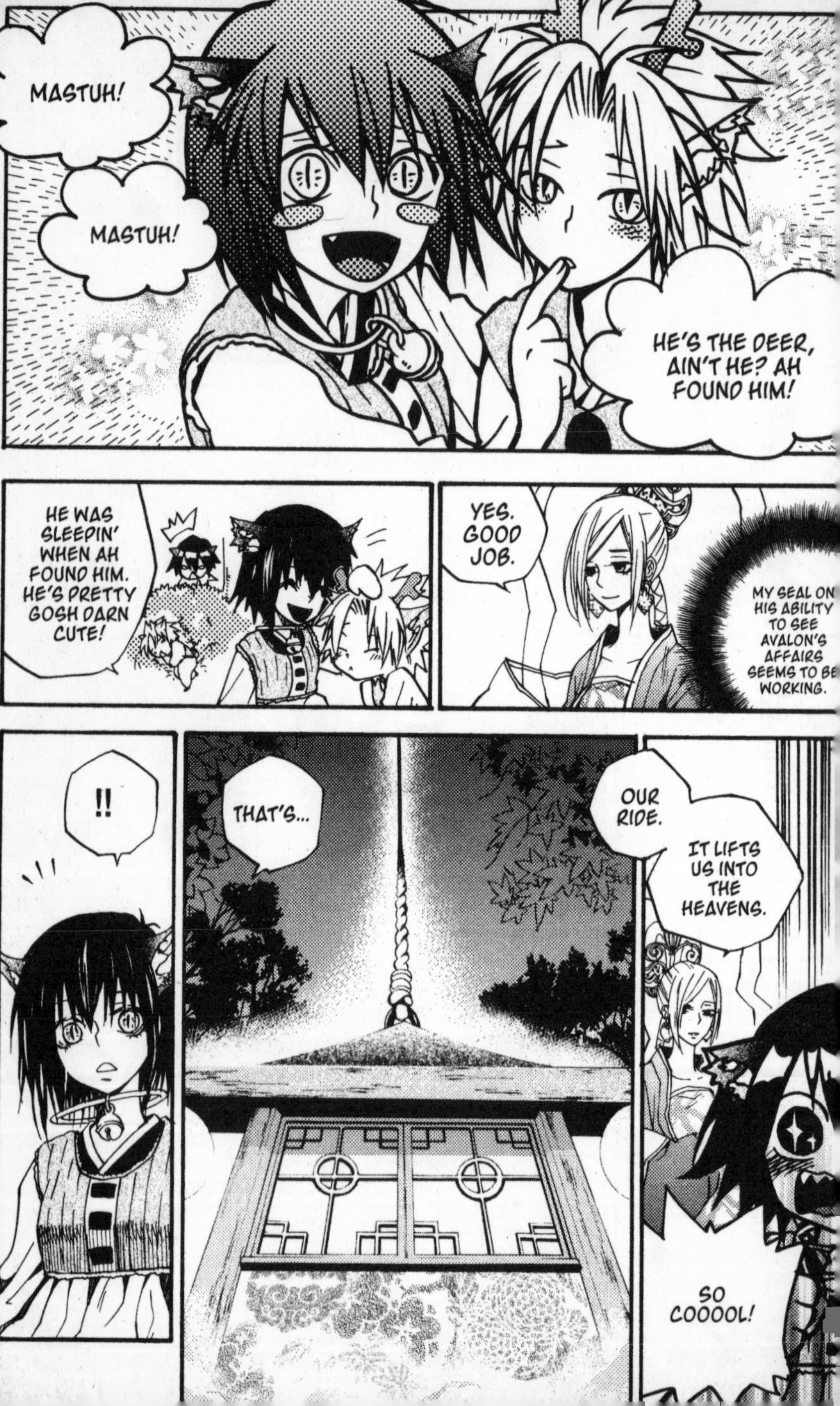
MASTUH!
MASTUH!
HE'S THE DEER, AIN'T HE? AH FOUND HIM!
HE WAS SLEEPIN' WHEN AH FOUND HIM. HE'S PRETTY GOSH DARN CUTE!
YES. GOOD JOB.
MY SEAL ON HIS ABILITY TO SEE AVALON'S AFFAIRS SEEMS TO BE WORKING.
!!
THAT'S...
OUR RIDE.
IT LIFTS US INTO THE HEAVENS.
SO COOOOL!

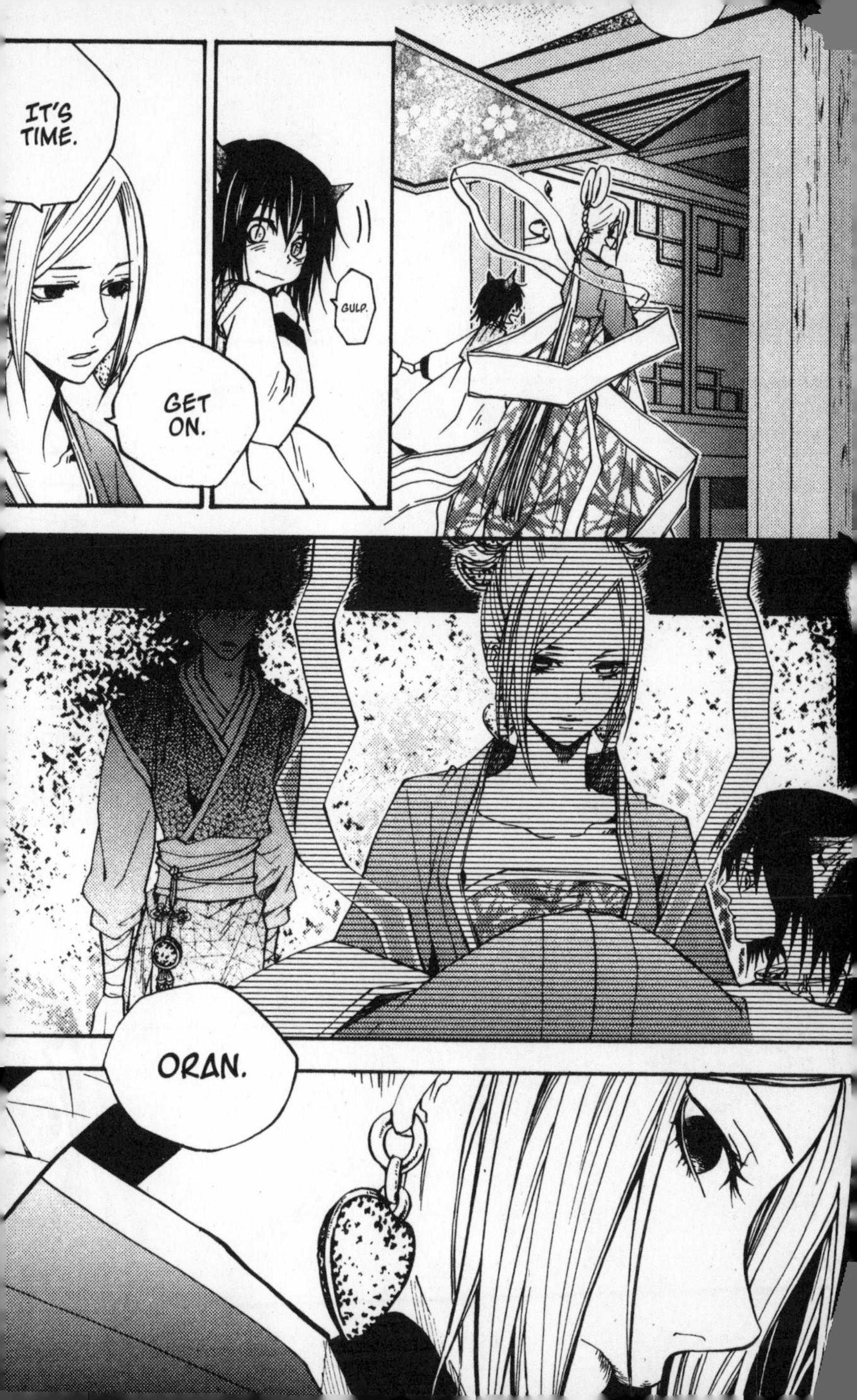
IT'S TIME.
GET ON.
GULP.
ORAN.

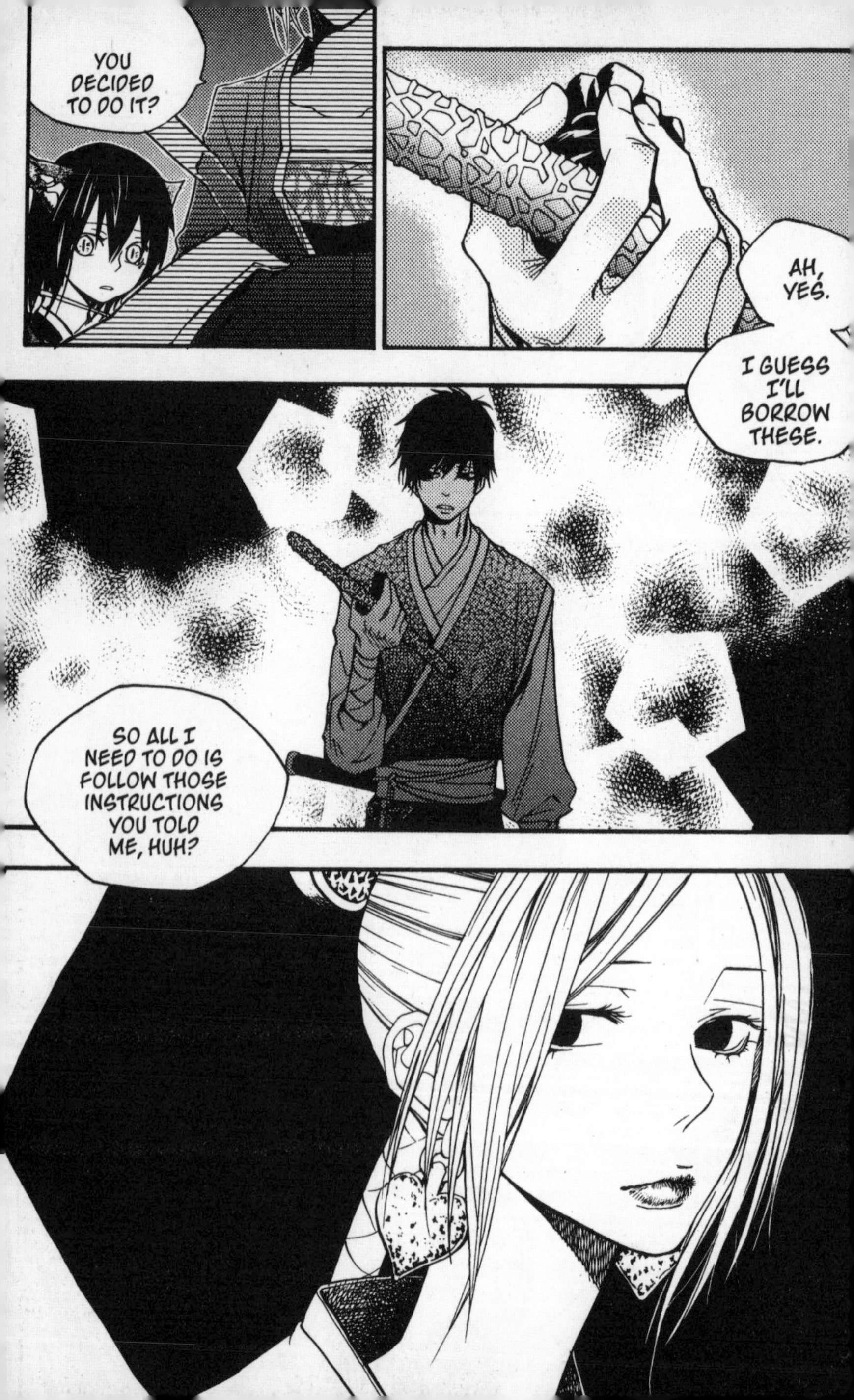
YOU DECIDED TO DO IT?
AH, YES.
I GUESS I'LL BORROW THESE.
SO ALL I NEED TO DO IS FOLLOW THOSE INSTRUCTIONS YOU TOLD ME, HUH?

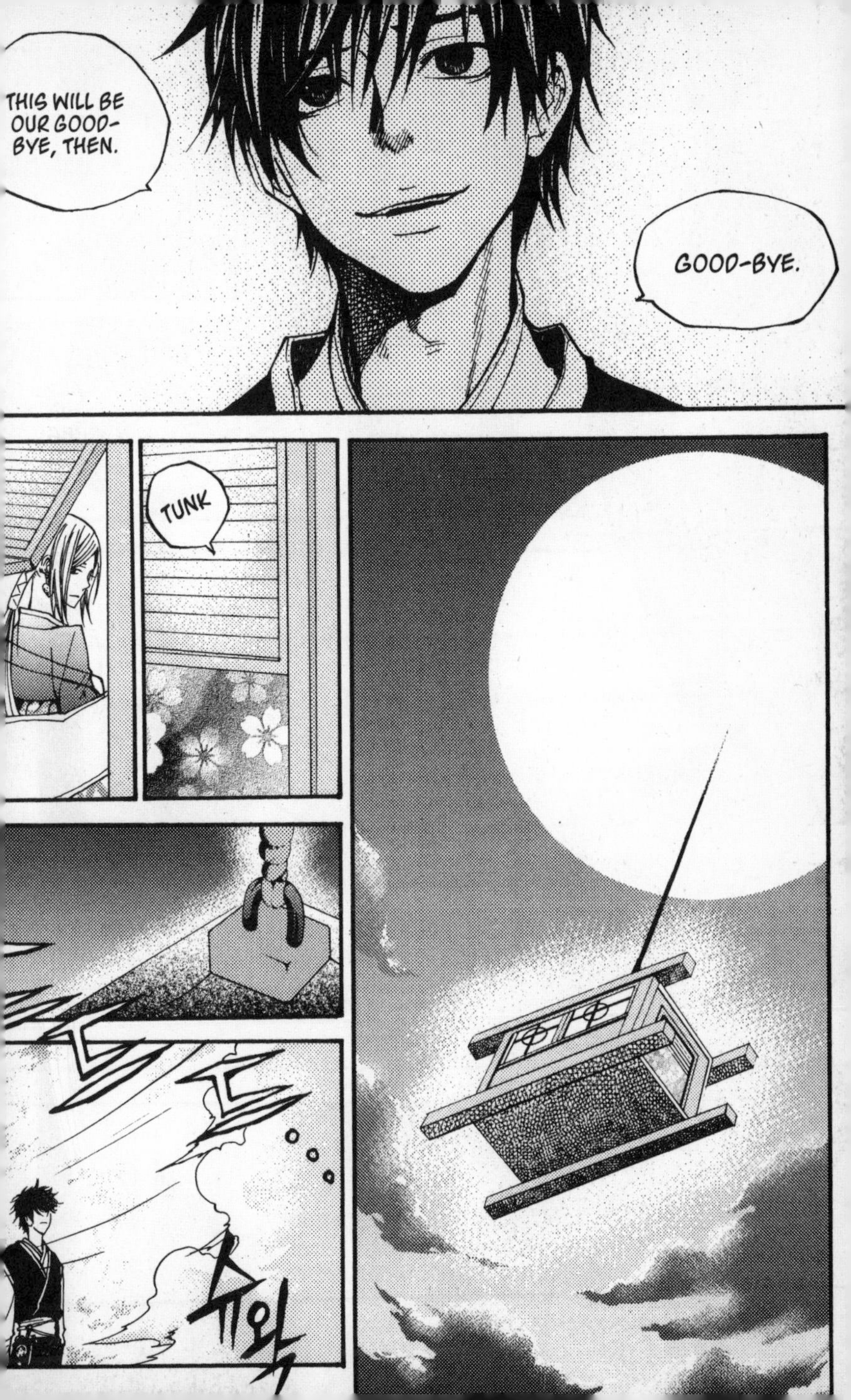
THIS WILL BE OUR GOOD-BYE, THEN.
GOOD-BYE.
TUNK

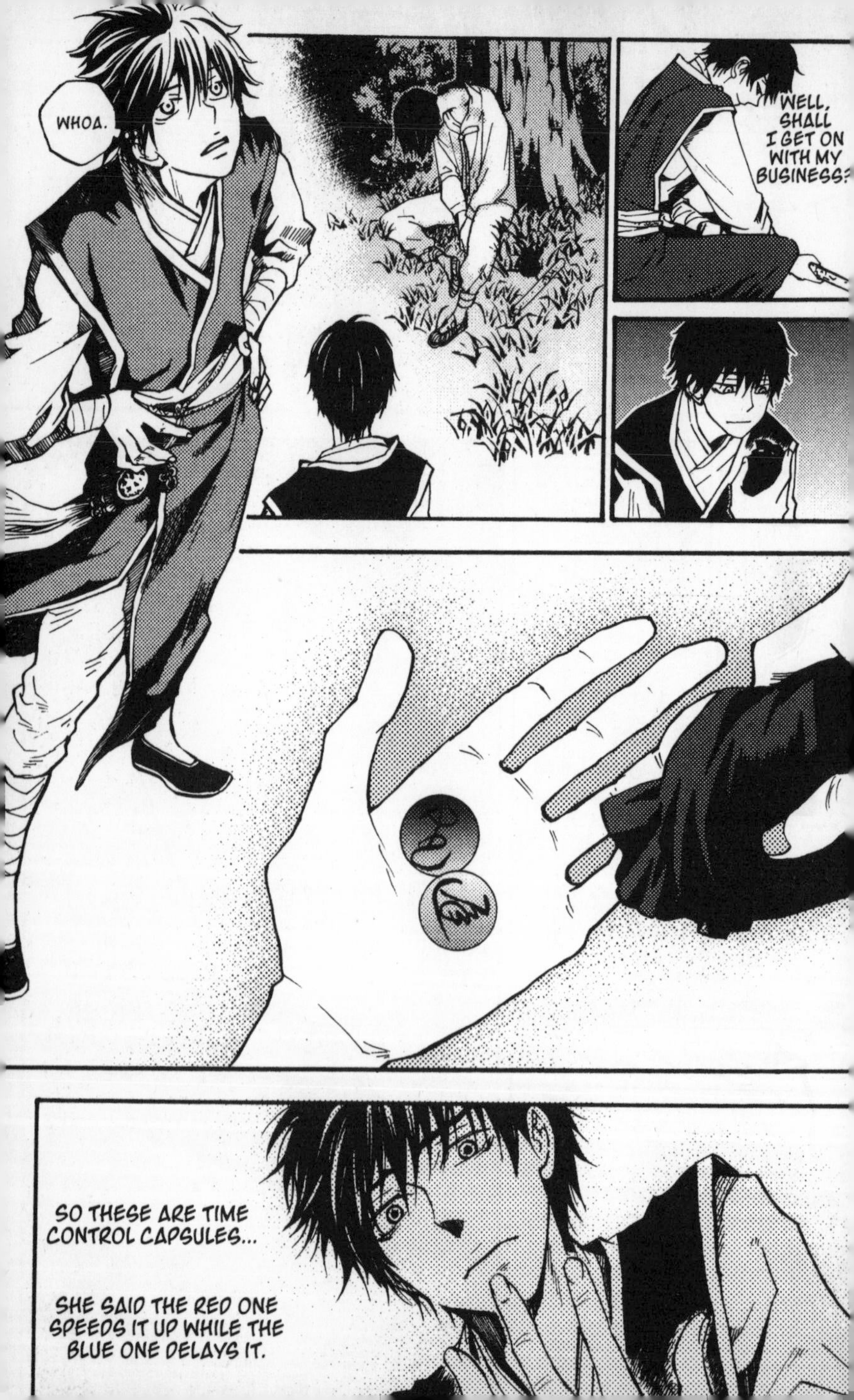
WHOA.
WELL, SHALL I GET ON WITH MY BUSINESS?
SO THESE ARE TIME CONTROL CAPSULES...
SHE SAID THE RED ONE SPEEDS IT UP WHILE THE BLUE ONE DELAYS IT.

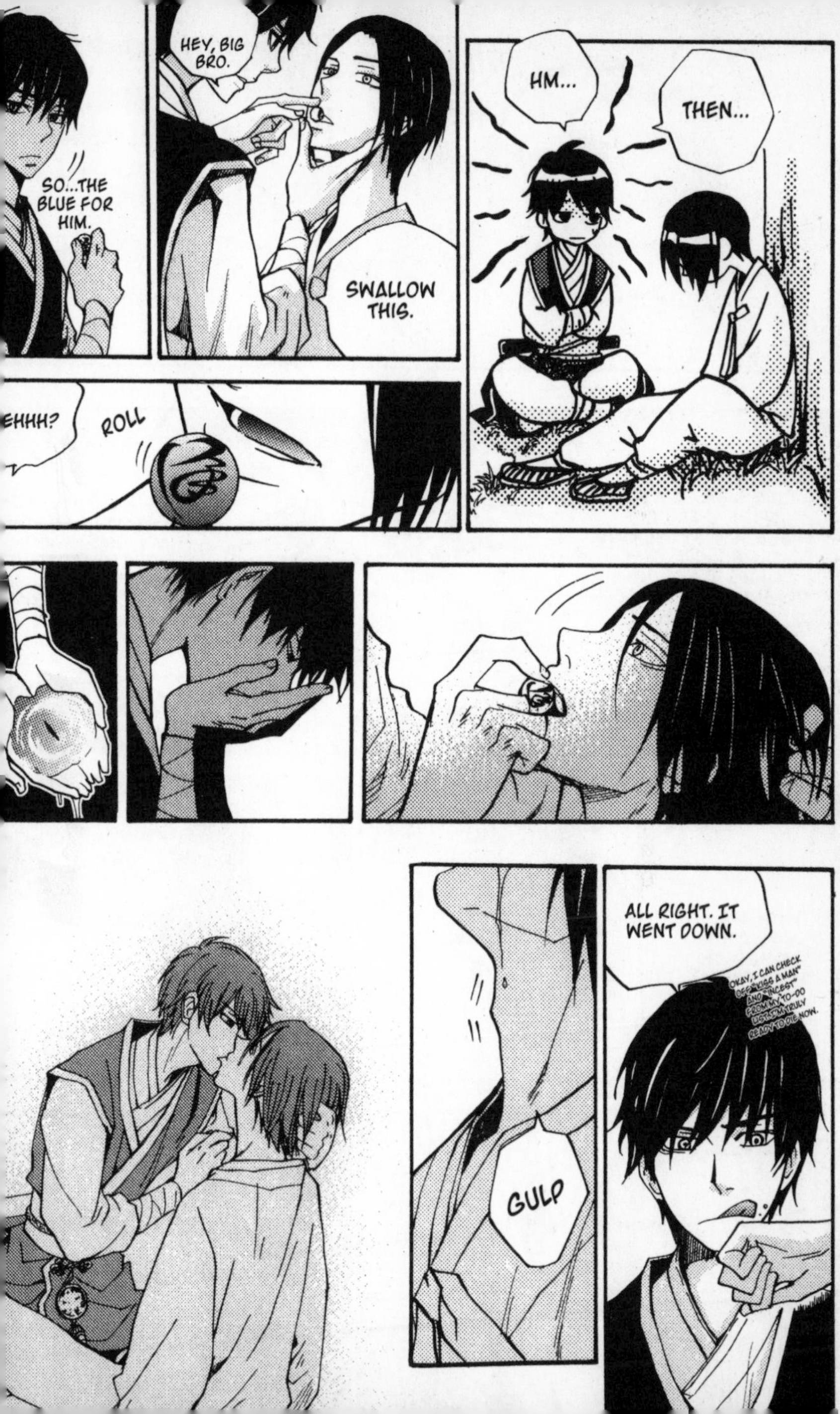

SO...THE BLUE FOR HIM.
HEY, BIG BRO.
SWALLOW THIS.
EHHH?
ROLL
HM...
THEN...
GULP
ALL RIGHT. IT WENT DOWN.
OKAY, I CAN CHECK OFF "KISS A MAN" AND "INCEST" FROM MY TO-DO LIST. I'M TRULY READY TO DIE NOW.

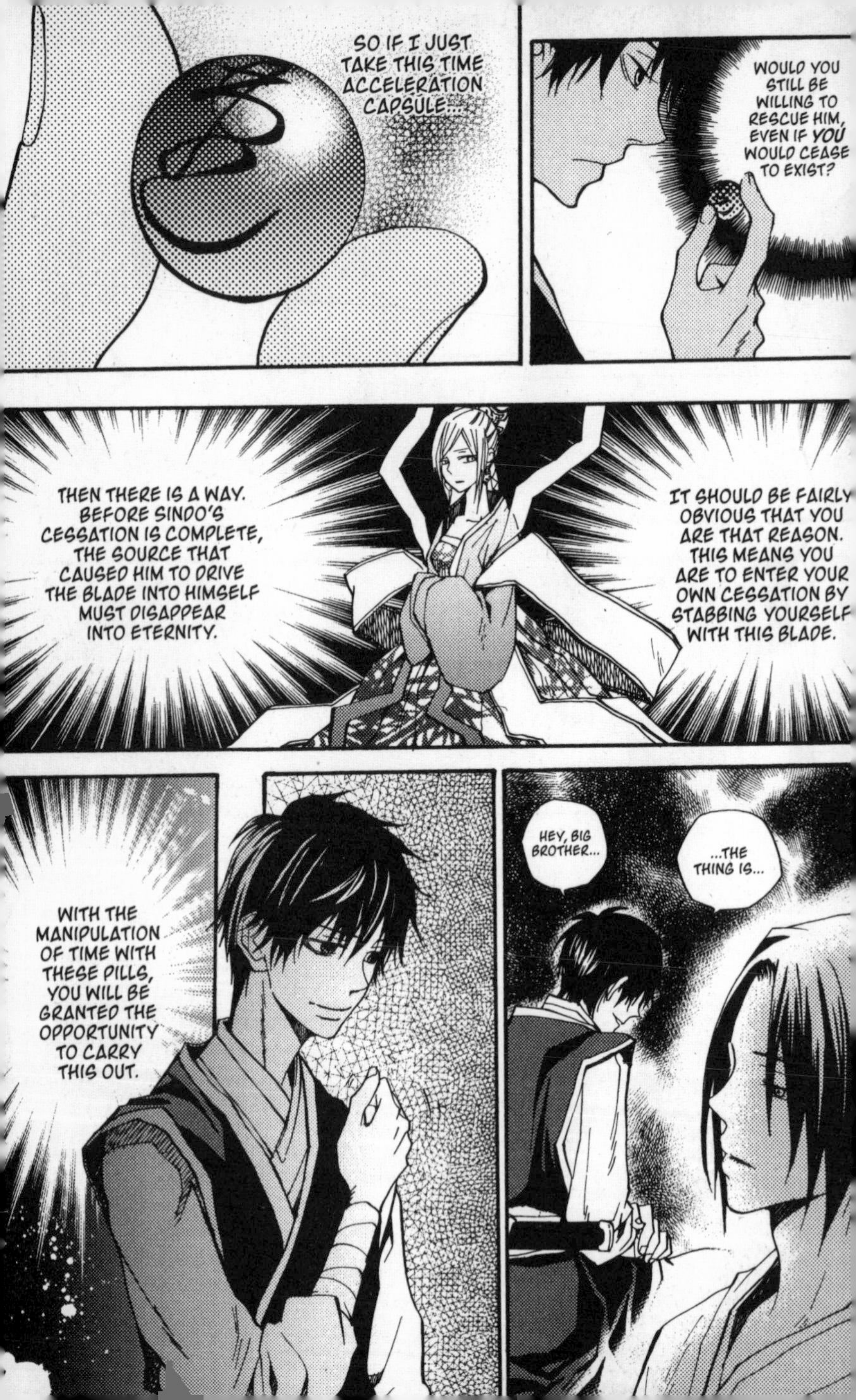
SO IF I JUST TAKE THIS TIME ACCELERATION CAPSULE...
WOULD YOU STILL BE WILLING TO RESCUE HIM, EVEN IF *YOU* WOULD CEASE TO EXIST?
THEN THERE IS A WAY. BEFORE SINDO'S CESSATION IS COMPLETE, THE SOURCE THAT CAUSED HIM TO DRIVE THE BLADE INTO HIMSELF MUST DISAPPEAR INTO ETERNITY.
IT SHOULD BE FAIRLY OBVIOUS THAT YOU ARE THAT REASON. THIS MEANS YOU ARE TO ENTER YOUR OWN CESSATION BY STABBING YOURSELF WITH THIS BLADE.
WITH THE MANIPULATION OF TIME WITH THESE PILLS, YOU WILL BE GRANTED THE OPPORTUNITY TO CARRY THIS OUT.
HEY, BIG BROTHER...
...THE THING IS...

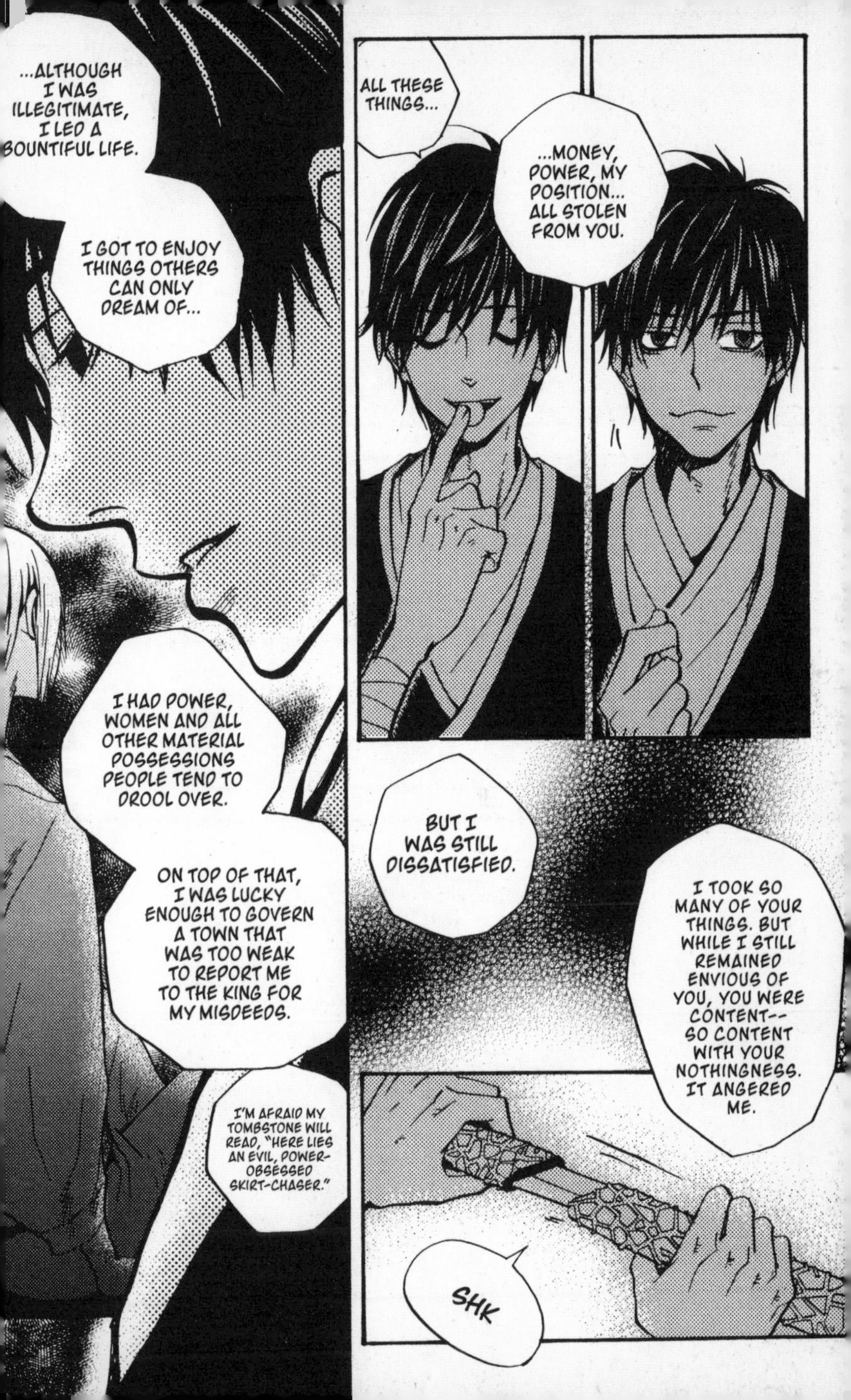
...ALTHOUGH I WAS ILLEGITIMATE, I LED A BOUNTIFUL LIFE.
I GOT TO ENJOY THINGS OTHERS CAN ONLY DREAM OF...
I HAD POWER, WOMEN AND ALL OTHER MATERIAL POSSESSIONS PEOPLE TEND TO DROOL OVER.
ON TOP OF THAT, I WAS LUCKY ENOUGH TO GOVERN A TOWN THAT WAS TOO WEAK TO REPORT ME TO THE KING FOR MY MISDEEDS.
I'M AFRAID MY TOMBSTONE WILL READ, "HERE LIES AN EVIL, POWER-OBSESSED SKIRT-CHASER."
ALL THESE THINGS...
...MONEY, POWER, MY POSITION... ALL STOLEN FROM YOU.
BUT I WAS STILL DISSATISFIED.
I TOOK SO MANY OF YOUR THINGS. BUT WHILE I STILL REMAINED ENVIOUS OF YOU, YOU WERE CONTENT--SO CONTENT WITH YOUR NOTHINGNESS. IT ANGERED ME.
SHK

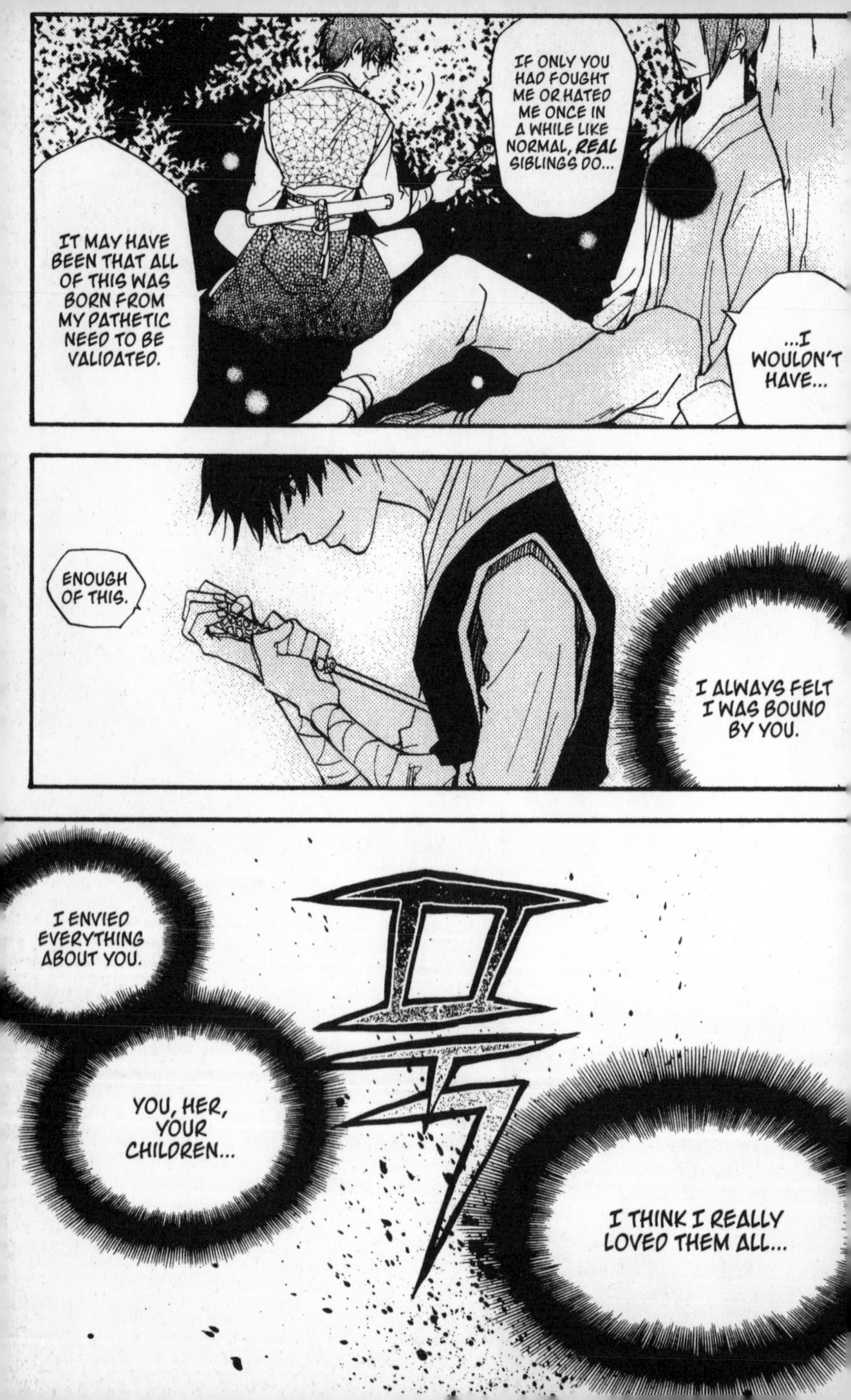
IT MAY HAVE BEEN THAT ALL OF THIS WAS BORN FROM MY PATHETIC NEED TO BE VALIDATED.
IF ONLY YOU HAD FOUGHT ME OR HATED ME ONCE IN A WHILE LIKE NORMAL, **REAL** SIBLINGS DO...
...I WOULDN'T HAVE...
ENOUGH OF THIS.
I ALWAYS FELT I WAS BOUND BY YOU.
I ENVIED EVERYTHING ABOUT YOU.
YOU, HER, YOUR CHILDREN...
I THINK I REALLY LOVED THEM ALL...

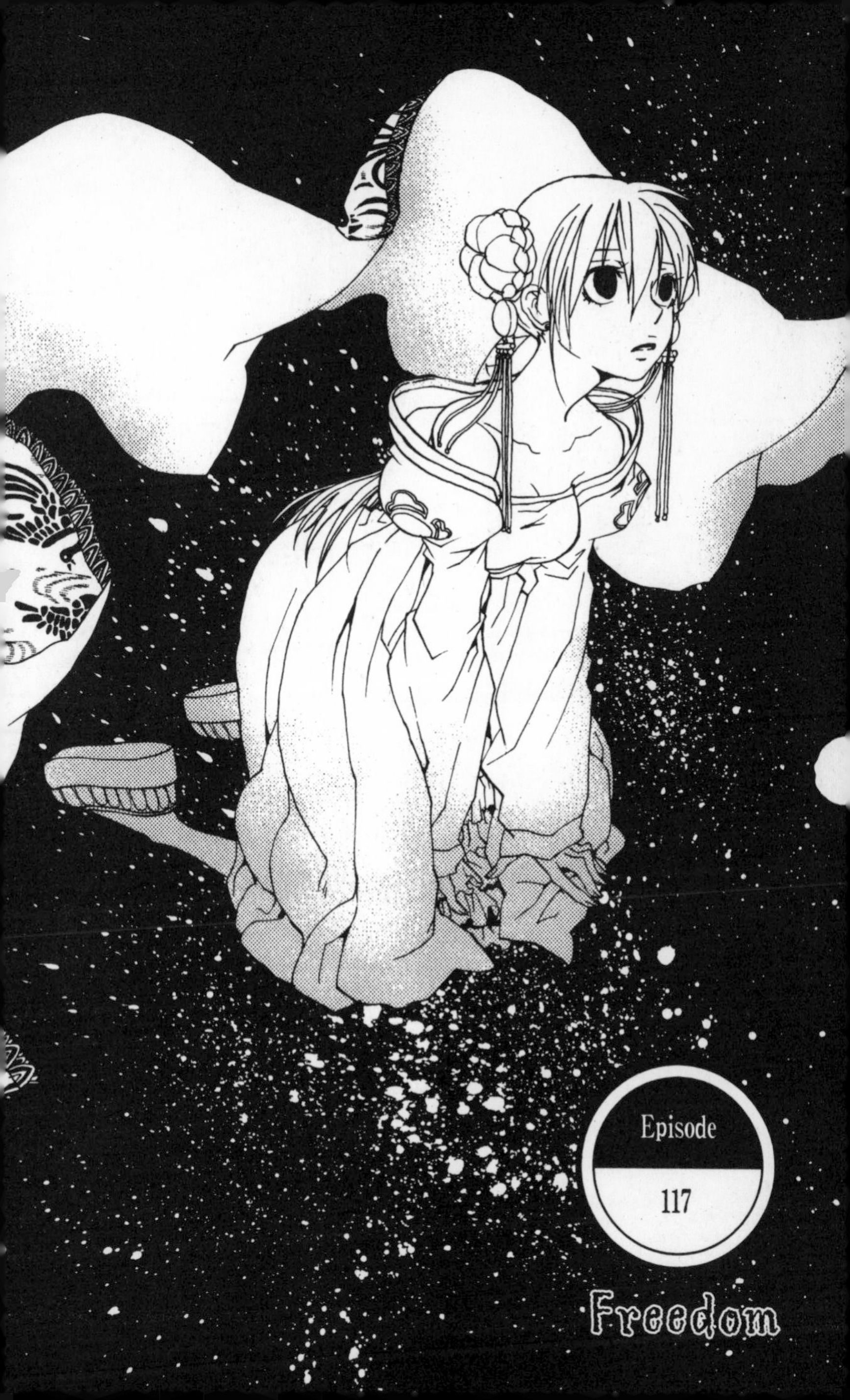
Episode
117
Freedom

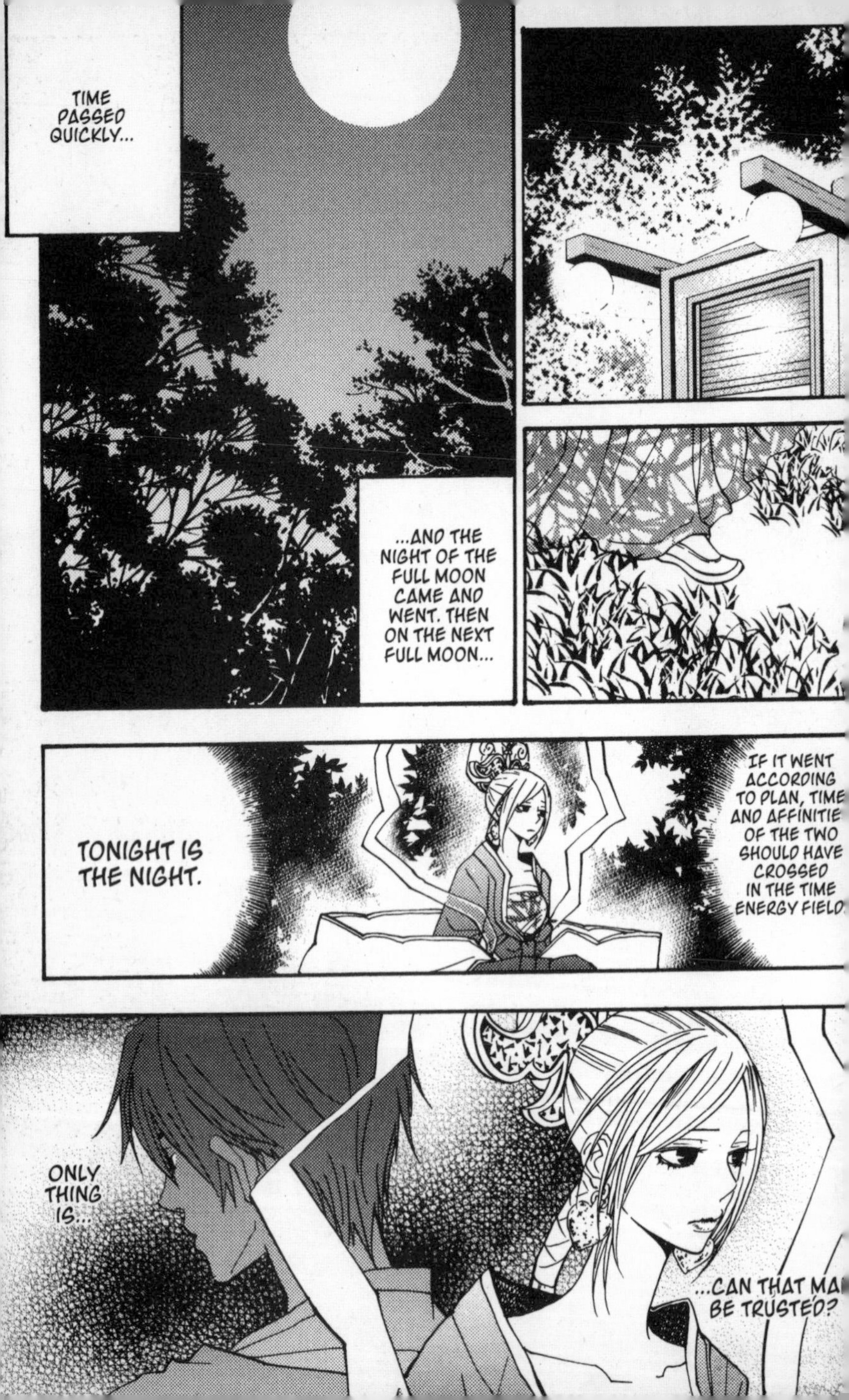
TIME PASSED QUICKLY...
...AND THE NIGHT OF THE FULL MOON CAME AND WENT. THEN ON THE NEXT FULL MOON...
TONIGHT IS THE NIGHT.
IF IT WENT ACCORDING TO PLAN, TIME AND AFFINITIE OF THE TWO SHOULD HAVE CROSSED IN THE TIME ENERGY FIELD.
ONLY THING IS...
...CAN THAT MA BE TRUSTED?

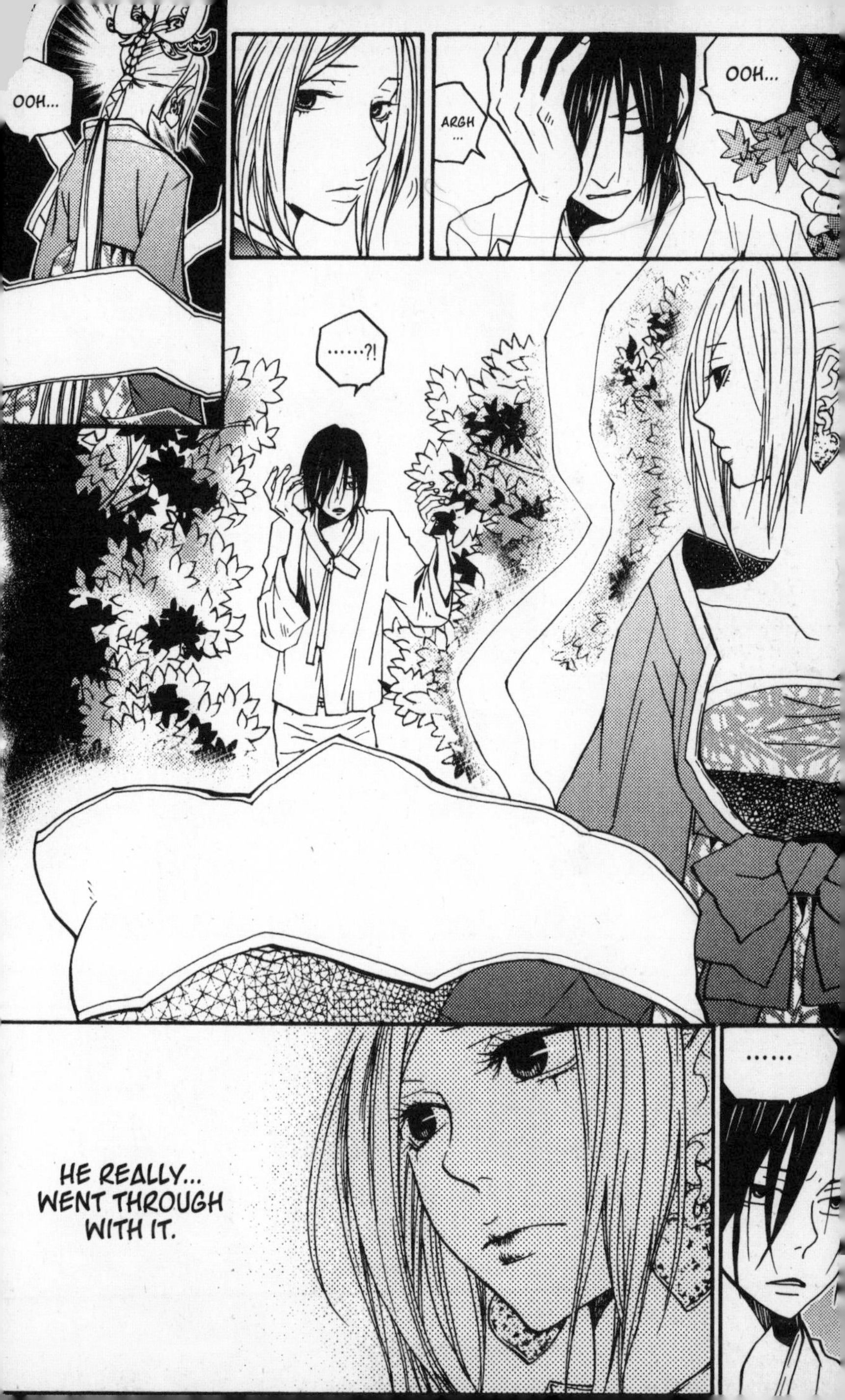
OOH...
ARGH ...
OOH...
......?!
HE REALLY... WENT THROUGH WITH IT.
......

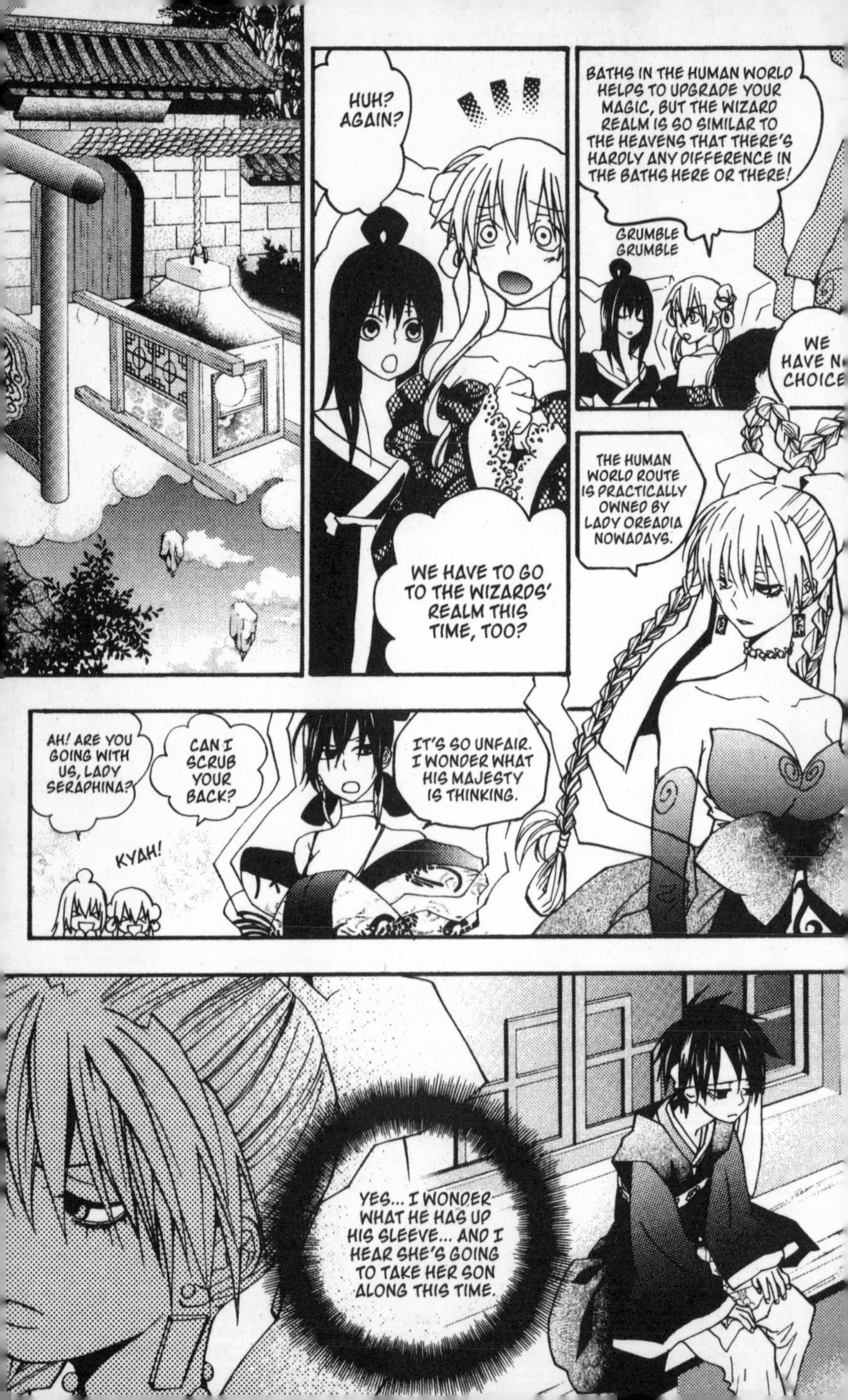
HUH? AGAIN?
WE HAVE TO GO TO THE WIZARDS' REALM THIS TIME, TOO?
BATHS IN THE HUMAN WORLD HELPS TO UPGRADE YOUR MAGIC, BUT THE WIZARD REALM IS SO SIMILAR TO THE HEAVENS THAT THERE'S HARDLY ANY DIFFERENCE IN THE BATHS HERE OR THERE!
GRUMBLE GRUMBLE
WE HAVE N CHOICE
THE HUMAN WORLD ROUTE IS PRACTICALLY OWNED BY LADY OREADIA NOWADAYS.
AH! ARE YOU GOING WITH US, LADY SERAPHINA?
CAN I SCRUB YOUR BACK?
KYAH!
IT'S SO UNFAIR. I WONDER WHAT HIS MAJESTY IS THINKING.
YES... I WONDER WHAT HE HAS UP HIS SLEEVE... AND I HEAR SHE'S GOING TO TAKE HER SON ALONG THIS TIME.

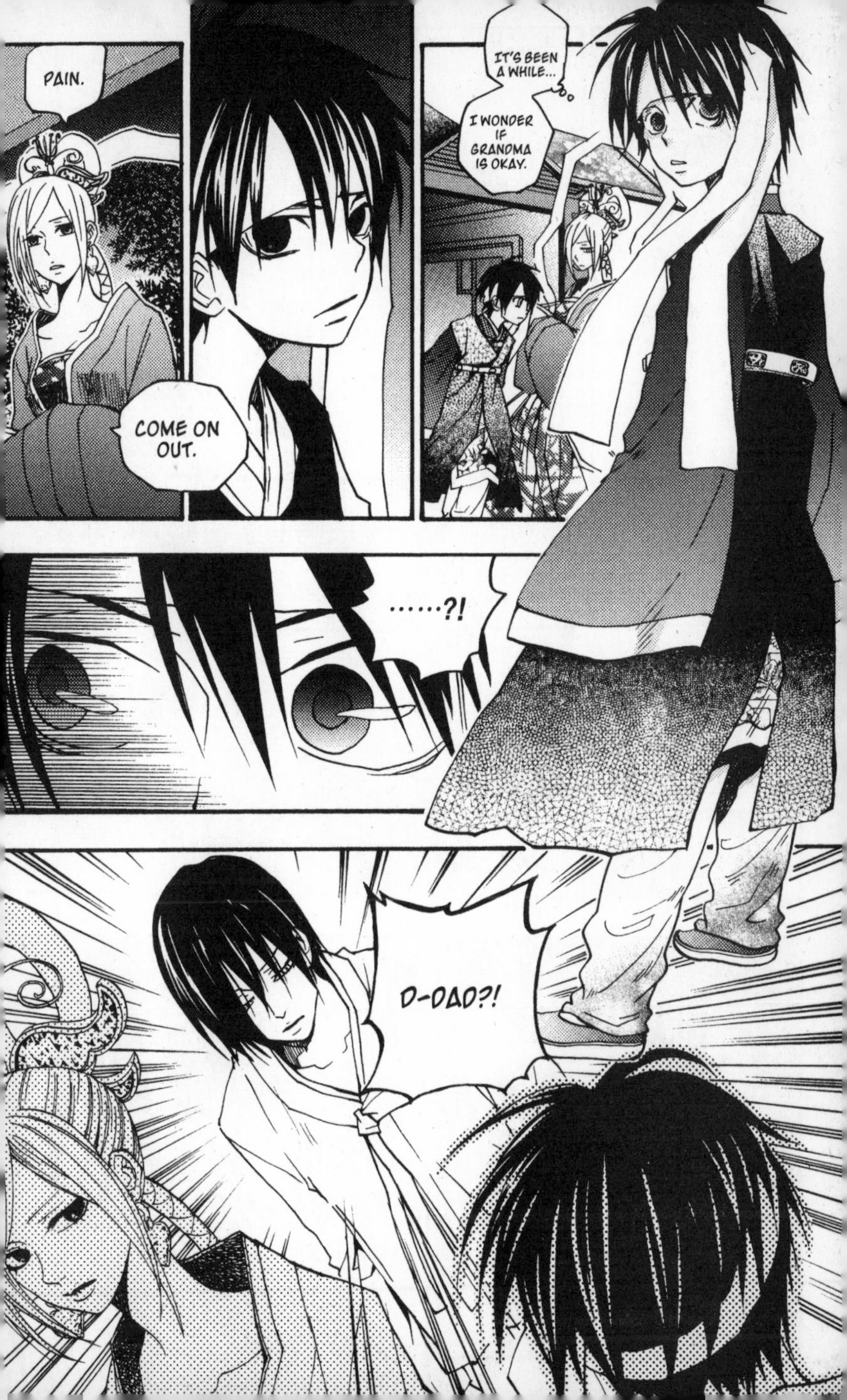
PAIN.
COME ON OUT.
IT'S BEEN A WHILE...
I WONDER IF GRANDMA IS OKAY.
......?!
D-DAD?!

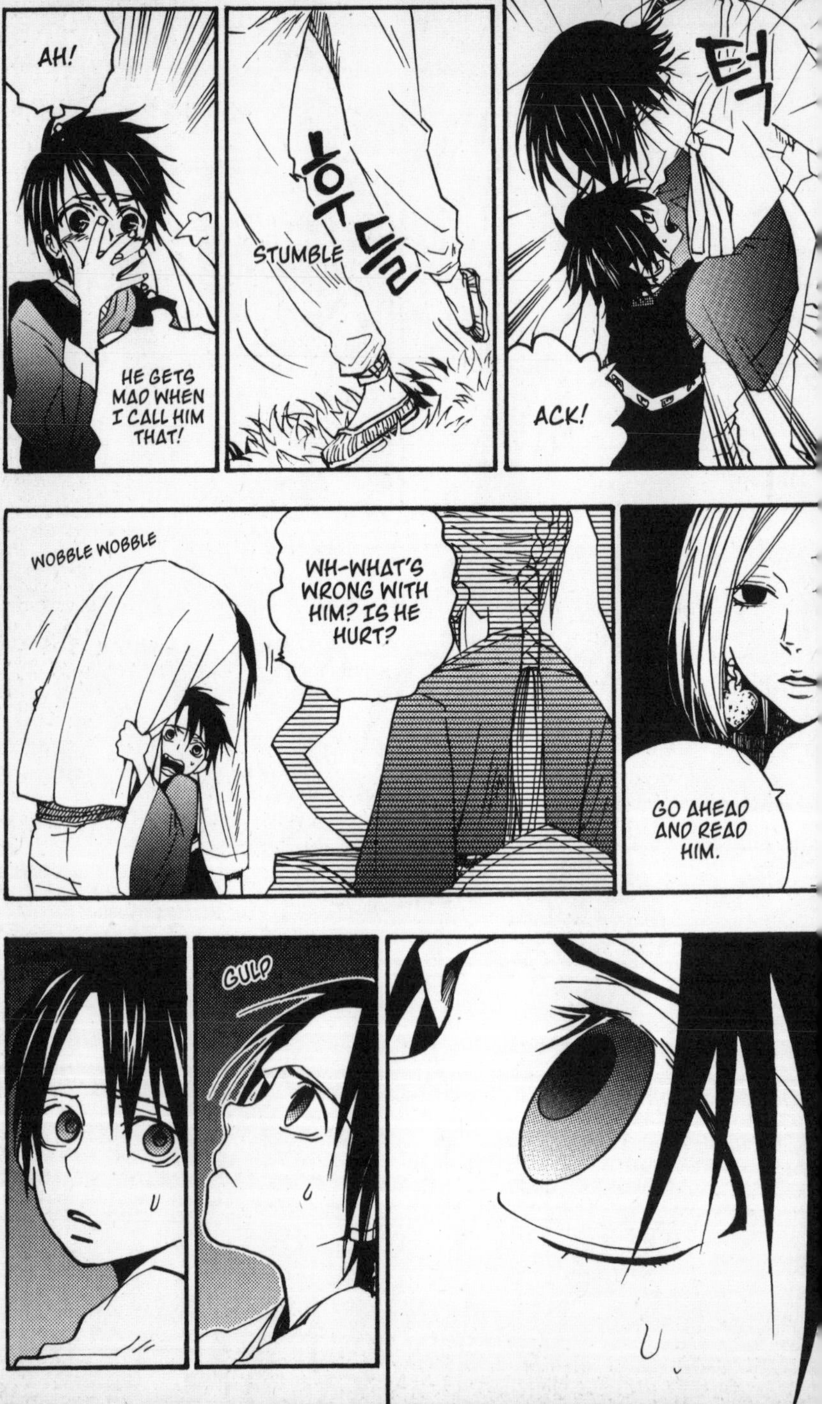
AH!
HE GETS MAD WHEN I CALL HIM THAT!
STUMBLE
턱
ACK!
WOBBLE WOBBLE
WH-WHAT'S WRONG WITH HIM? IS HE HURT?
GO AHEAD AND READ HIM.
GULP

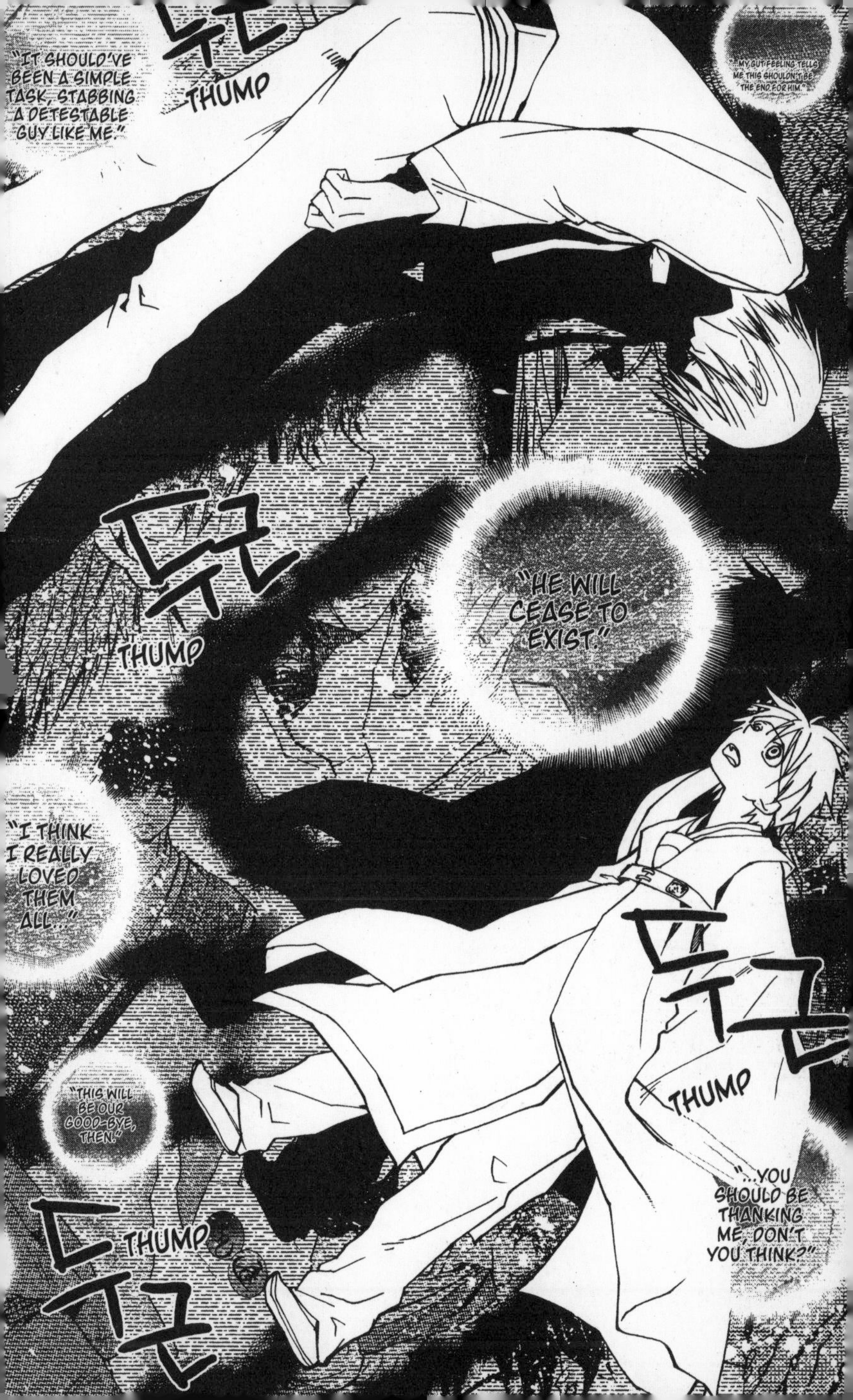

"IT SHOULD'VE BEEN A SIMPLE TASK, STABBING A DETESTABLE GUY LIKE ME."
THUMP
"MY GUT FEELING TELLS ME THIS SHOULDN'T BE THE END FOR HIM."
THUMP
"HE WILL CEASE TO EXIST."
"I THINK I REALLY LOVED THEM ALL..."
THUMP
"THIS WILL BE OUR GOOD-BYE, THEN."
THUMP
"...YOU SHOULD BE THANKING ME, DON'T YOU THINK?"

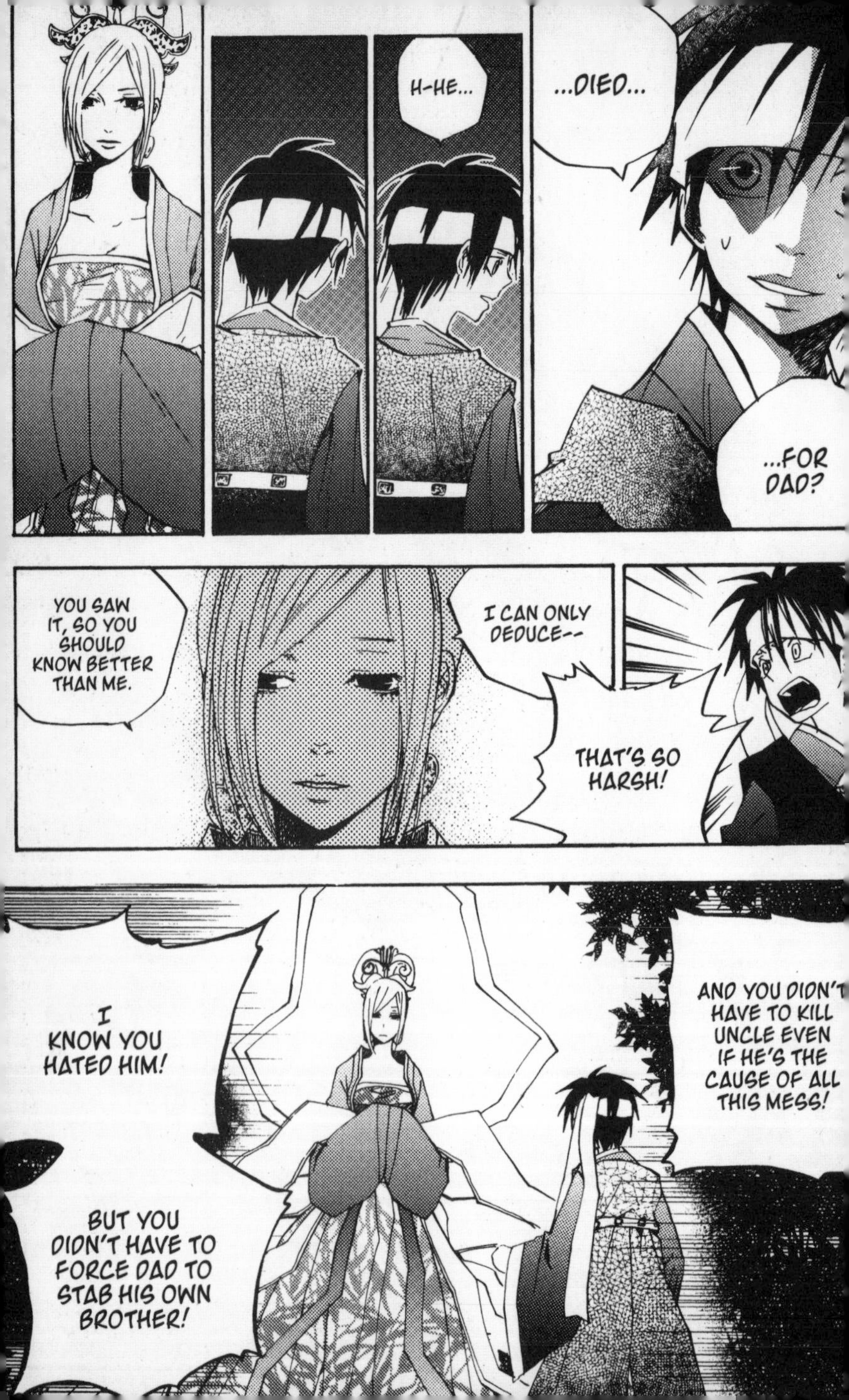
H-HE...
...DIED...
...FOR DAD?
YOU SAW IT, SO YOU SHOULD KNOW BETTER THAN ME.
I CAN ONLY DEDUCE--
THAT'S SO HARSH!
I KNOW YOU HATED HIM!
BUT YOU DIDN'T HAVE TO FORCE DAD TO STAB HIS OWN BROTHER!
AND YOU DIDN'T HAVE TO KILL UNCLE EVEN IF HE'S THE CAUSE OF ALL THIS MESS!

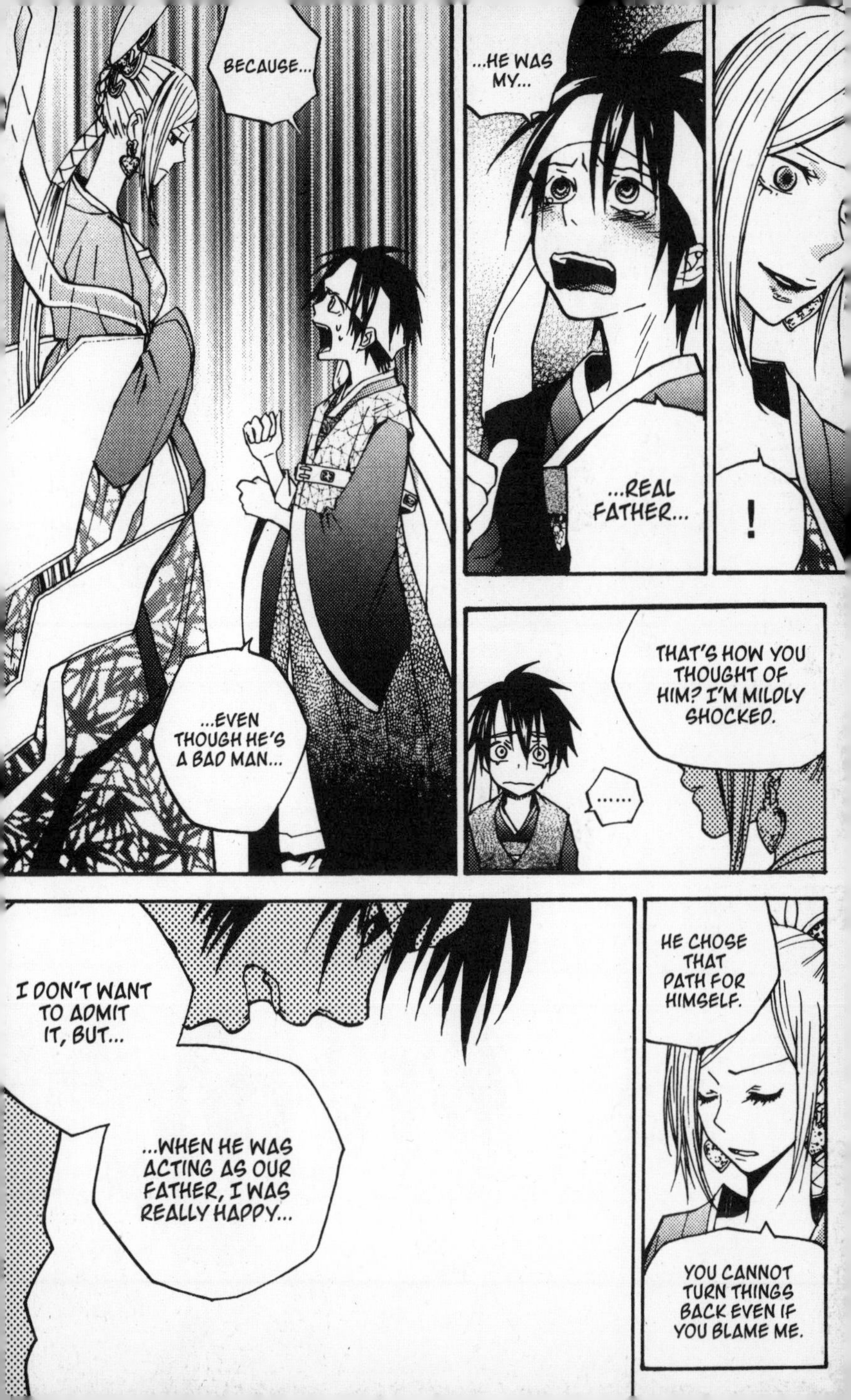
BECAUSE...
...EVEN THOUGH HE'S A BAD MAN...
...HE WAS MY...
...REAL FATHER...
!
THAT'S HOW YOU THOUGHT OF HIM? I'M MILDLY SHOCKED.
......
I DON'T WANT TO ADMIT IT, BUT...
...WHEN HE WAS ACTING AS OUR FATHER, I WAS REALLY HAPPY...
HE CHOSE THAT PATH FOR HIMSELF.
YOU CANNOT TURN THINGS BACK EVEN IF YOU BLAME ME.

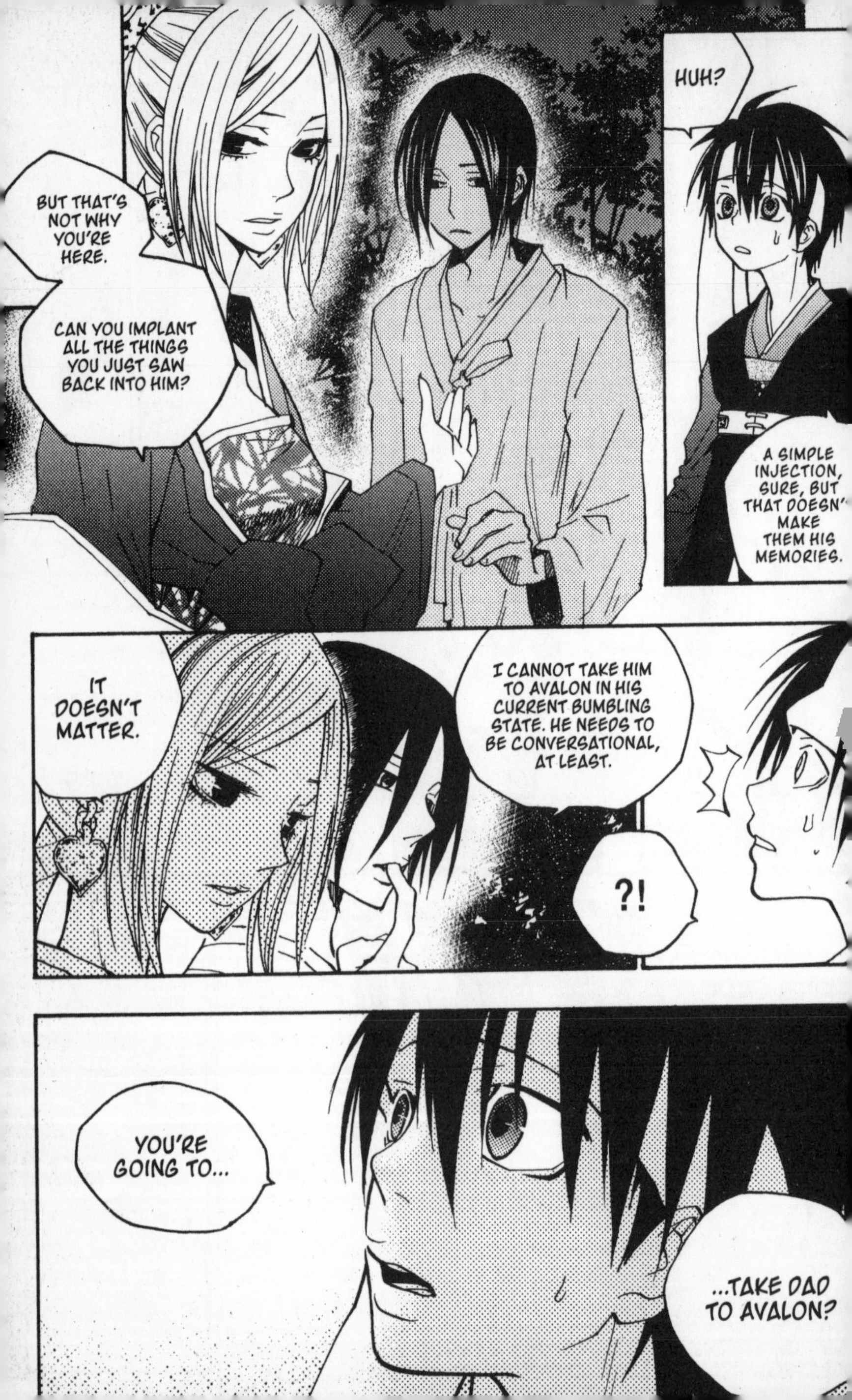
BUT THAT'S NOT WHY YOU'RE HERE.
CAN YOU IMPLANT ALL THE THINGS YOU JUST SAW BACK INTO HIM?
HUH?
A SIMPLE INJECTION, SURE, BUT THAT DOESN'T MAKE THEM HIS MEMORIES.
IT DOESN'T MATTER.
I CANNOT TAKE HIM TO AVALON IN HIS CURRENT BUMBLING STATE. HE NEEDS TO BE CONVERSATIONAL, AT LEAST.
?!
YOU'RE GOING TO...
...TAKE DAD TO AVALON?

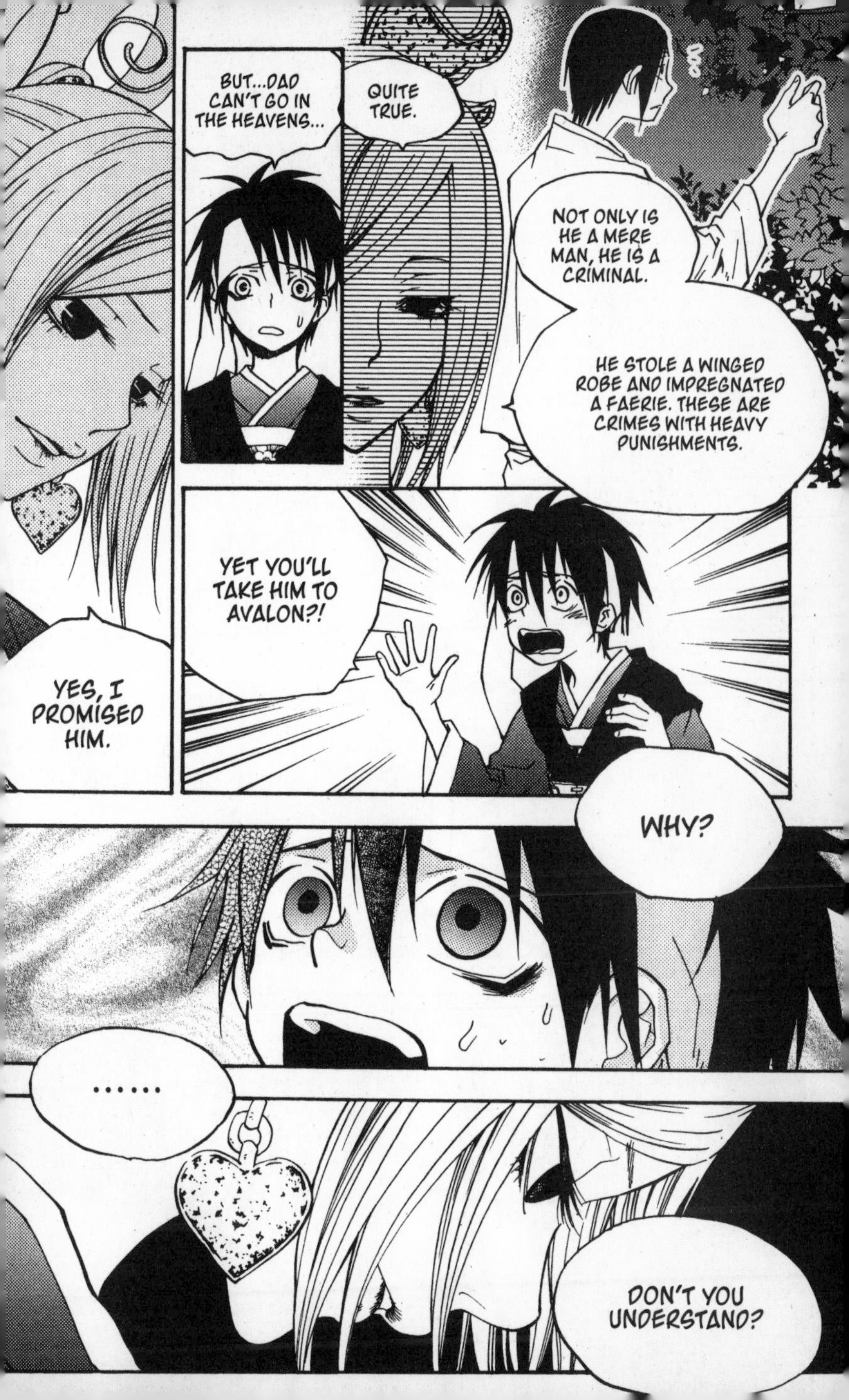
YES, I PROMISED HIM.
BUT...DAD CAN'T GO IN THE HEAVENS...
QUITE TRUE.
NOT ONLY IS HE A MERE MAN, HE IS A CRIMINAL.
HE STOLE A WINGED ROBE AND IMPREGNATED A FAERIE. THESE ARE CRIMES WITH HEAVY PUNISHMENTS.
YET YOU'LL TAKE HIM TO AVALON?!
WHY?
......
DON'T YOU UNDERSTAND?

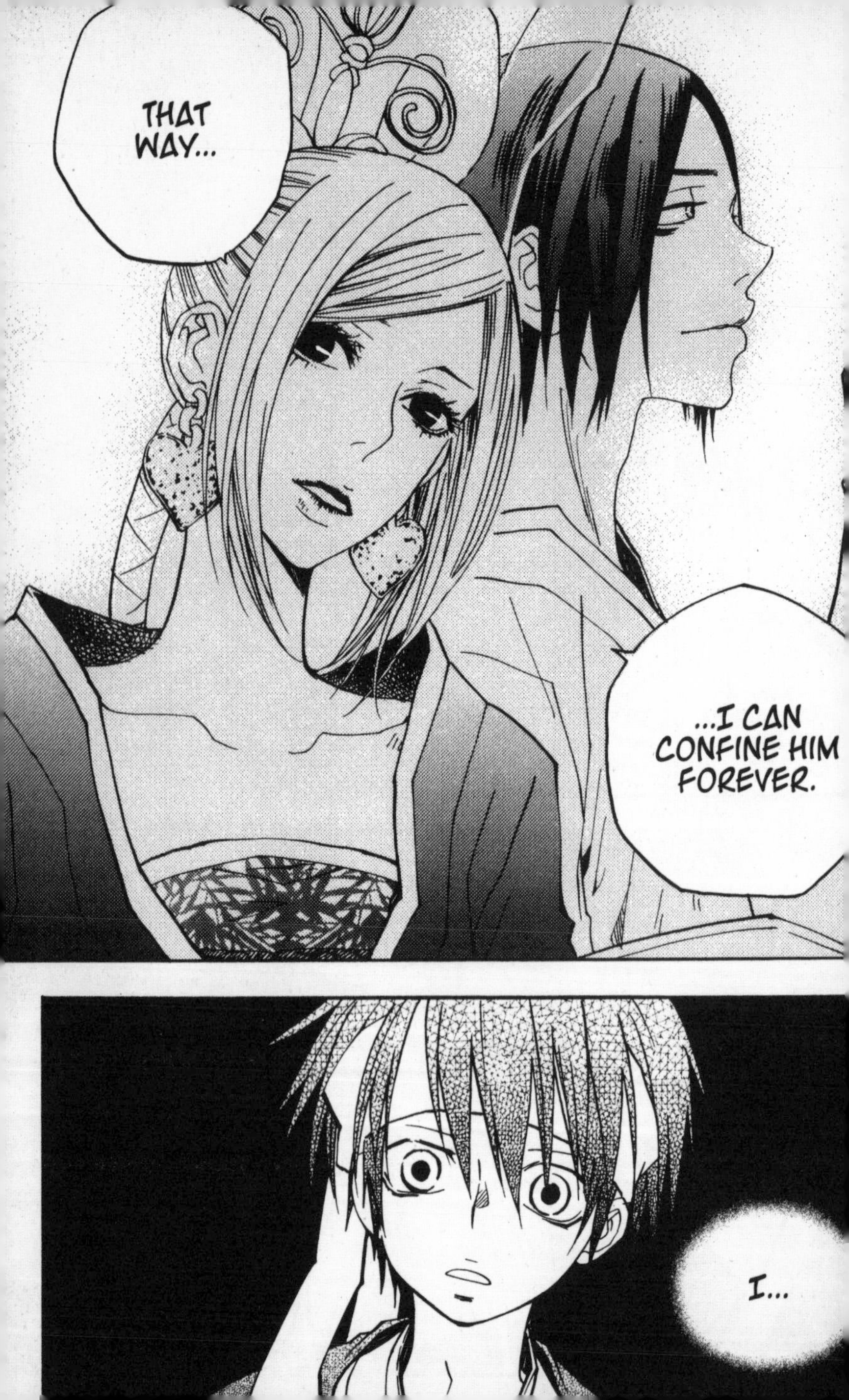
THAT WAY...
...I CAN CONFINE HIM FOREVER.
I...

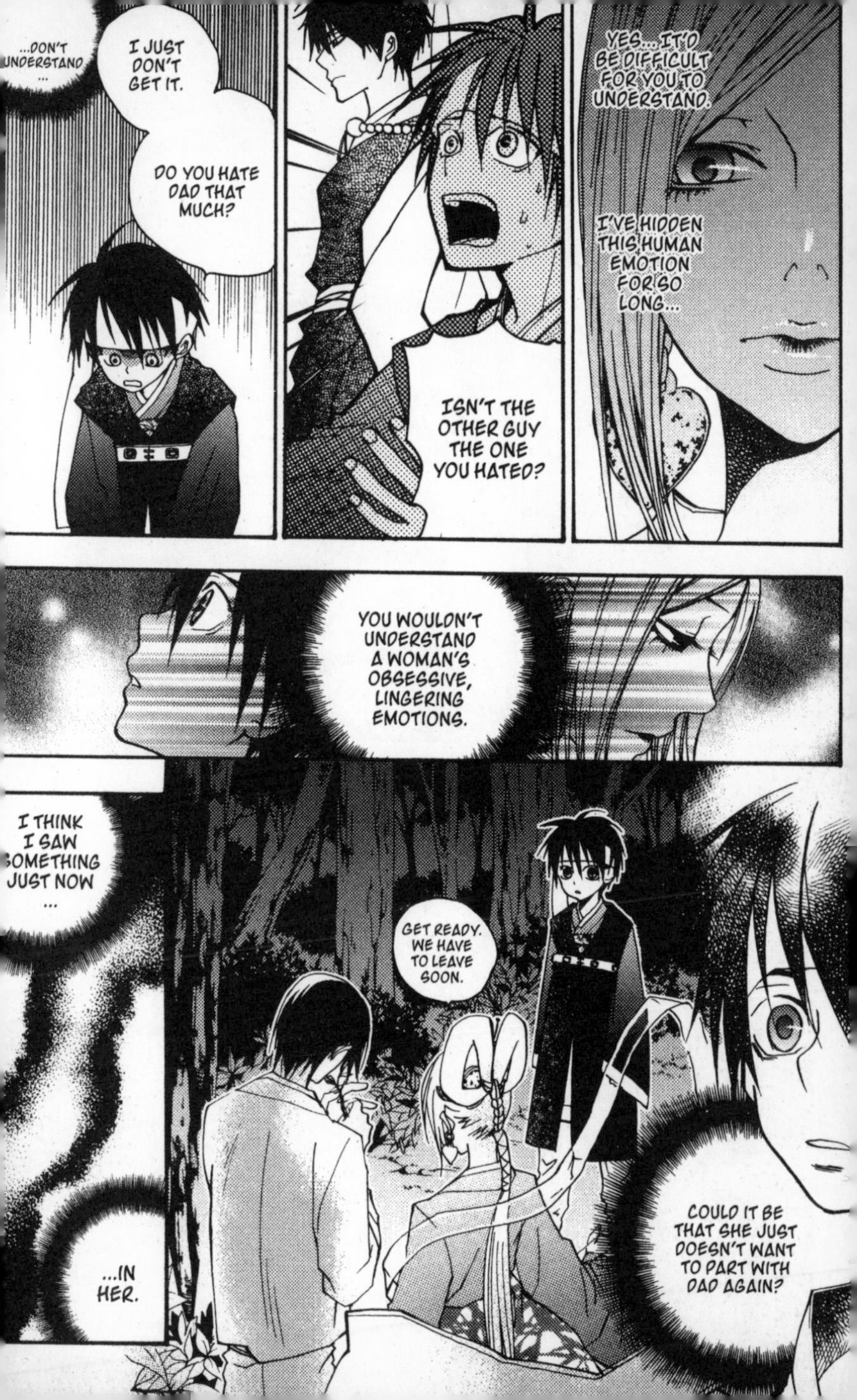
...DON'T UNDERSTAND ...
I JUST DON'T GET IT.
DO YOU HATE DAD THAT MUCH?
ISN'T THE OTHER GUY THE ONE YOU HATED?
YES... IT'D BE DIFFICULT FOR YOU TO UNDERSTAND.
I'VE HIDDEN THIS HUMAN EMOTION FOR SO LONG...
YOU WOULDN'T UNDERSTAND A WOMAN'S OBSESSIVE, LINGERING EMOTIONS.
I THINK I SAW SOMETHING JUST NOW ...
...IN HER.
GET READY. WE HAVE TO LEAVE SOON.
COULD IT BE THAT SHE JUST DOESN'T WANT TO PART WITH DAD AGAIN?

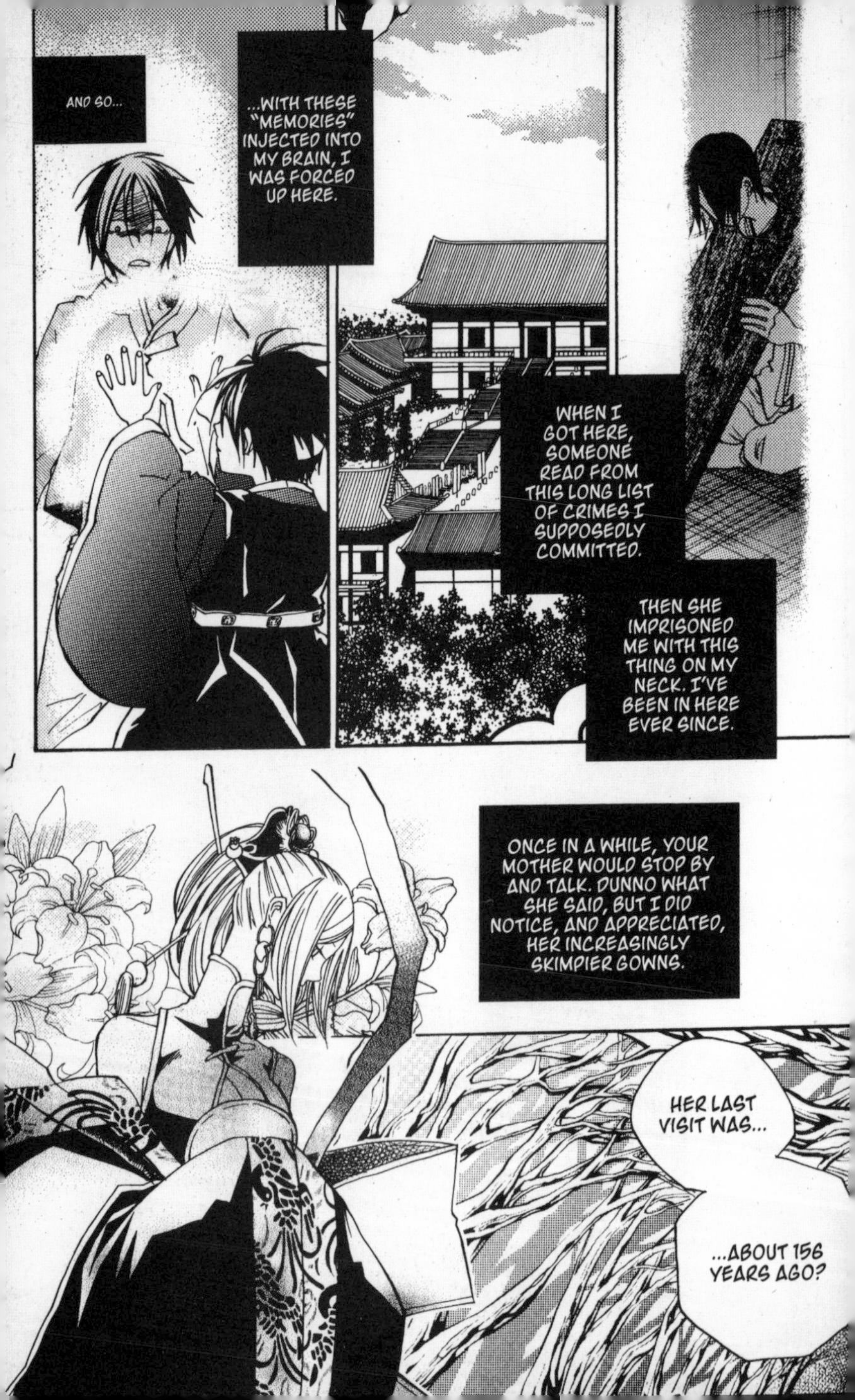
AND SO...
...WITH THESE "MEMORIES" INJECTED INTO MY BRAIN, I WAS FORCED UP HERE.
WHEN I GOT HERE, SOMEONE READ FROM THIS LONG LIST OF CRIMES I SUPPOSEDLY COMMITTED.
THEN SHE IMPRISONED ME WITH THIS THING ON MY NECK. I'VE BEEN IN HERE EVER SINCE.
ONCE IN A WHILE, YOUR MOTHER WOULD STOP BY AND TALK. DUNNO WHAT SHE SAID, BUT I DID NOTICE, AND APPRECIATED, HER INCREASINGLY SKIMPIER GOWNS.
HER LAST VISIT WAS...
...ABOUT 156 YEARS AGO?

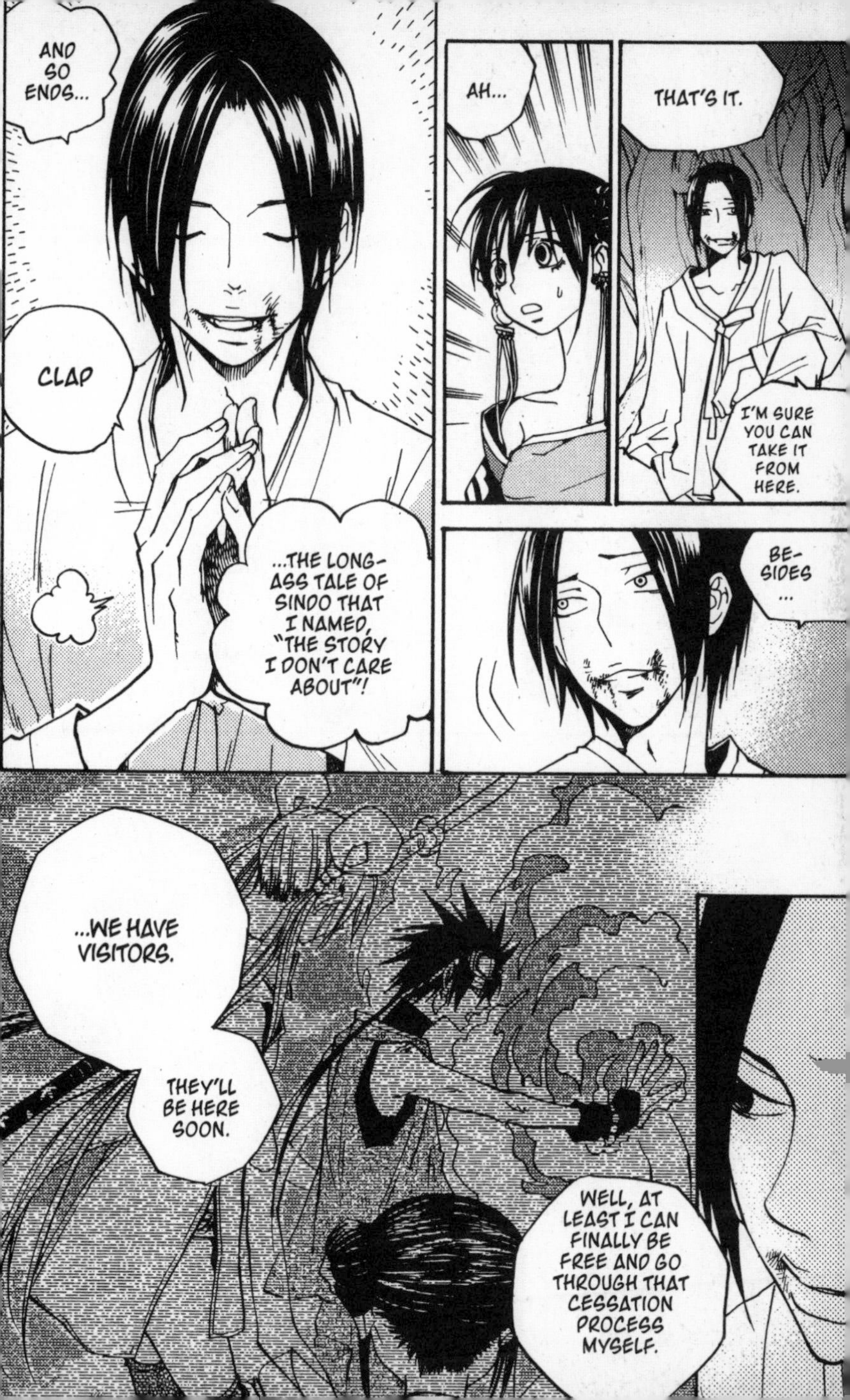
AND SO ENDS...
CLAP
...THE LONG-ASS TALE OF SINDO THAT I NAMED, "THE STORY I DON'T CARE ABOUT"!
AH...
THAT'S IT.
I'M SURE YOU CAN TAKE IT FROM HERE.
BE-SIDES...
...WE HAVE VISITORS.
THEY'LL BE HERE SOON.
WELL, AT LEAST I CAN FINALLY BE FREE AND GO THROUGH THAT CESSATION PROCESS MYSELF.

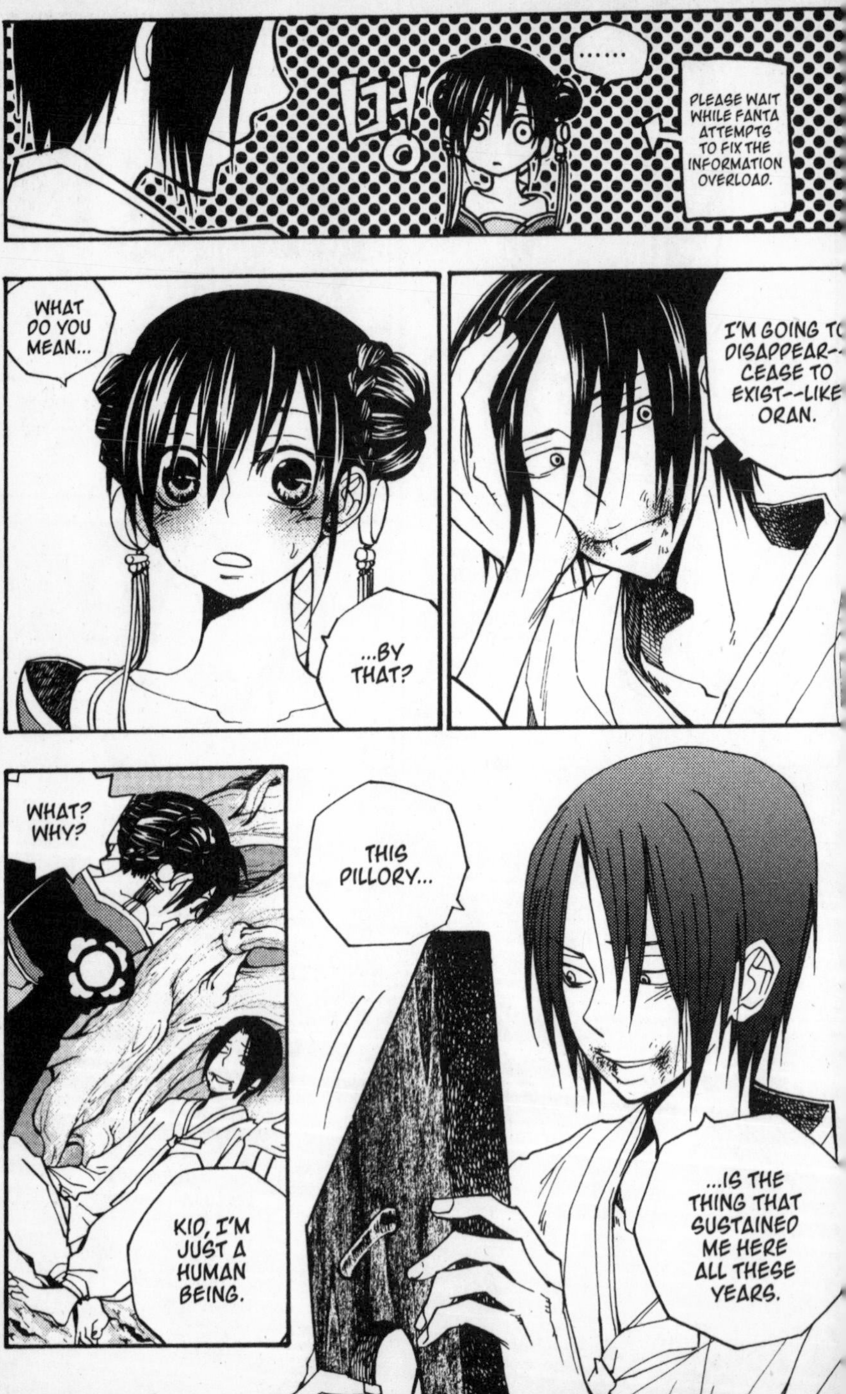
....
PLEASE WAIT WHILE FANTA ATTEMPTS TO FIX THE INFORMATION OVERLOAD.
WHAT DO YOU MEAN...
...BY THAT?
I'M GOING TO DISAPPEAR--CEASE TO EXIST--LIKE ORAN.
WHAT? WHY?
KID, I'M JUST A HUMAN BEING.
THIS PILLORY...
...IS THE THING THAT SUSTAINED ME HERE ALL THESE YEARS.

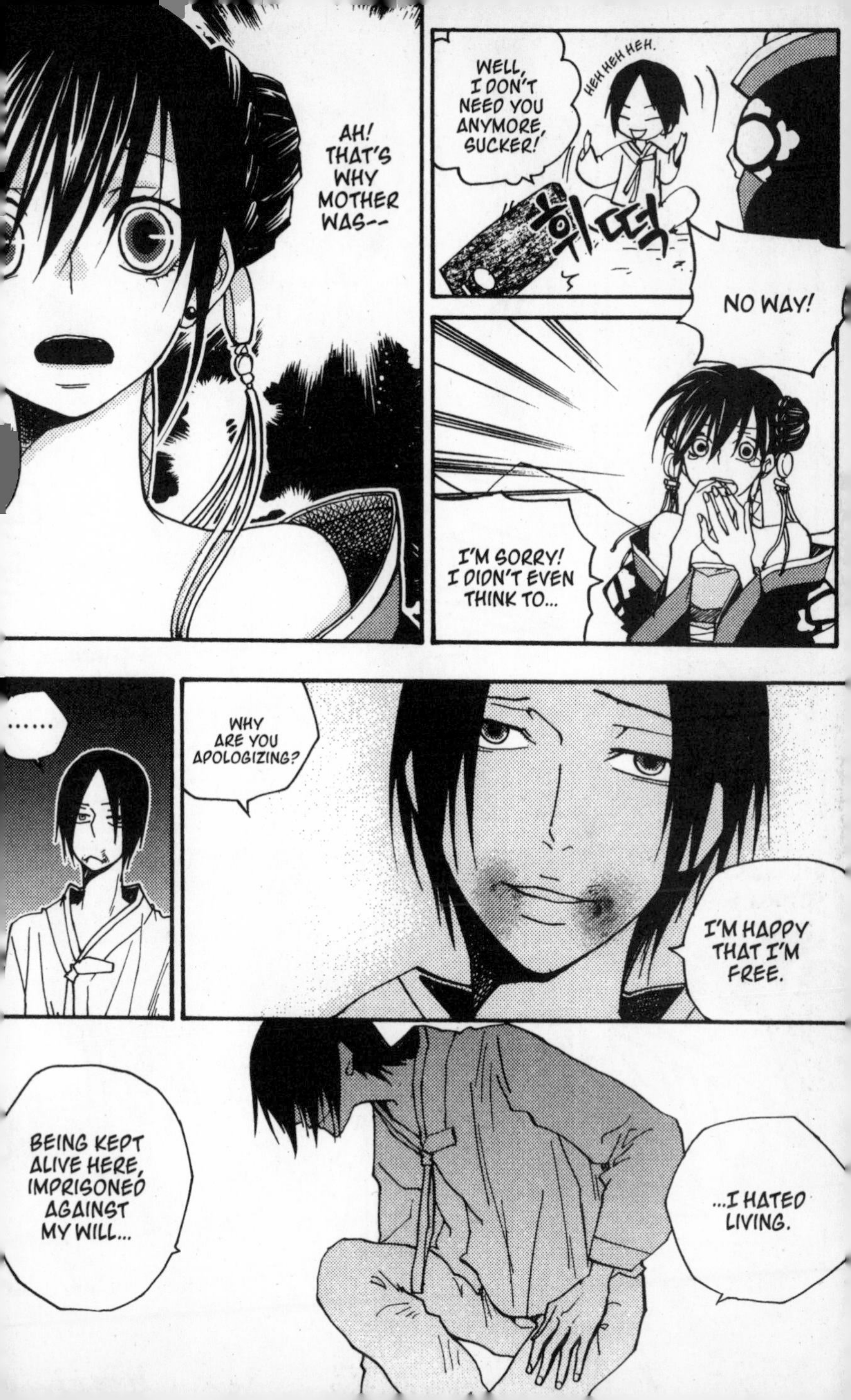
AH! THAT'S WHY MOTHER WAS--
WELL, I DON'T NEED YOU ANYMORE, SUCKER!
HEH HEH HEH.
휘떡
NO WAY!
I'M SORRY! I DIDN'T EVEN THINK TO...
....
WHY ARE YOU APOLOGIZING?
I'M HAPPY THAT I'M FREE.
BEING KEPT ALIVE HERE, IMPRISONED AGAINST MY WILL...
...I HATED LIVING.

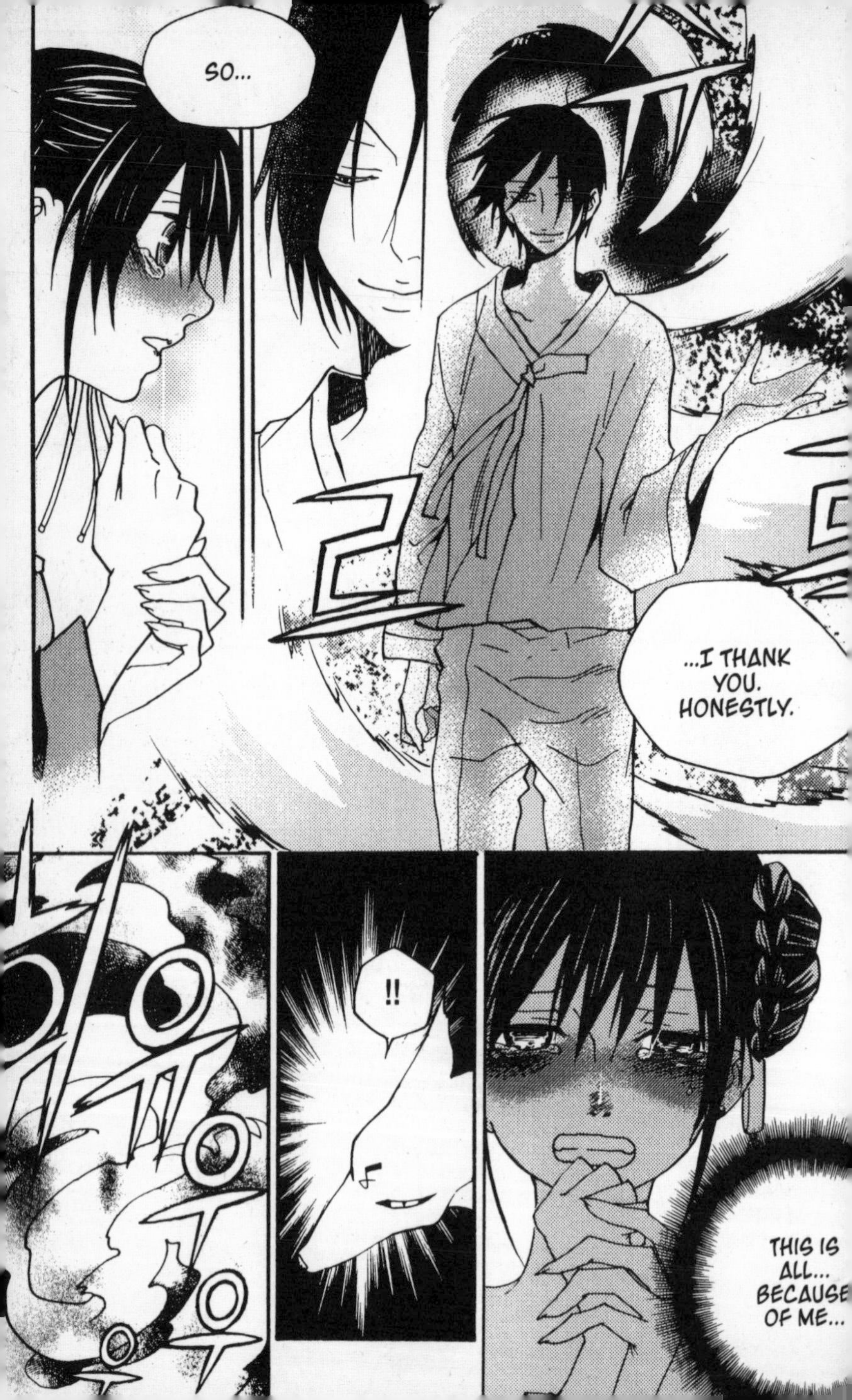
SO...
...I THANK YOU. HONESTLY.
!!
THIS IS ALL... BECAUSE OF ME...

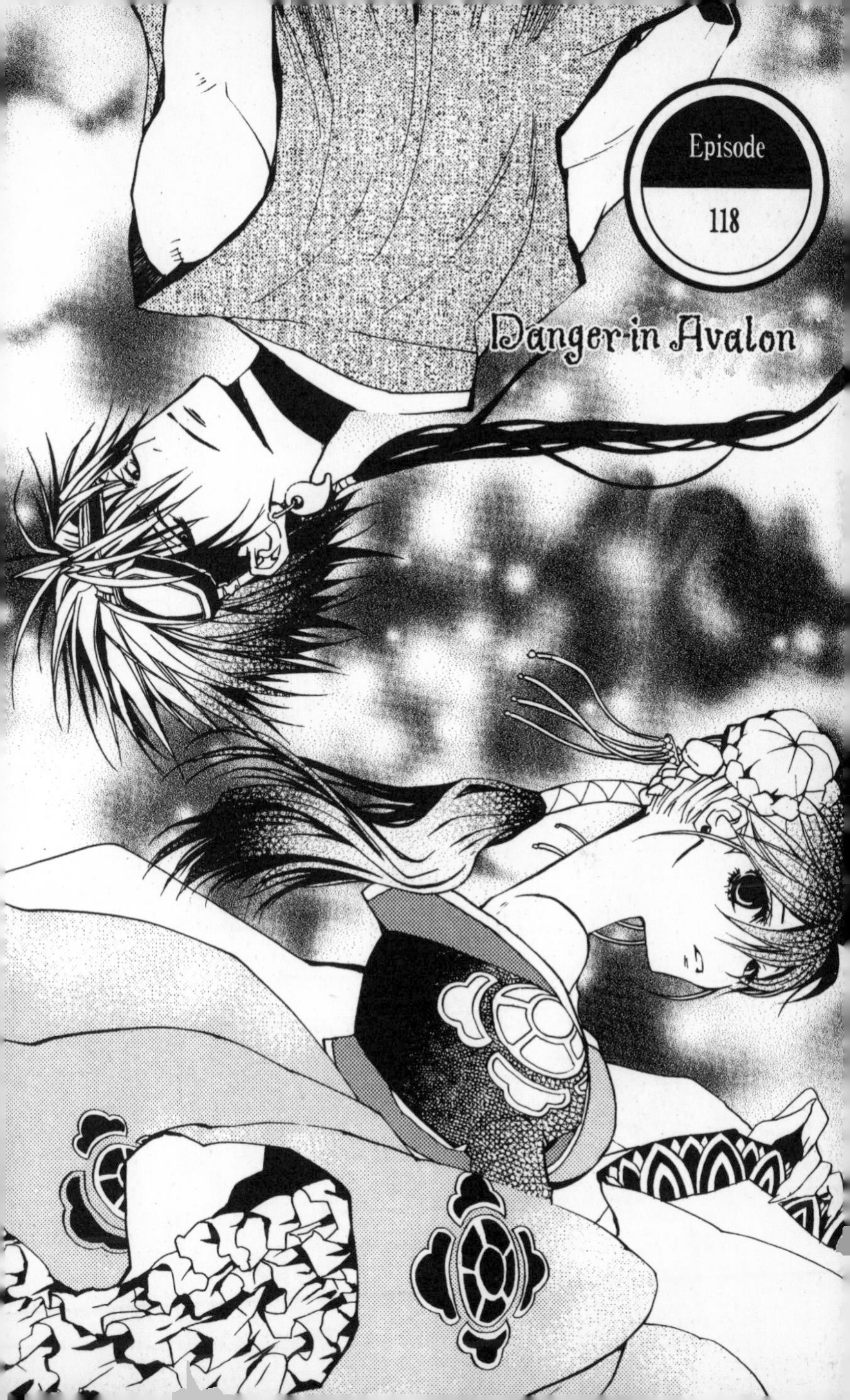
Episode
118
Danger in Avalon

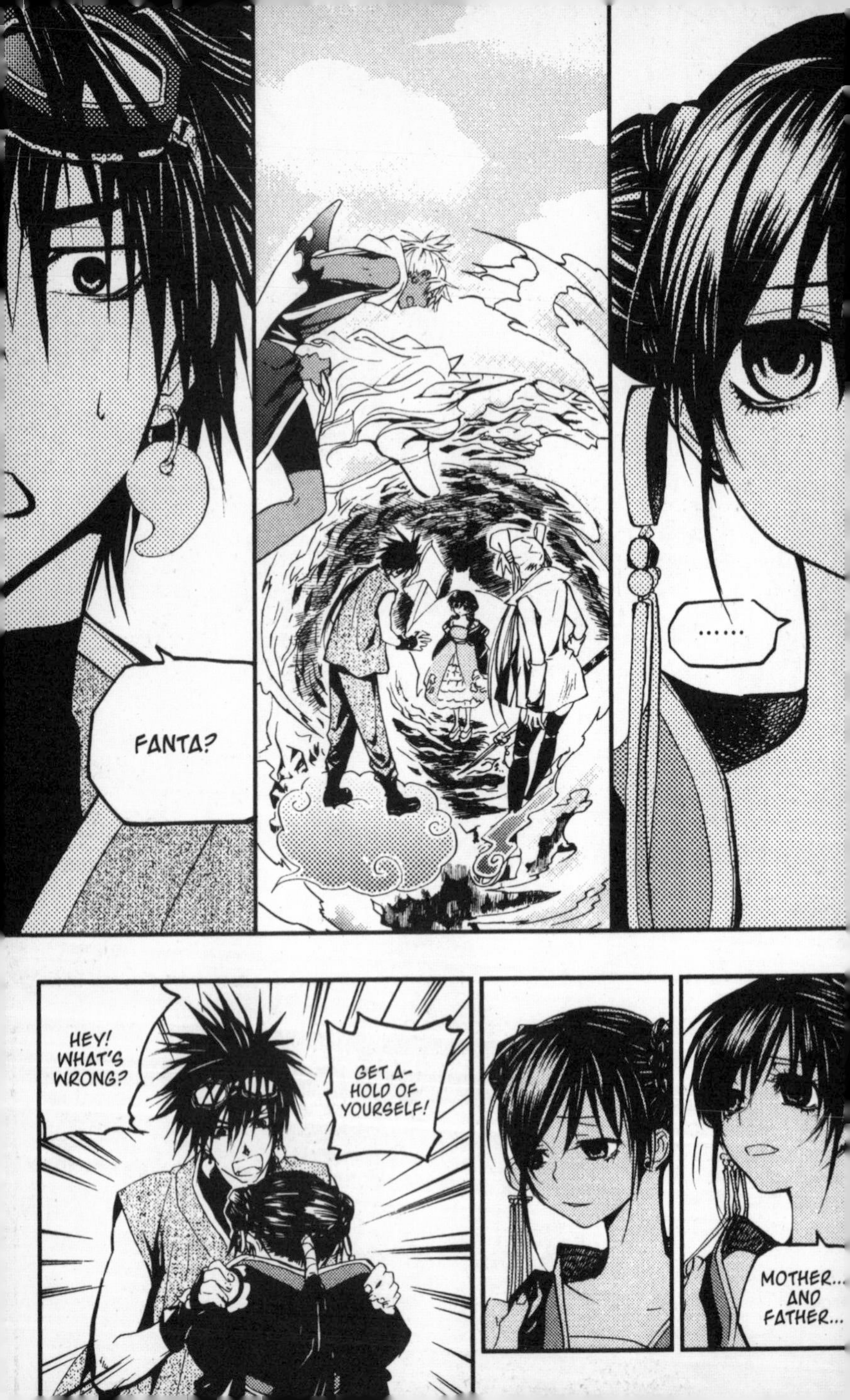
FANTA?
......
HEY! WHAT'S WRONG?
GET A-HOLD OF YOURSELF!
MOTHER... AND FATHER...

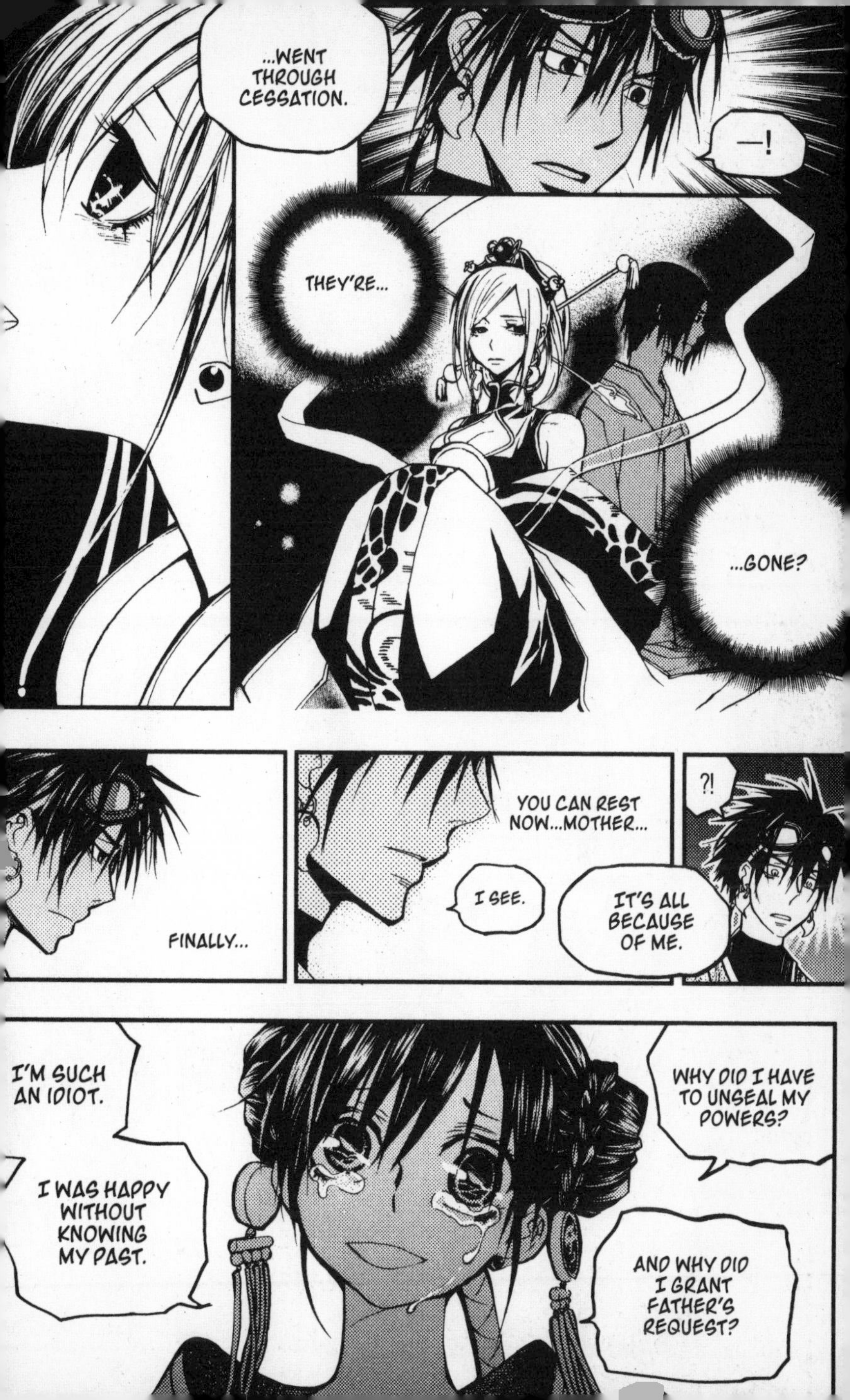
...WENT THROUGH CESSATION.
—!
THEY'RE...
...GONE?
FINALLY...
YOU CAN REST NOW...MOTHER...
I SEE.
IT'S ALL BECAUSE OF ME.
?!
I'M SUCH AN IDIOT.
I WAS HAPPY WITHOUT KNOWING MY PAST.
WHY DID I HAVE TO UNSEAL MY POWERS?
AND WHY DID I GRANT FATHER'S REQUEST?

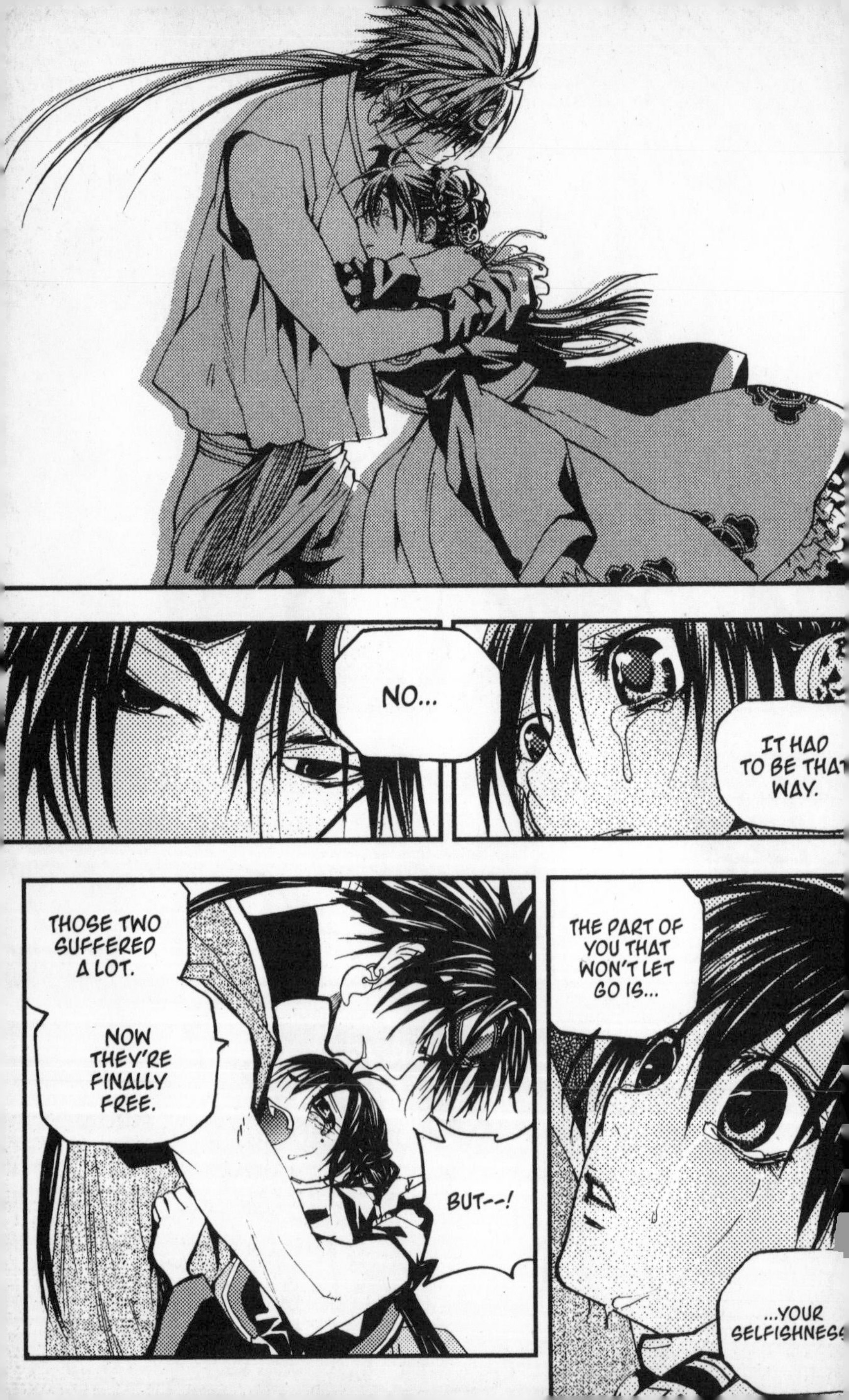
NO...
IT HAD TO BE THAT WAY.
THOSE TWO SUFFERED A LOT.
NOW THEY'RE FINALLY FREE.
BUT--!
THE PART OF YOU THAT WON'T LET GO IS...
...YOUR SELFISHNESS

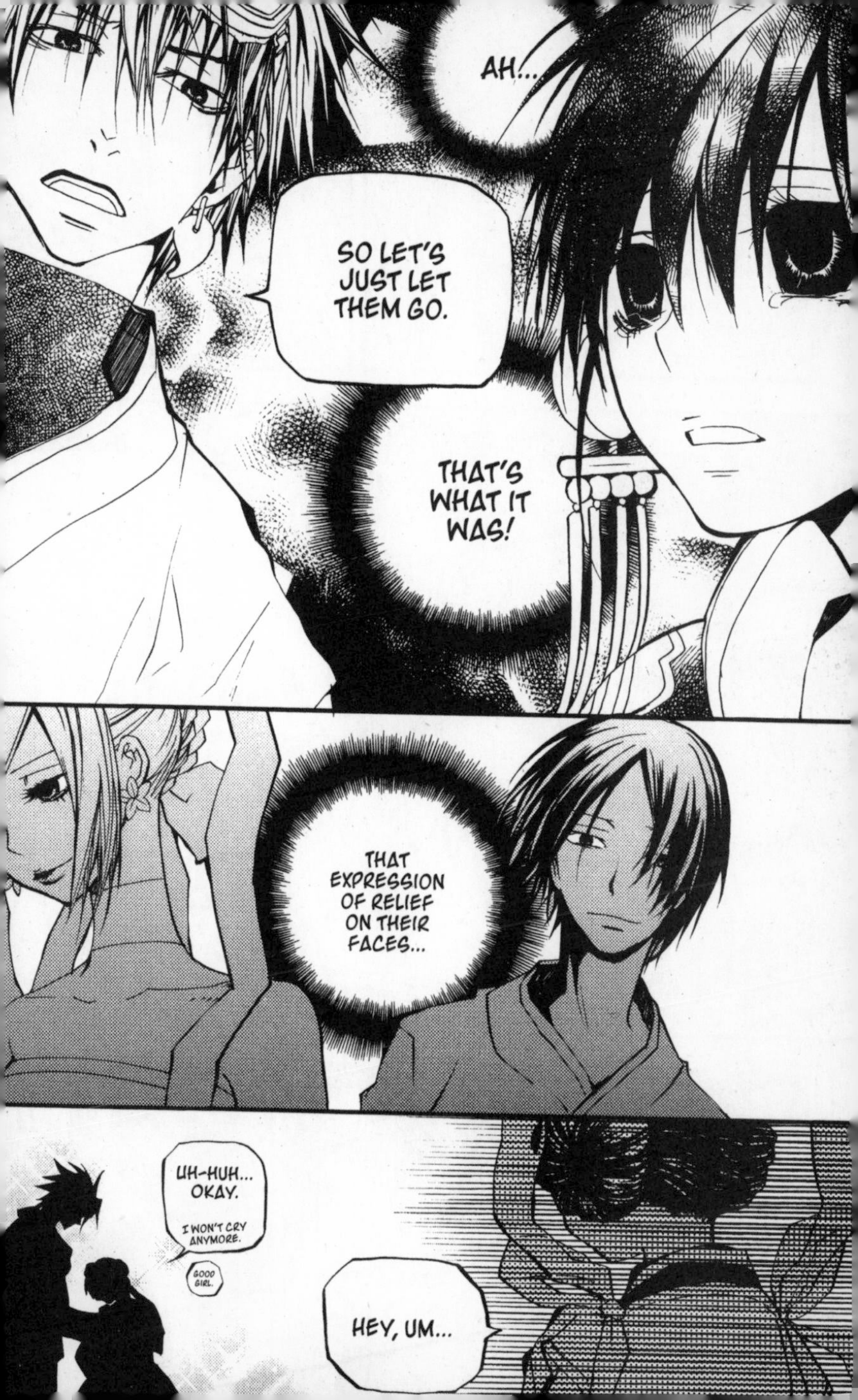
AH...
SO LET'S JUST LET THEM GO.
THAT'S WHAT IT WAS!
THAT EXPRESSION OF RELIEF ON THEIR FACES...
UH-HUH... OKAY.
I WON'T CRY ANYMORE.
GOOD GIRL.
HEY, UM...

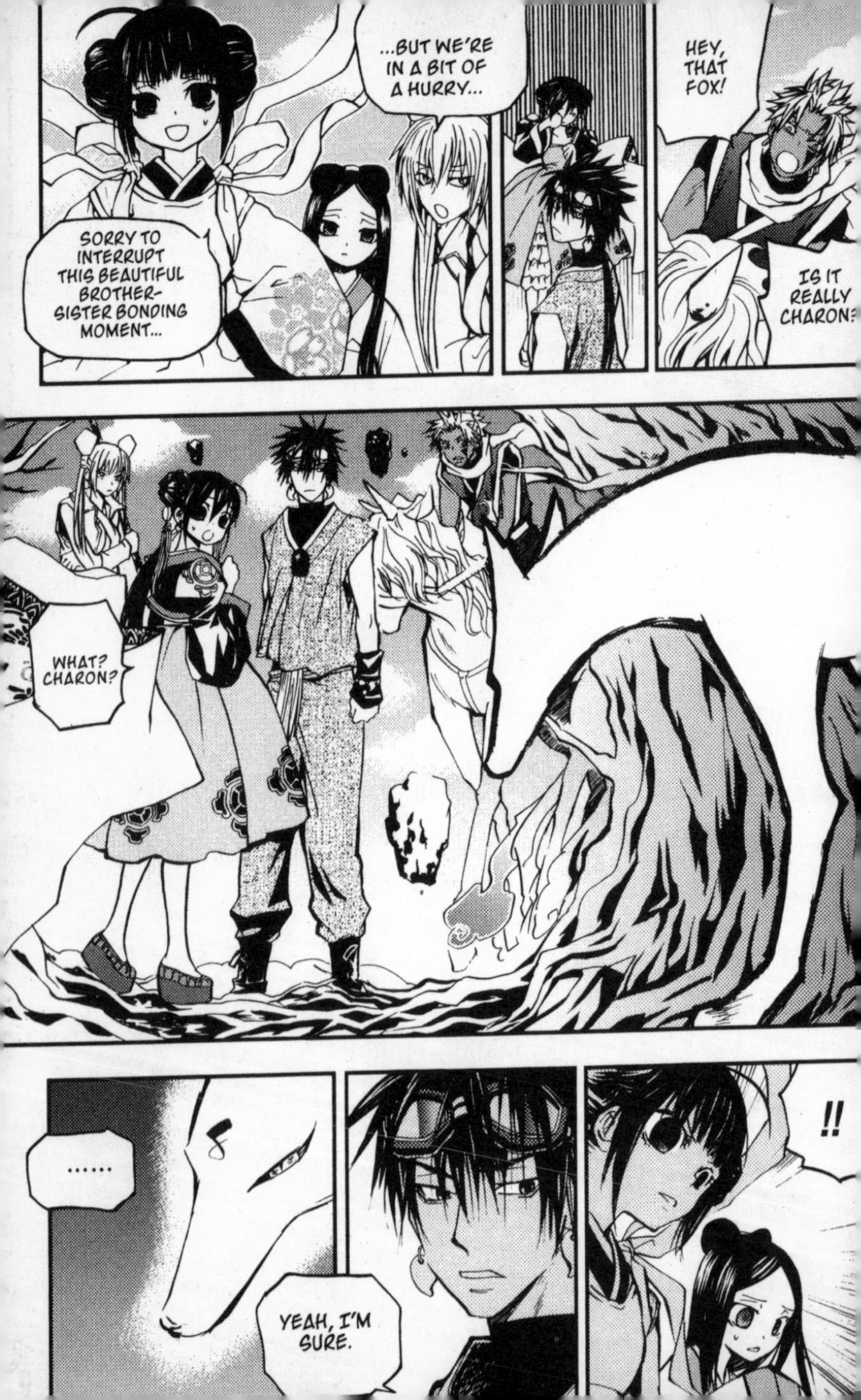
SORRY TO INTERRUPT THIS BEAUTIFUL BROTHER-SISTER BONDING MOMENT...
...BUT WE'RE IN A BIT OF A HURRY...
HEY, THAT FOX!
IS IT REALLY CHARON?
WHAT? CHARON?
......
YEAH, I'M SURE.
!!

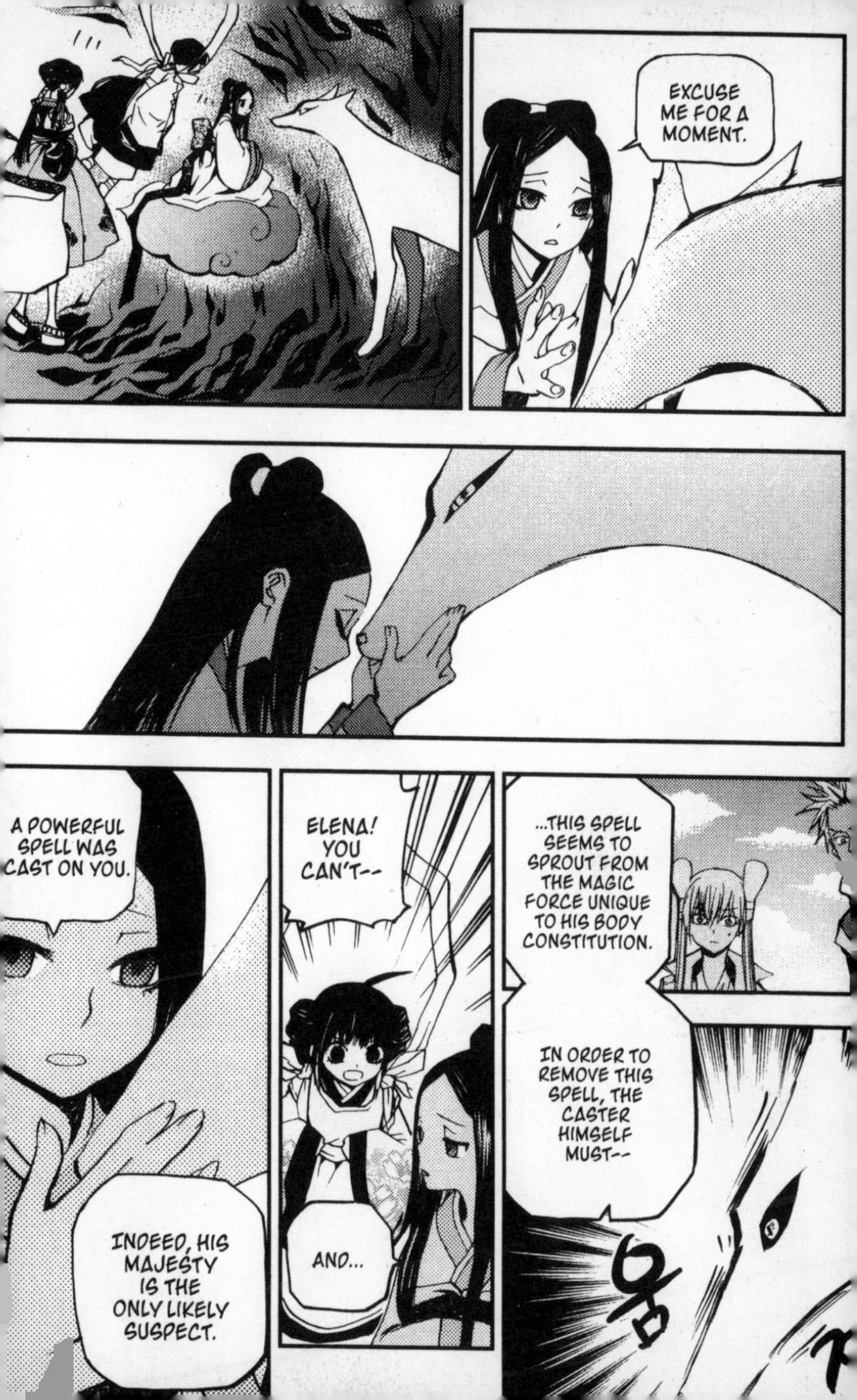
EXCUSE ME FOR A MOMENT.
A POWERFUL SPELL WAS CAST ON YOU.
INDEED, HIS MAJESTY IS THE ONLY LIKELY SUSPECT.
ELENA! YOU CAN'T--
AND...
...THIS SPELL SEEMS TO SPROUT FROM THE MAGIC FORCE UNIQUE TO HIS BODY CONSTITUTION.
IN ORDER TO REMOVE THIS SPELL, THE CASTER HIMSELF MUST--

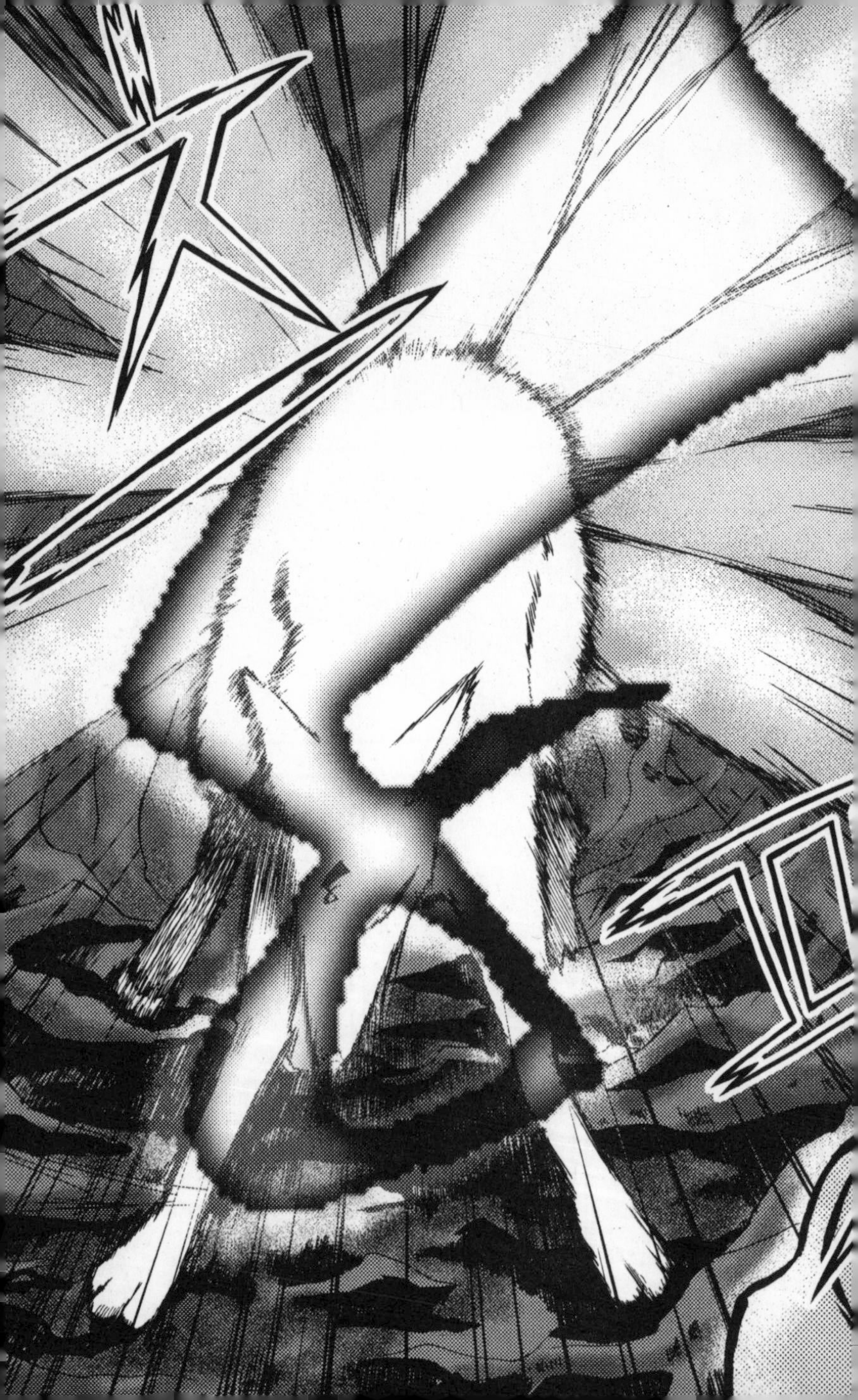
ズ

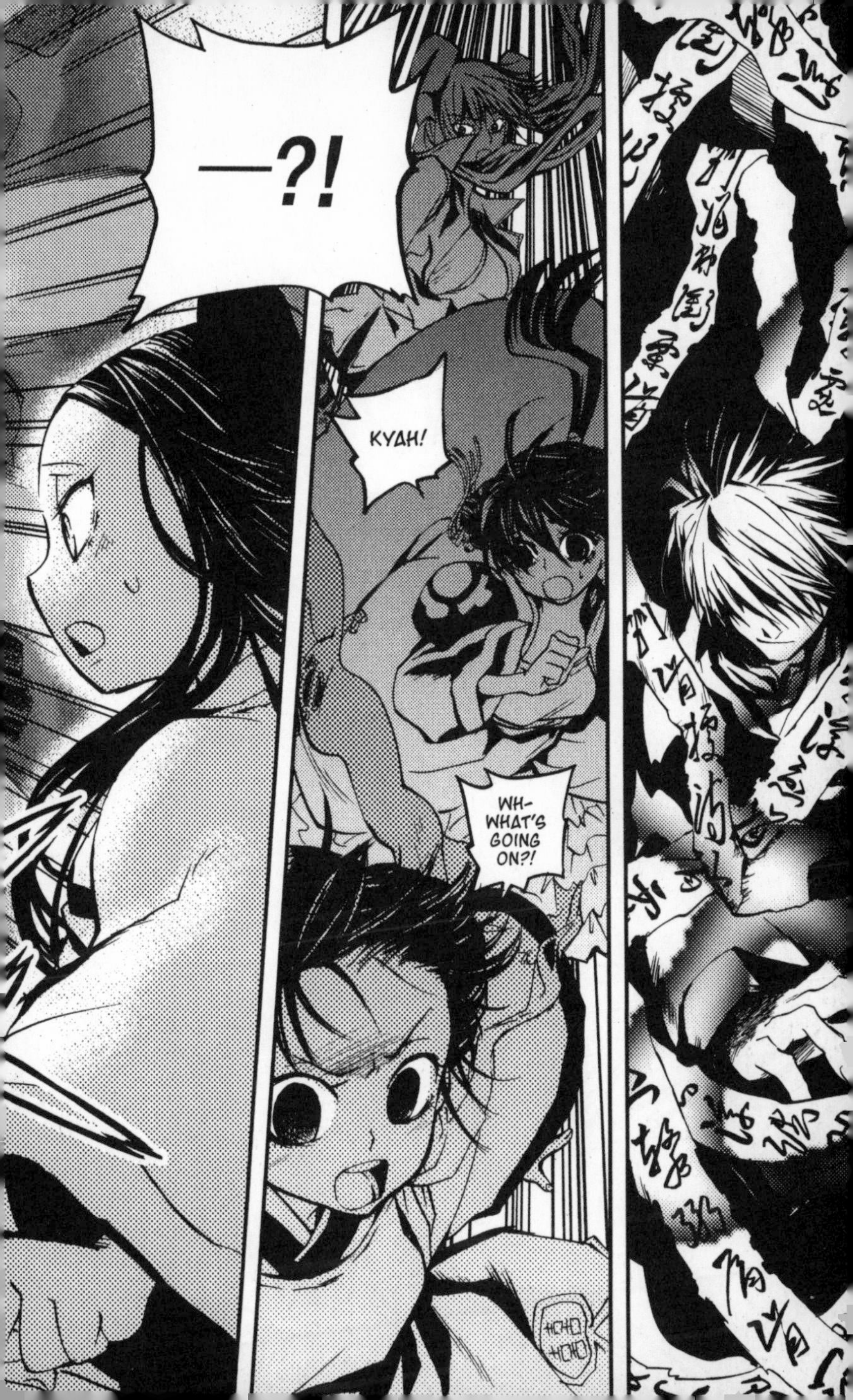
—?!
KYAH!
WH-WHAT'S GOING ON?!

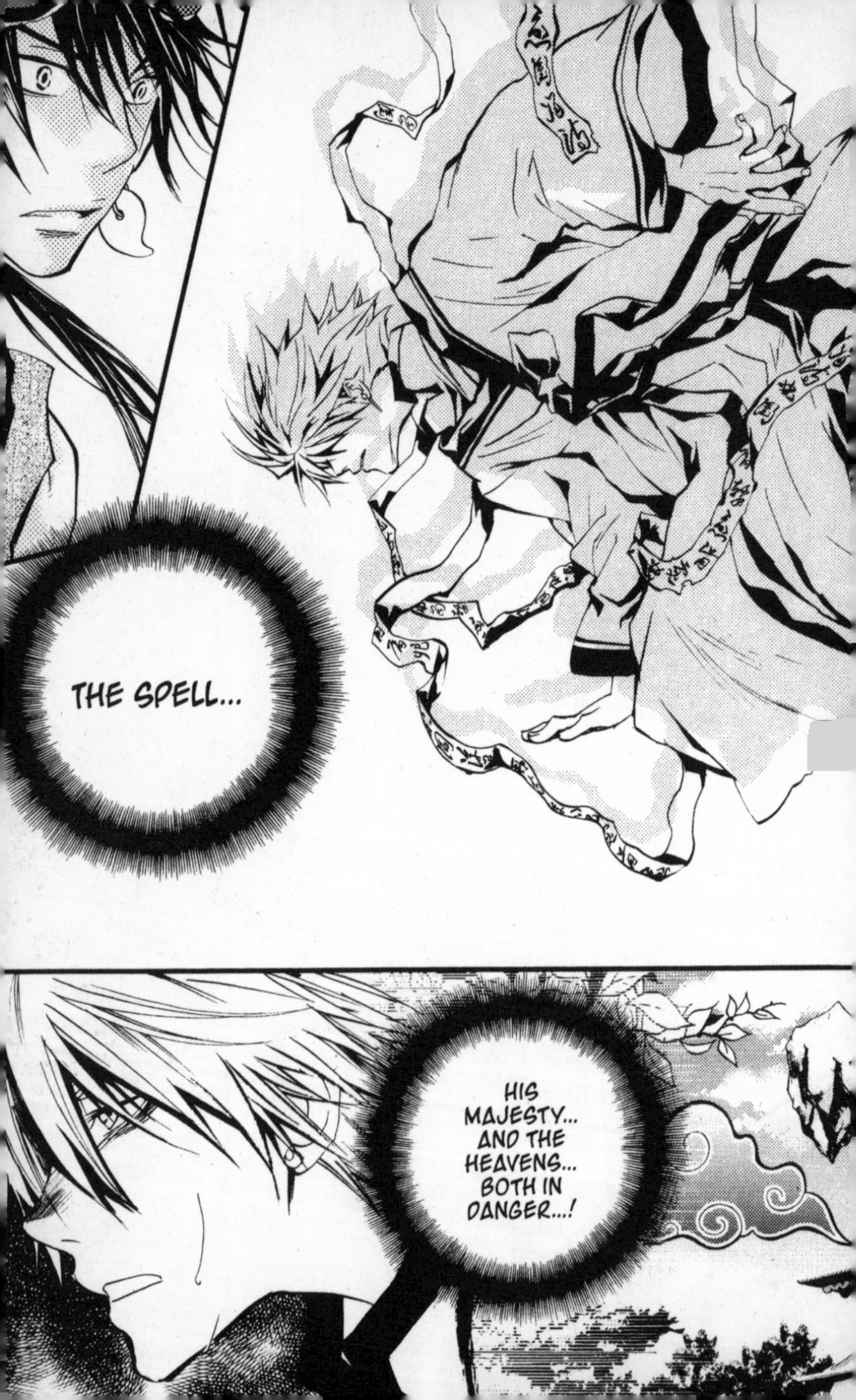
THE SPELL...
HIS MAJESTY... AND THE HEAVENS... BOTH IN DANGER...!

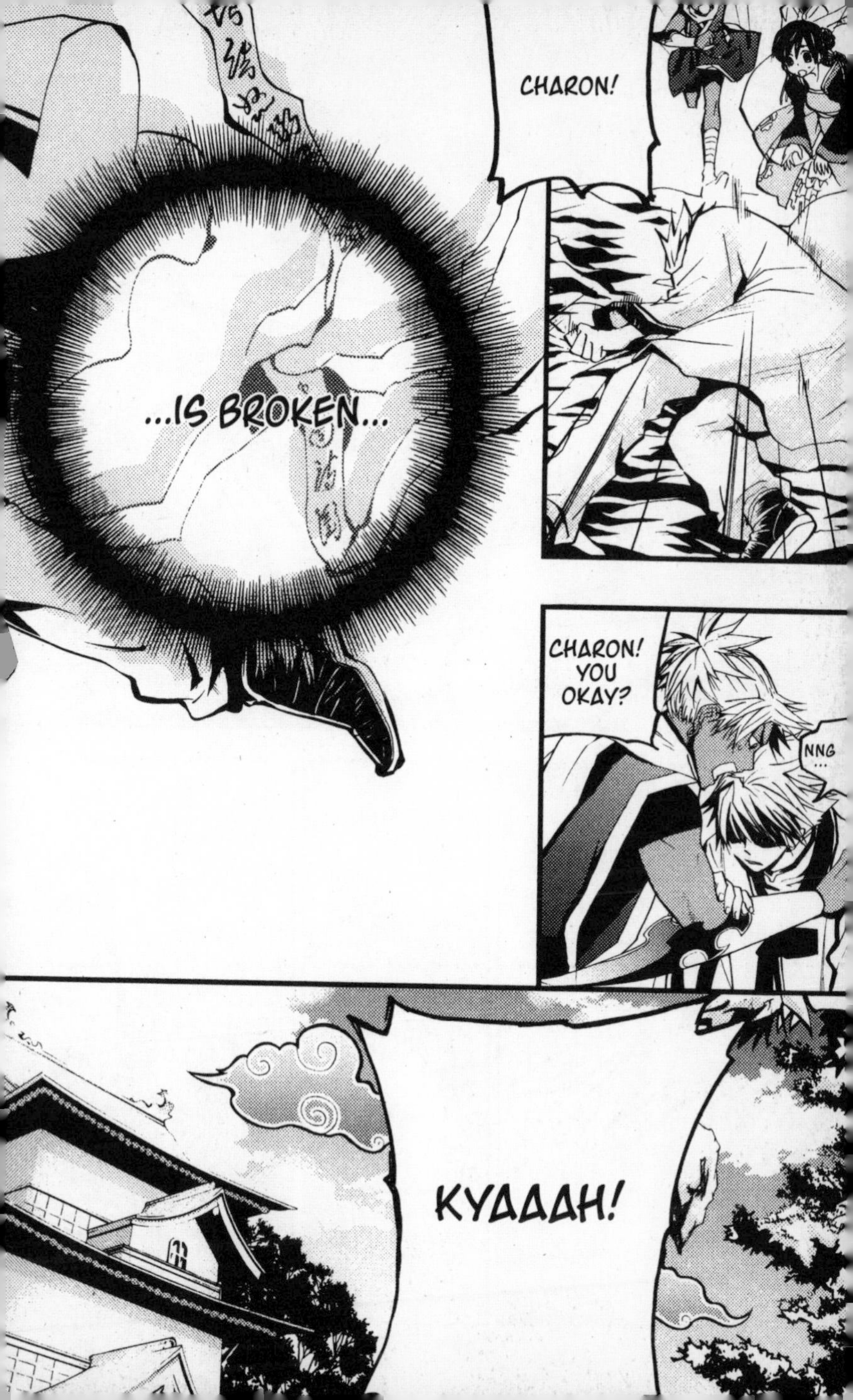
...IS BROKEN...
CHARON!
CHARON! YOU OKAY?
NNG...
KYAAAH!

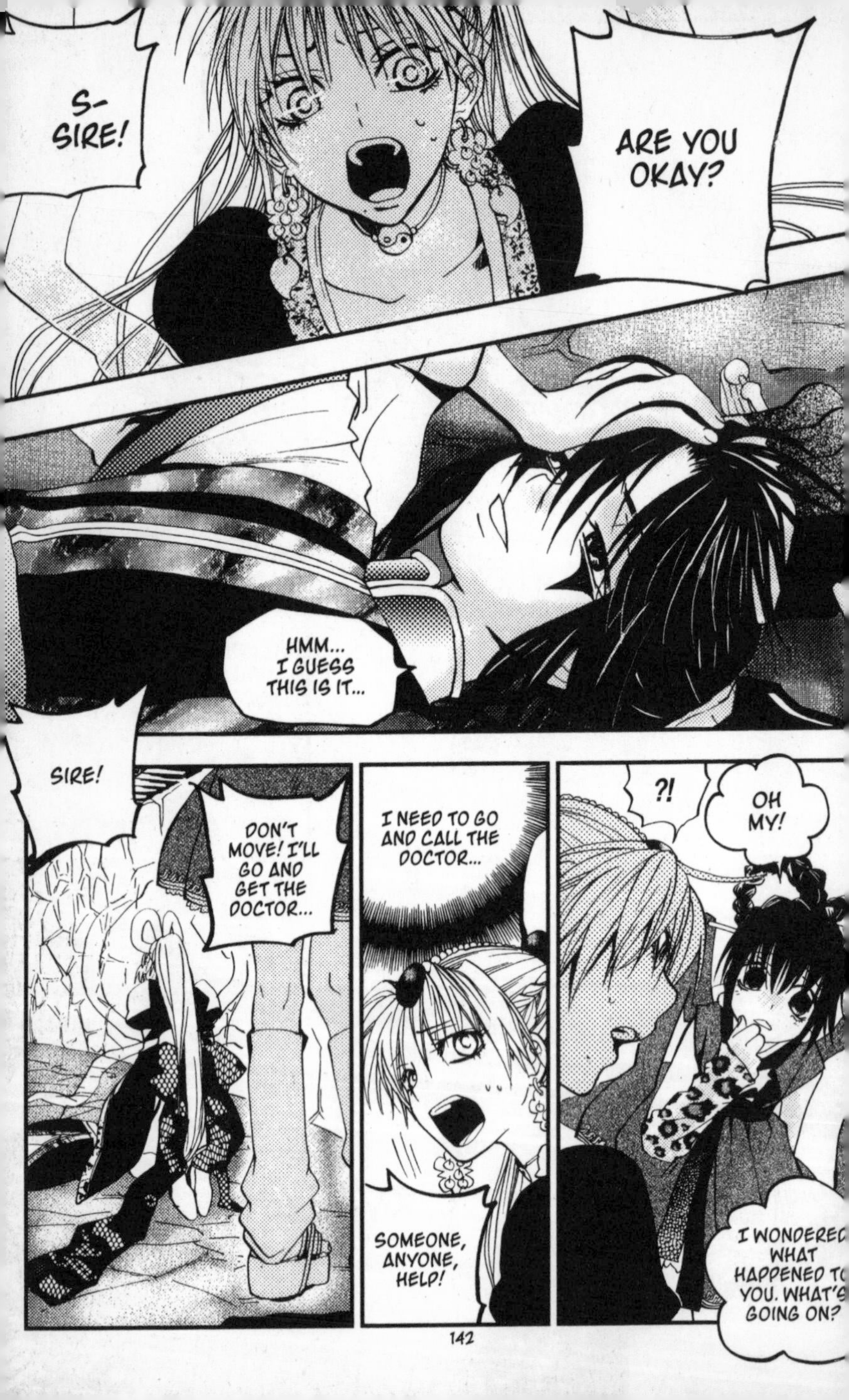

S-SIRE!
ARE YOU OKAY?
HMM... I GUESS THIS IS IT...
SIRE!
DON'T MOVE! I'LL GO AND GET THE DOCTOR...
I NEED TO GO AND CALL THE DOCTOR...
SOMEONE, ANYONE, HELP!
?!
OH MY!
I WONDERED WHAT HAPPENED TO YOU. WHAT'S GOING ON?

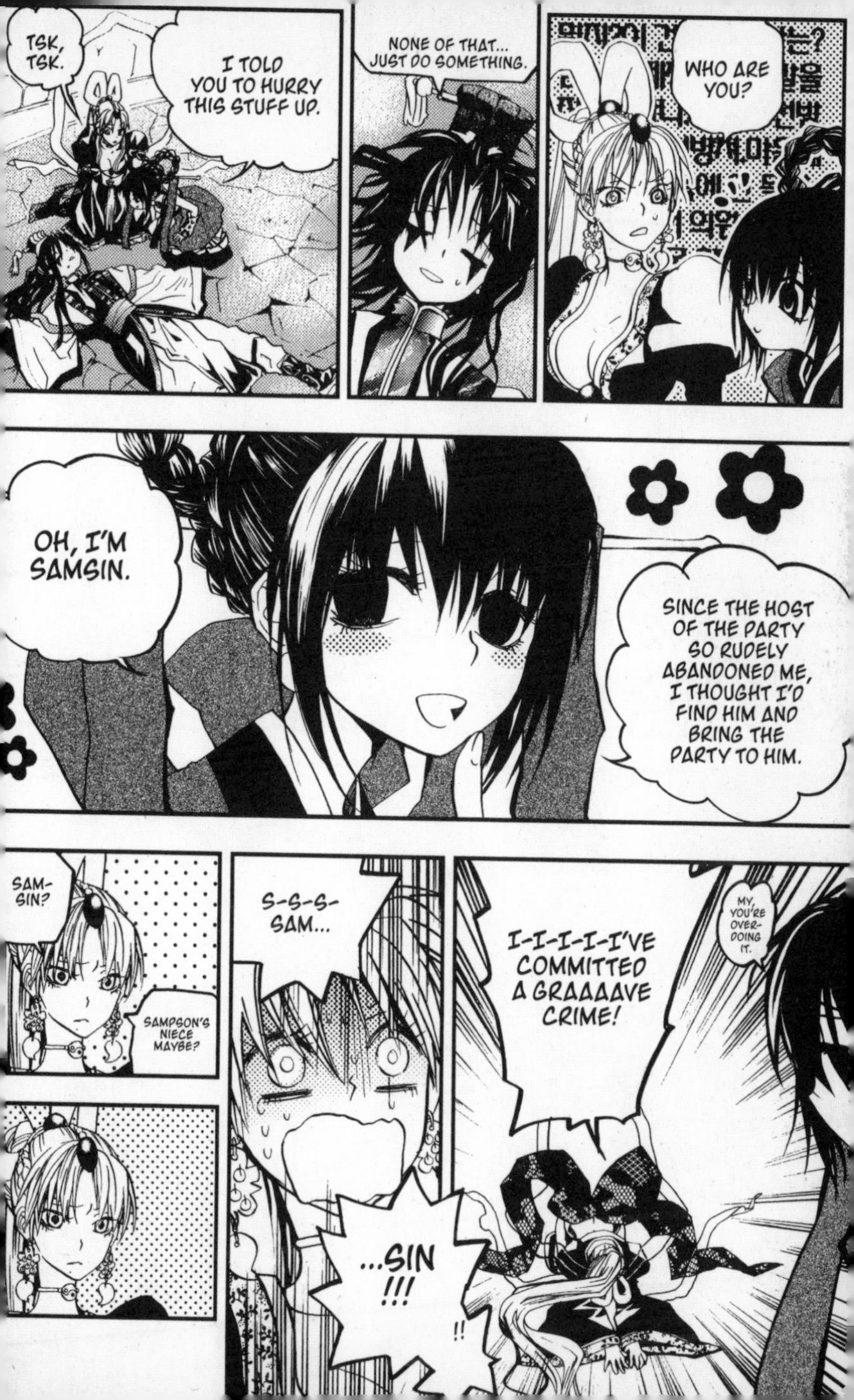
TSK, TSK.
I TOLD YOU TO HURRY THIS STUFF UP.
NONE OF THAT... JUST DO SOMETHING.
WHO ARE YOU?
OH, I'M SAMSIN.
SINCE THE HOST OF THE PARTY SO RUDELY ABANDONED ME, I THOUGHT I'D FIND HIM AND BRING THE PARTY TO HIM.
SAM-SIN?
SAMPSON'S NIECE MAYBE?
S-S-S-SAM...
...SIN !!!
!!
I-I-I-I-I'VE COMMITTED A GRAAAAVE CRIME!
MY, YOU'RE OVER-DOING IT.

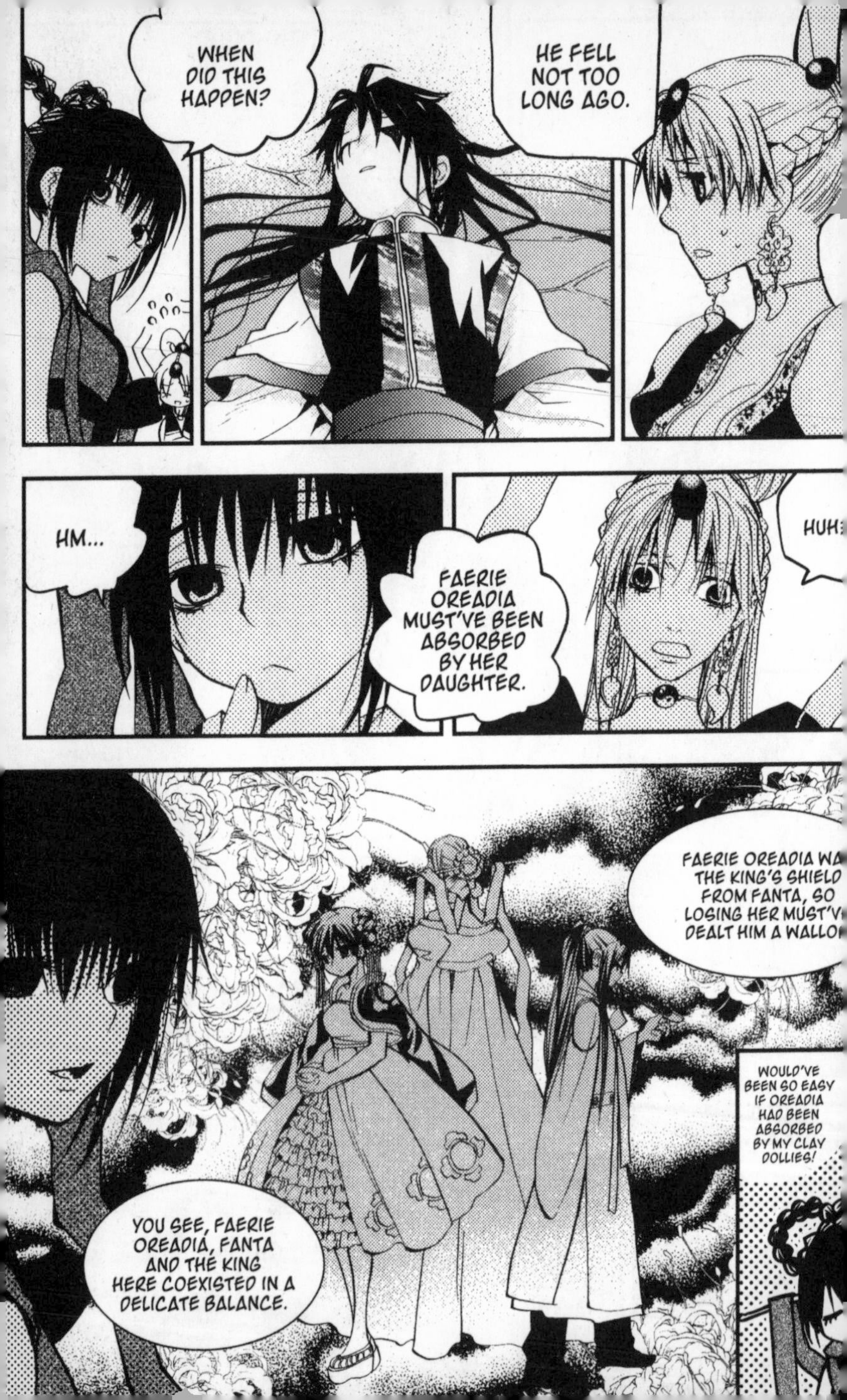
WHEN DID THIS HAPPEN?
HE FELL NOT TOO LONG AGO.
HM...
FAERIE OREADIA MUST'VE BEEN ABSORBED BY HER DAUGHTER.
HUH?
FAERIE OREADIA WA THE KING'S SHIELD FROM FANTA, SO LOSING HER MUST'V DEALT HIM A WALLO
YOU SEE, FAERIE OREADIA, FANTA AND THE KING HERE COEXISTED IN A DELICATE BALANCE.
WOULD'VE BEEN SO EASY IF OREADIA HAD BEEN ABSORBED BY MY CLAY DOLLIES!

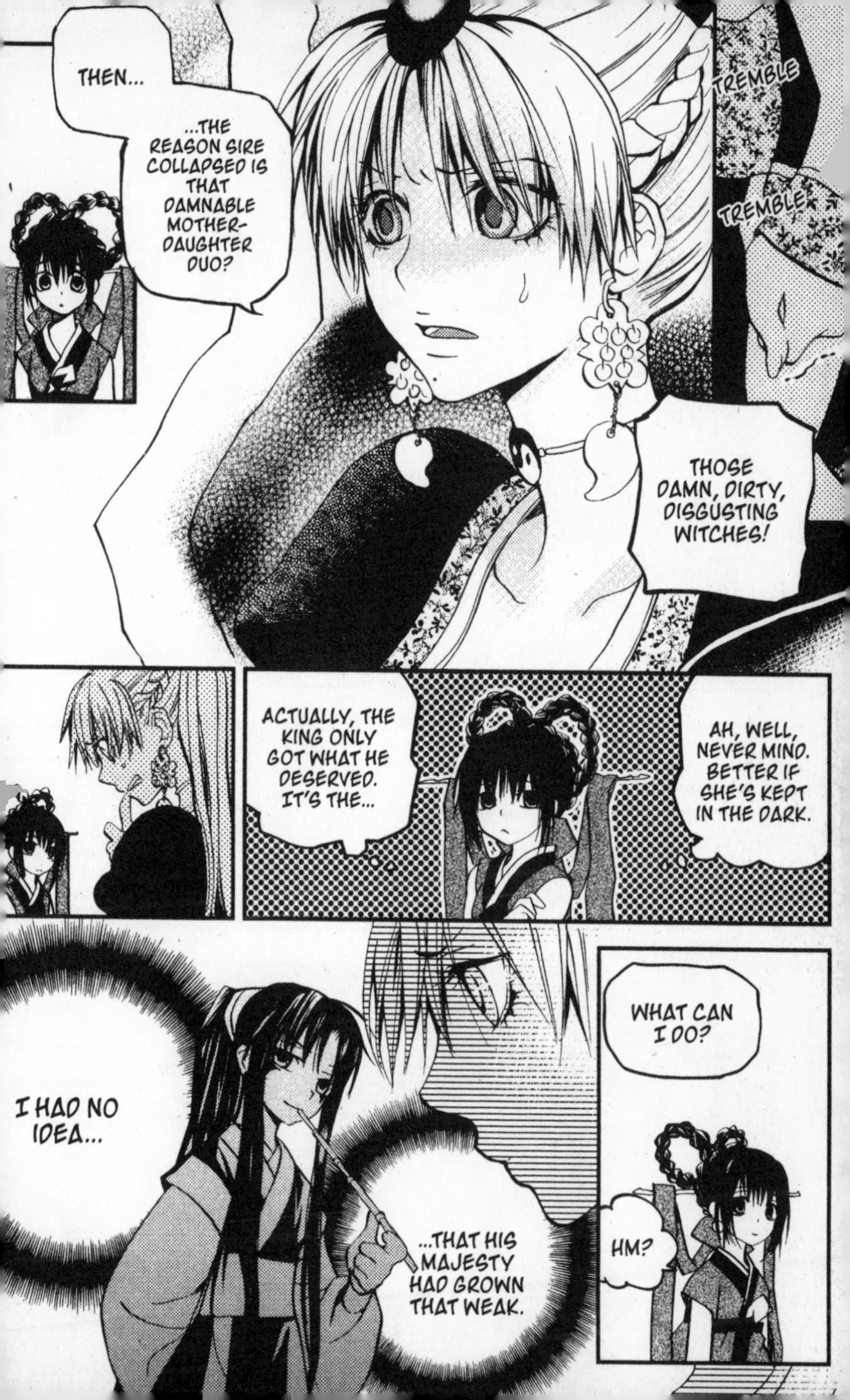
THEN...
...THE REASON SIRE COLLAPSED IS THAT DAMNABLE MOTHER-DAUGHTER DUO?
TREMBLE
TREMBLE
THOSE DAMN, DIRTY, DISGUSTING WITCHES!
ACTUALLY, THE KING ONLY GOT WHAT HE DESERVED. IT'S THE...
AH, WELL, NEVER MIND. BETTER IF SHE'S KEPT IN THE DARK.
I HAD NO IDEA...
...THAT HIS MAJESTY HAD GROWN THAT WEAK.
WHAT CAN I DO?
HM?

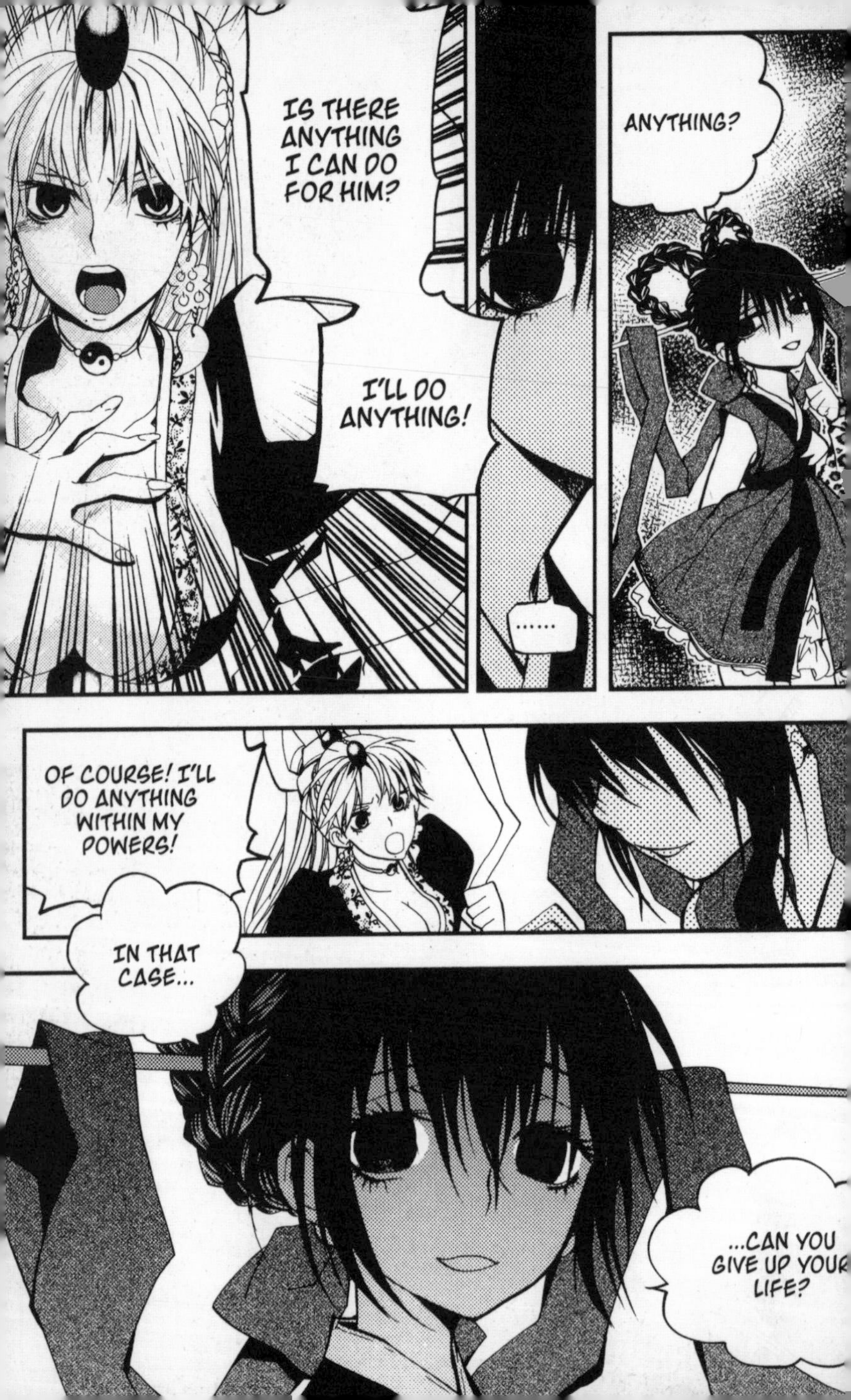
IS THERE ANYTHING I CAN DO FOR HIM?
I'LL DO ANYTHING!
......
ANYTHING?
OF COURSE! I'LL DO ANYTHING WITHIN MY POWERS!
IN THAT CASE...
...CAN YOU GIVE UP YOUR LIFE?

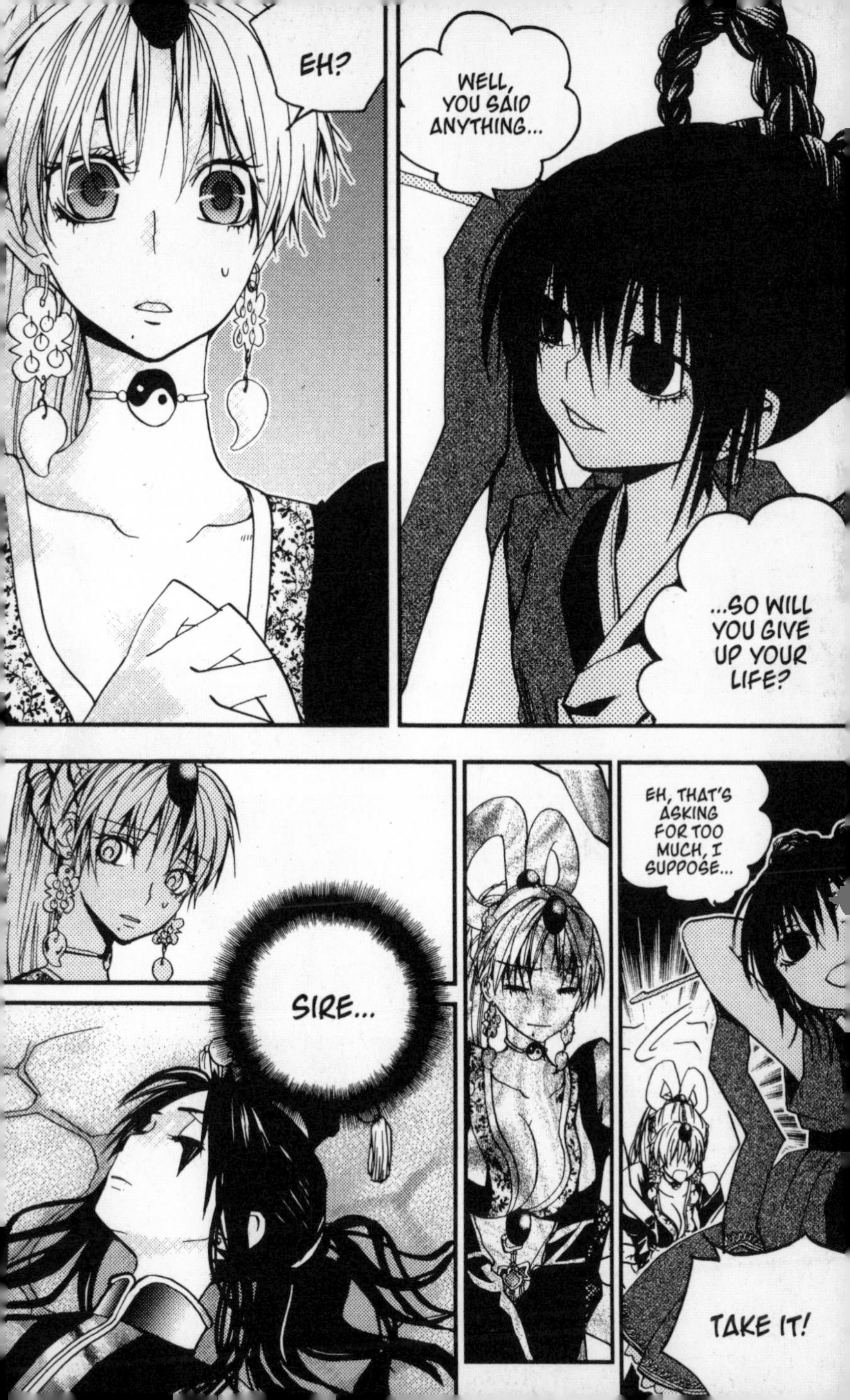
EH?
WELL, YOU SAID ANYTHING...
...SO WILL YOU GIVE UP YOUR LIFE?
SIRE...
EH, THAT'S ASKING FOR TOO MUCH, I SUPPOSE...
TAKE IT!

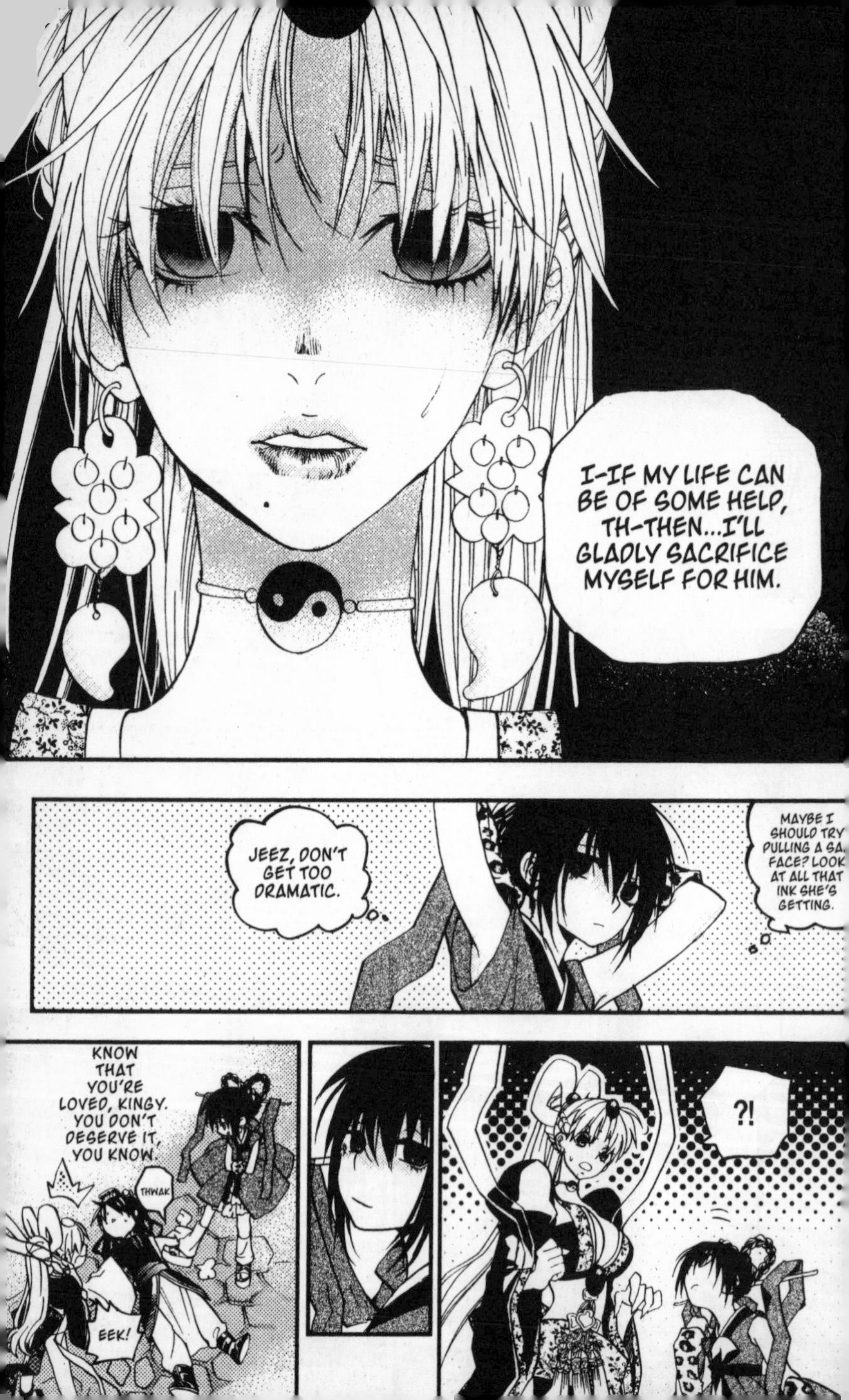
I-IF MY LIFE CAN BE OF SOME HELP, TH-THEN...I'LL GLADLY SACRIFICE MYSELF FOR HIM.
JEEZ, DON'T GET TOO DRAMATIC.
MAYBE I SHOULD TRY PULLING A SA FACE? LOOK AT ALL THAT INK SHE'S GETTING.
KNOW THAT YOU'RE LOVED, KINGY. YOU DON'T DESERVE IT, YOU KNOW.
THWAK
EEK!
?!

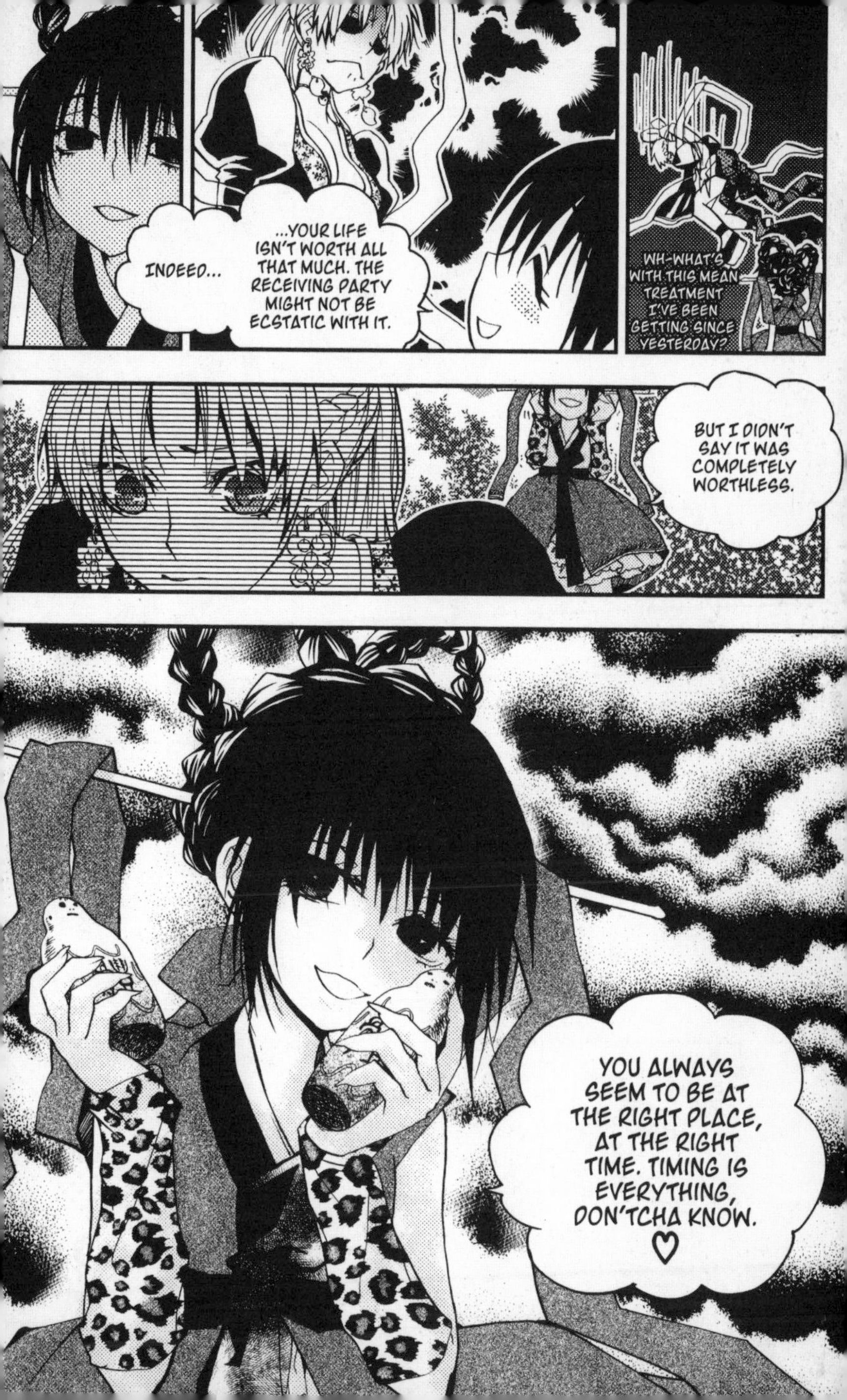
INDEED...
...YOUR LIFE ISN'T WORTH ALL THAT MUCH. THE RECEIVING PARTY MIGHT NOT BE ECSTATIC WITH IT.
WH-WHAT'S WITH THIS MEAN TREATMENT I'VE BEEN GETTING SINCE YESTERDAY?
BUT I DIDN'T SAY IT WAS COMPLETELY WORTHLESS.
YOU ALWAYS SEEM TO BE AT THE RIGHT PLACE, AT THE RIGHT TIME. TIMING IS EVERYTHING, DON'TCHA KNOW. ♡

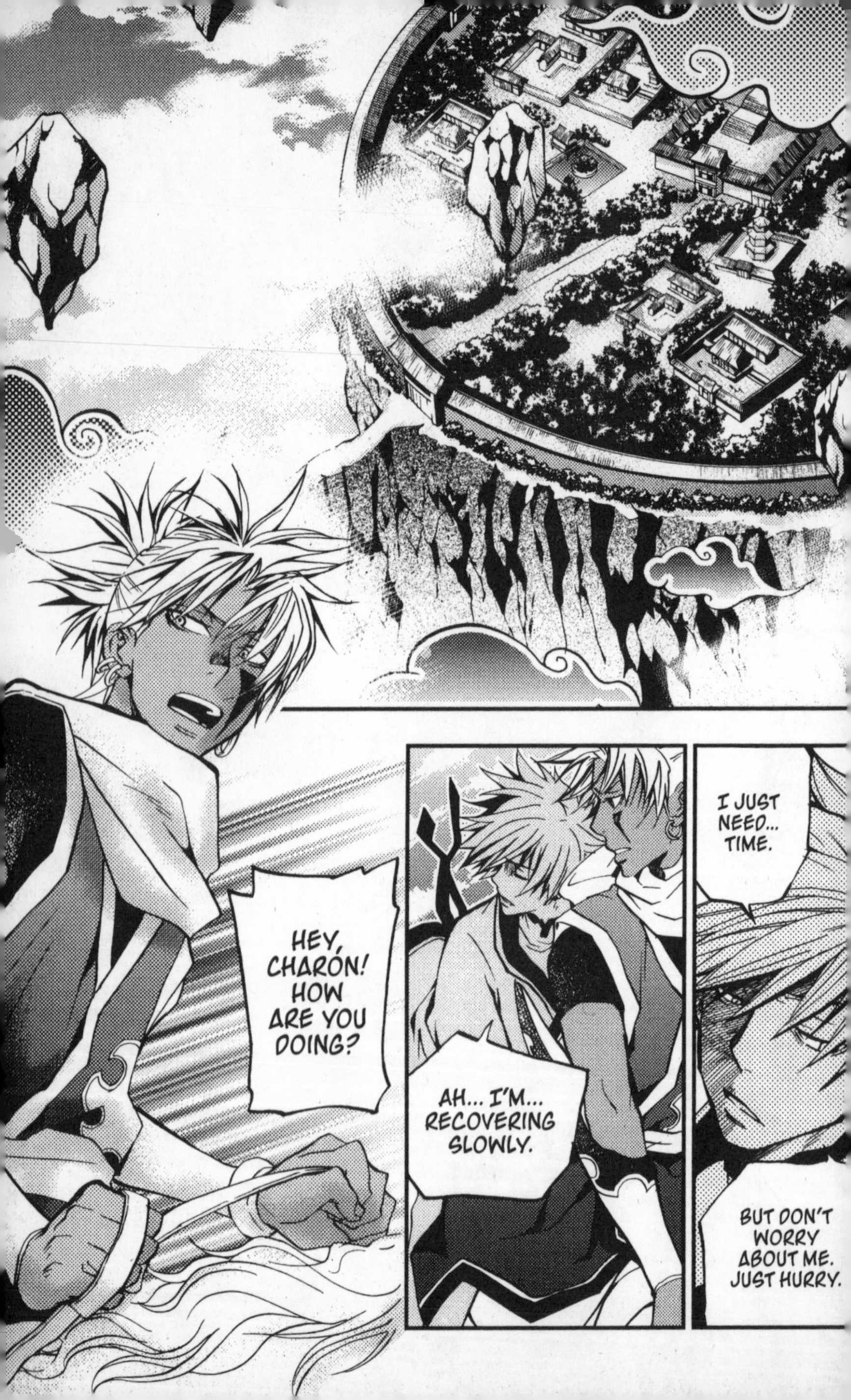
HEY, CHARÓN! HOW ARE YOU DOING?
AH... I'M... RECOVERING SLOWLY.
I JUST NEED... TIME.
BUT DON'T WORRY ABOUT ME. JUST HURRY.

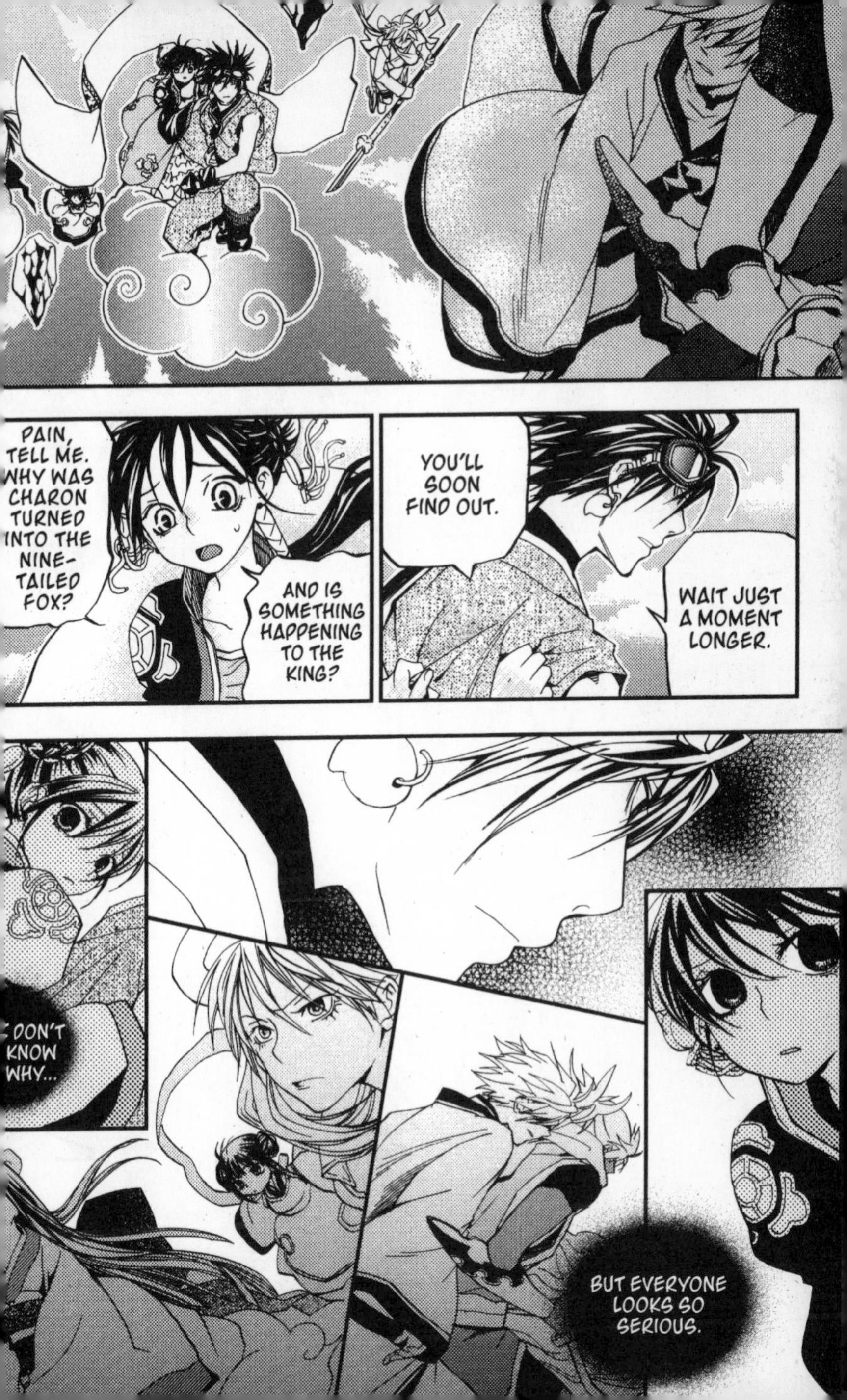
PAIN, TELL ME. WHY WAS CHARON TURNED INTO THE NINE-TAILED FOX?
AND IS SOMETHING HAPPENING TO THE KING?
YOU'LL SOON FIND OUT.
WAIT JUST A MOMENT LONGER.
DON'T KNOW WHY...
BUT EVERYONE LOOKS SO SERIOUS.

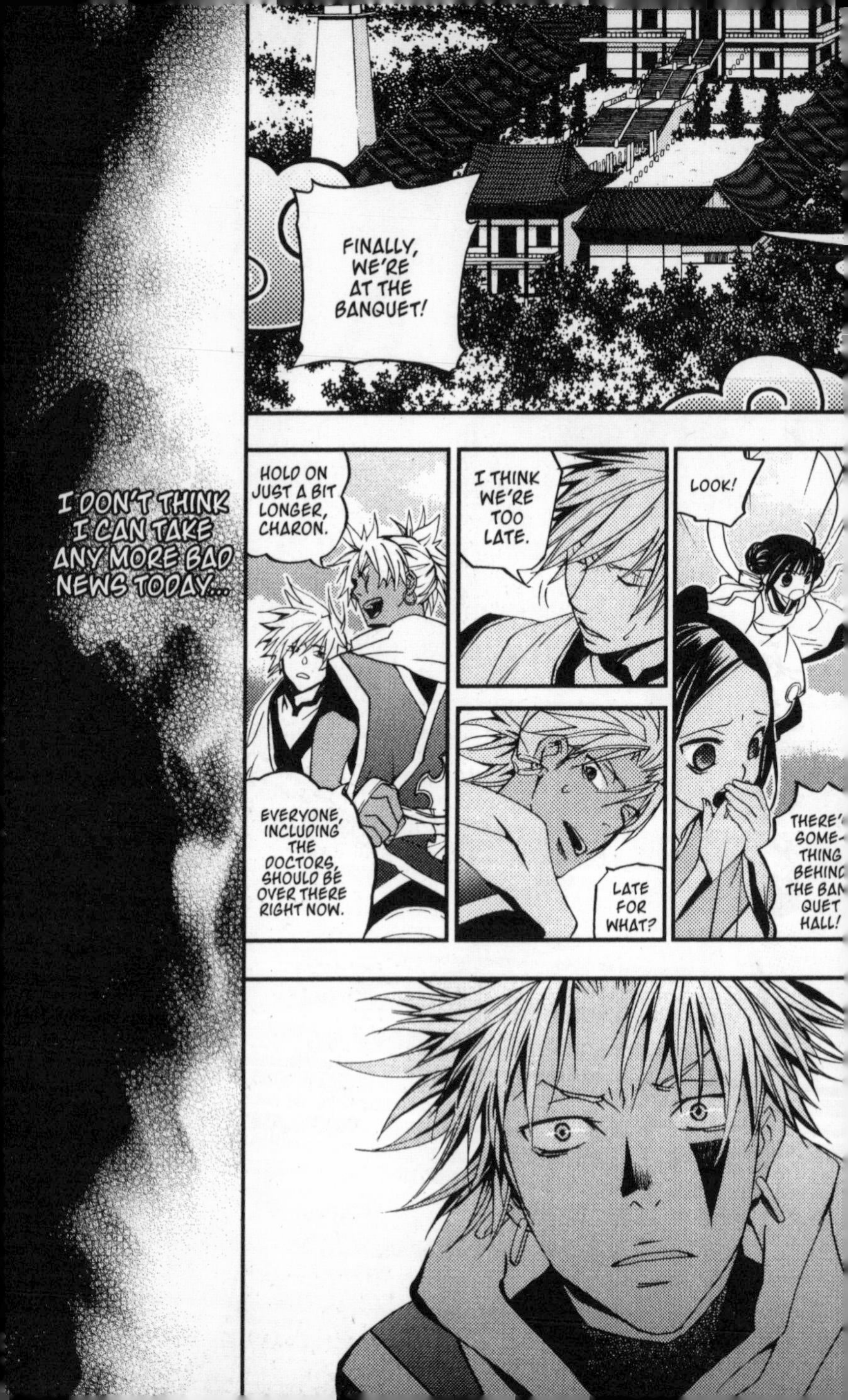
I DON'T THINK I CAN TAKE ANY MORE BAD NEWS TODAY...
FINALLY, WE'RE AT THE BANQUET!
HOLD ON JUST A BIT LONGER, CHARON.
EVERYONE, INCLUDING THE DOCTORS, SHOULD BE OVER THERE RIGHT NOW.
I THINK WE'RE TOO LATE.
LATE FOR WHAT?
LOOK!
THERE' SOME-THING BEHIN THE BAN QUET HALL!

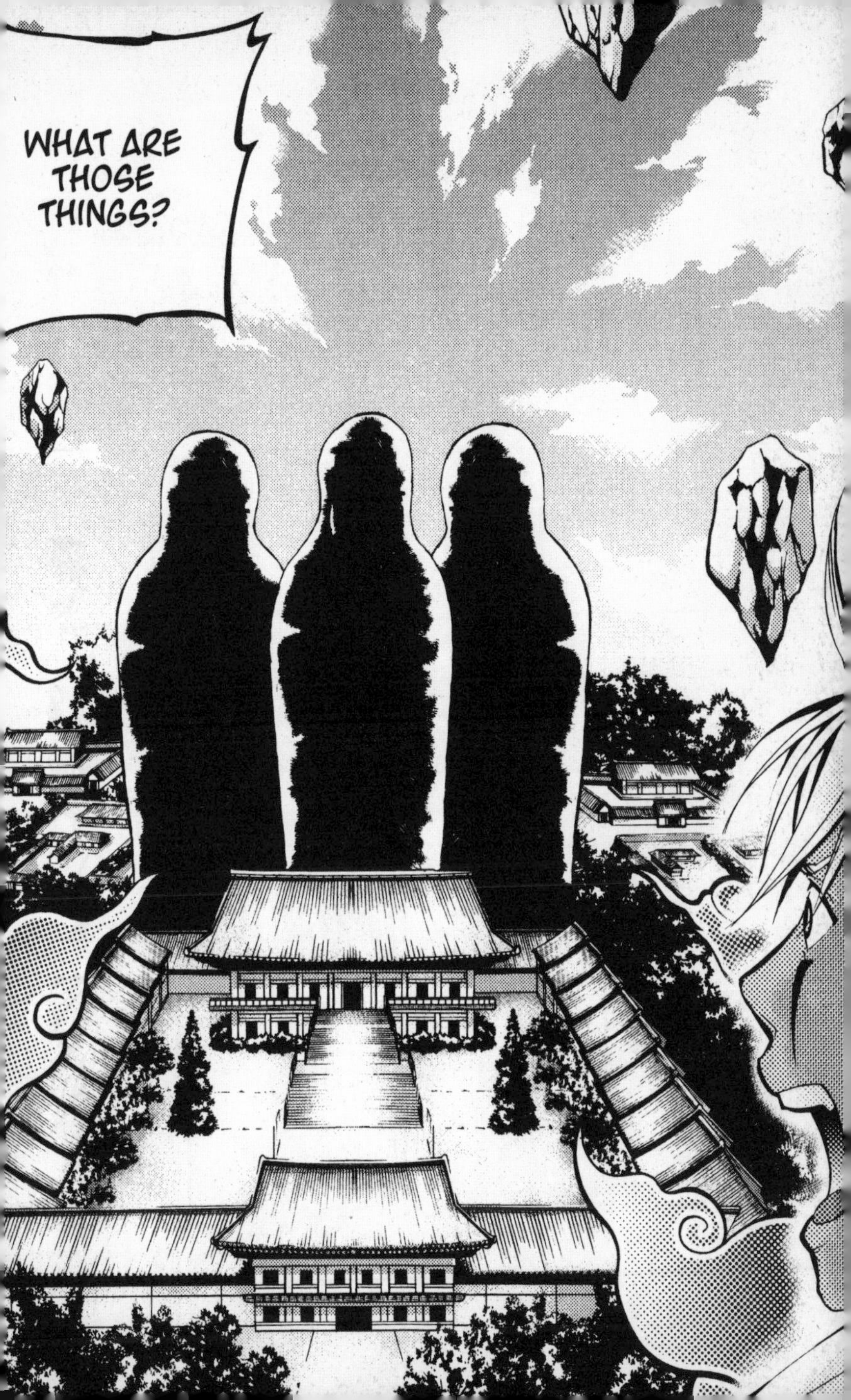
WHAT ARE THOSE THINGS?

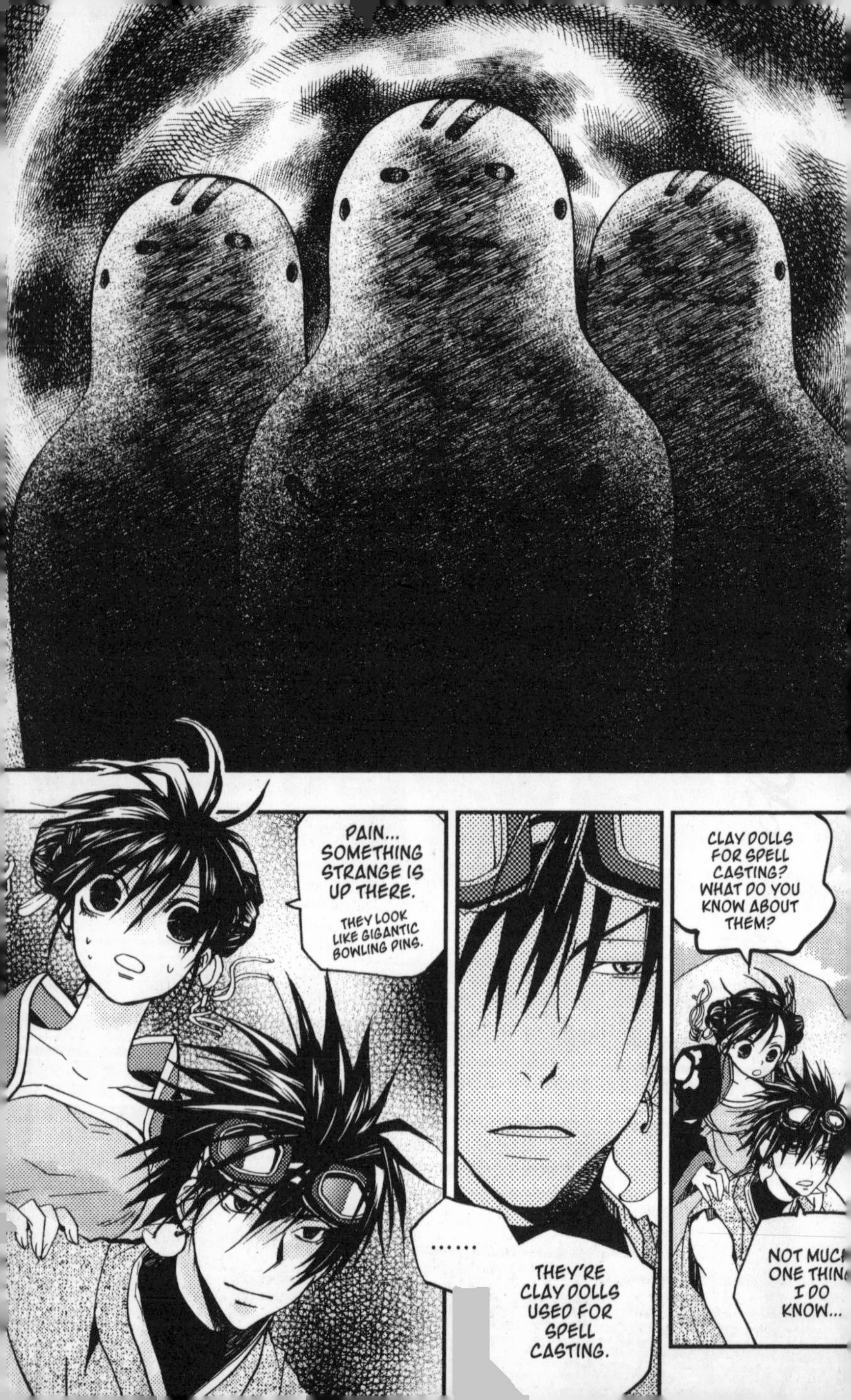
PAIN... SOMETHING STRANGE IS UP THERE.
THEY LOOK LIKE GIGANTIC BOWLING PINS.
......
THEY'RE CLAY DOLLS USED FOR SPELL CASTING.
CLAY DOLLS FOR SPELL CASTING? WHAT DO YOU KNOW ABOUT THEM?
NOT MUC ONE THIN I DO KNOW...

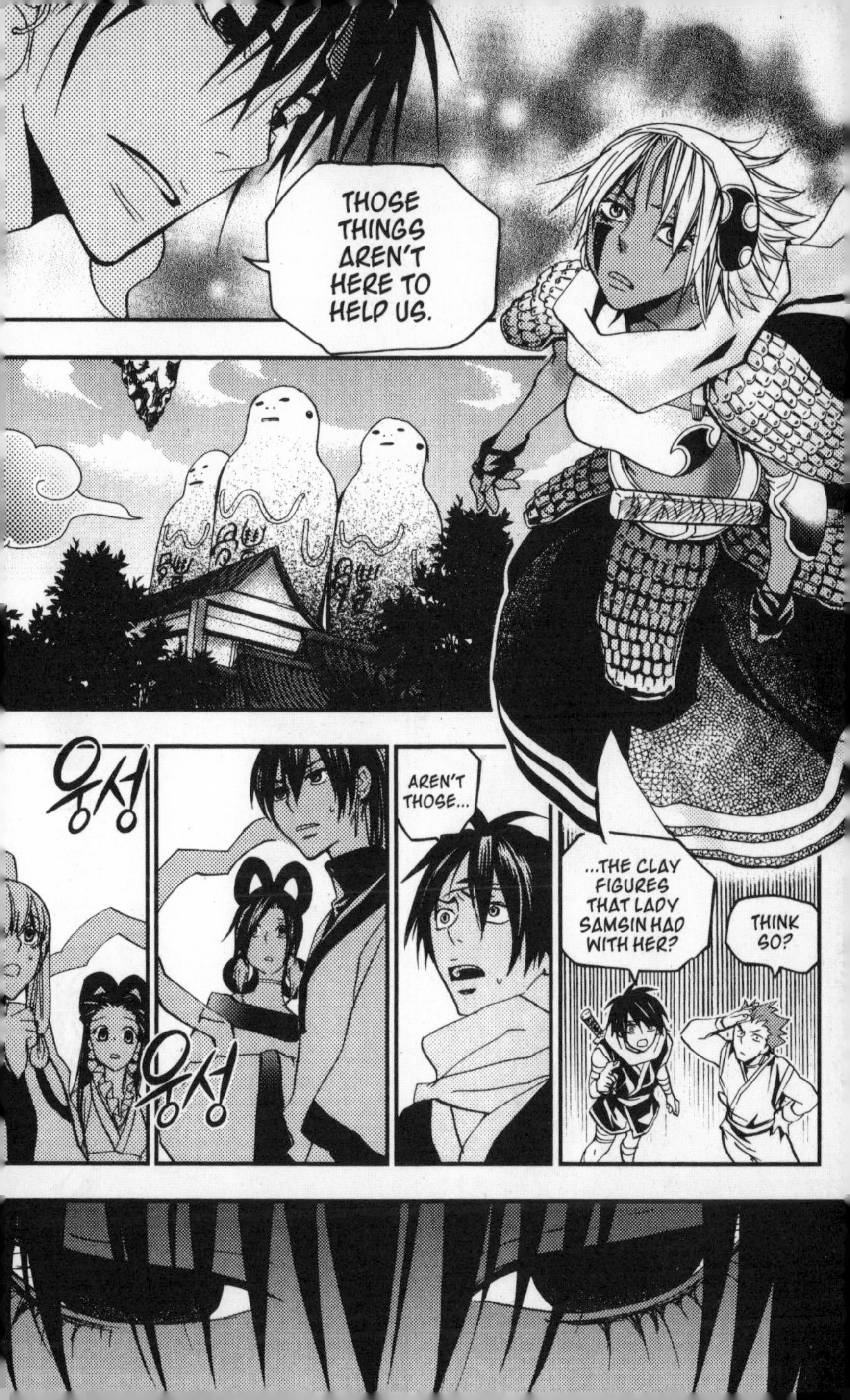
THOSE THINGS AREN'T HERE TO HELP US.
웅성!
웅성!
AREN'T THOSE...
...THE CLAY FIGURES THAT LADY SAMSIN HAD WITH HER?
THINK SO?

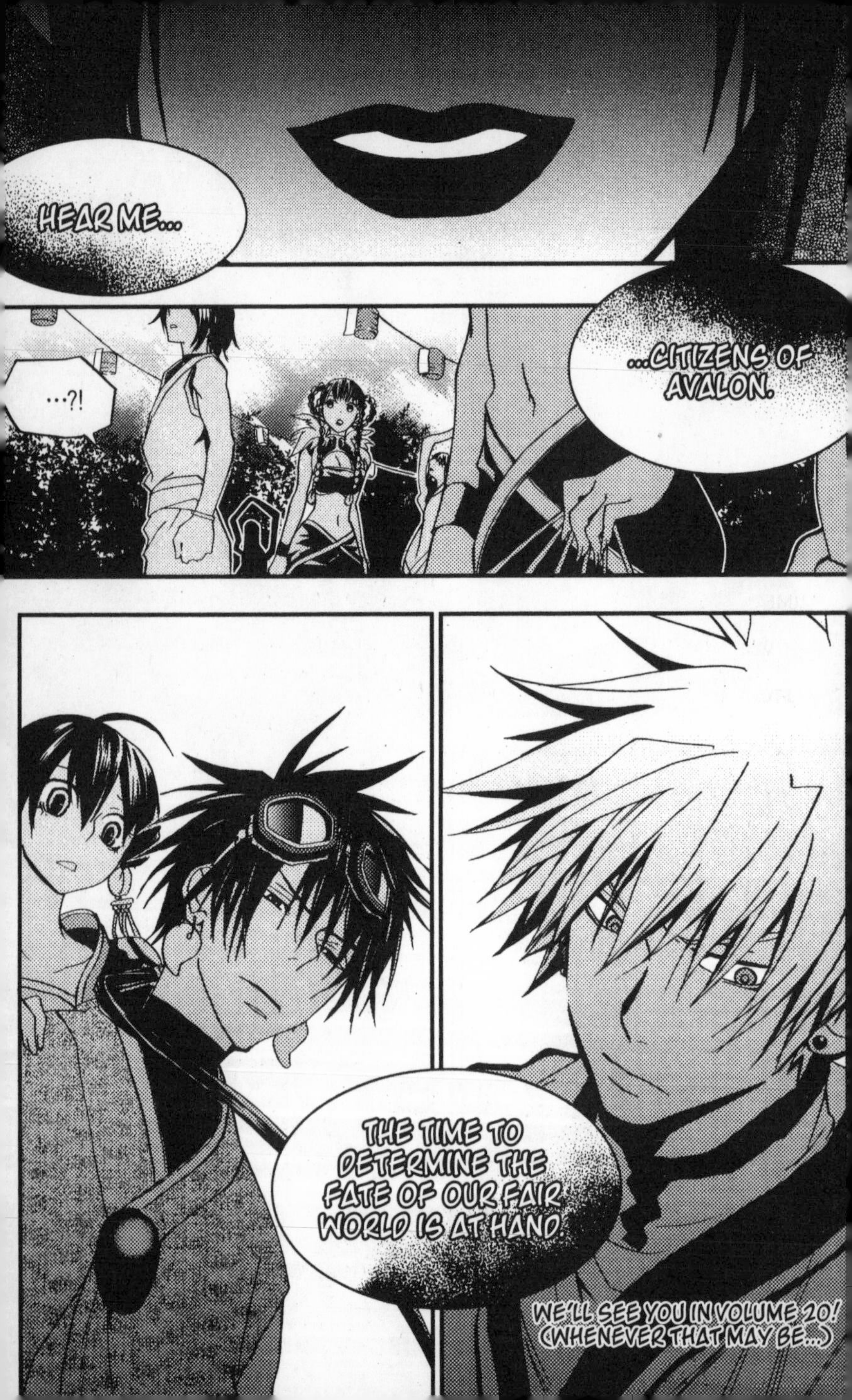
HEAR ME...
...?!
...CITIZENS OF AVALON.
THE TIME TO DETERMINE THE FATE OF OUR FAIR WORLD IS AT HAND.
WE'LL SEE YOU IN VOLUME 20! (WHENEVER THAT MAY BE...)

ON BEHALF OF EVERYONE HERE AT TOKYOPOP, THE EDITORS OF FAERIES'
LANDING WOULD LIKE TO EXTEND OUR HEARTFELT CONDOLENCES TO FANTA
AND PAIN FOR THEIR TRAGIC LOSS. WE ARE, OF COURSE, TALKING ABOUT
THE CESSATION OF THEIR MOTHER (AND THEIR FATHER, TOO, I GUESS...).
FOR OUR FAIR FAERIE OREADIA, WE HAVE COMPILED THIS FABULOUS
OUTLINE OF HER FANTASTIC CONTRIBUTIONS TO FAERIES' LANDING:

EPISODES 1-46: COMPLETE AND UTTER ABSENCE OF OREADIA. INSTEAD,
WE HAD THE TOTALLY HOT, CHEERY, UNASSUMING MS. YUN IN ALL
HER CAMOUFLAGE-LOVING GLORY. AH...GOOD TIMES...

EPISODE 47: ONLY AFTER SEVEN SHORT VOLUMES, OUR OREADIA MADE
HER DEBUT WITH THIS HEART STOPPING LINE: "IT'S BEEN A LONG TIME."

EPISODE 55: GONE AGAIN AFTER DELIVERING THAT COMPELLING
LINE, OREADIA ATTEMPTED A COMEBACK BY "PURIFYING" AN
EVIL AFFINITY. (ACTUALLY, SHE FRIED HIS GIZZARDS.)

EPISODE 63: FAILING TO MAKE A SPLASH IN EPISODE 55, OREADIA ONCE AGAIN
DARED TO GET MORE INK BY SLICING A GUARD FAERIE DOWN IN AVALON. THEN
SHE REVEALED HERSELF TO BE THE PUPPETEER BEHIND THE FORCES THAT TRIED
TO KILL FANTA. IT WORKED. SHE DIDN'T GO AWAY FROM THIS POINT ON.

VOLUME 10: GRACED THE COVER OF THIS VOLUME...DID NOTHING MUCH OTHERWISE.

VOLUME 12: ANOTHER COVER FOR OUR OREADIA. SHE ALSO MUST'VE
USED HER MANIPULATION SPELL ON OUR AUTHOR TO CHUCK THE
STORYLINE OF DISPELLING THE 108 AFFINITIES. SHE EMERGED AS THE MAIN
CHARACTER AS WE TIME-TRAVELED BACK TO ANCIENT KOREA...

VOLUME 13-16: STILL IN ANCIENT KOREA, WE LEARNED OREADIA
WAS RAPED, HAD KIDS AND BECAME ORAN.

EPISODE 97: BACK TO THE PRESENT TIME, OREADIA LEVELED
DOWN AND HER WINGED DRESS GOT SKIMPIER.

THIS VOLUME: GONE! DECEASED! DEAD! CESSATED! (NO
SUCH WORD, YOU SAY? THERE IS NOW!)

AS SOON AS THE JOYOUS CHORUS OF "DING-DONG THE (W)
ITCH IS DEAD!" SUBSIDES, WE'LL BE BACK WITH MORE...

FAERIES' LANDING

Volume 20 Coming Soon

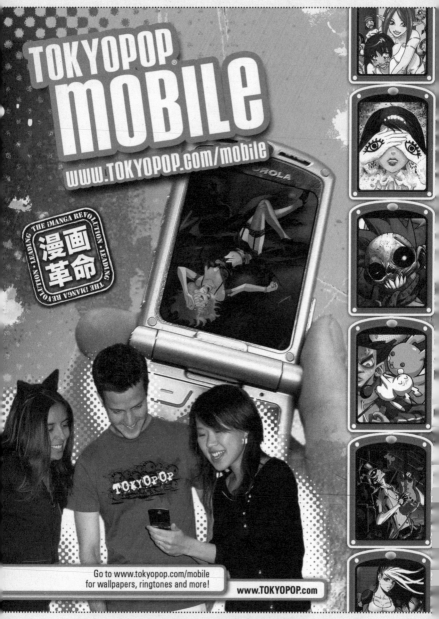

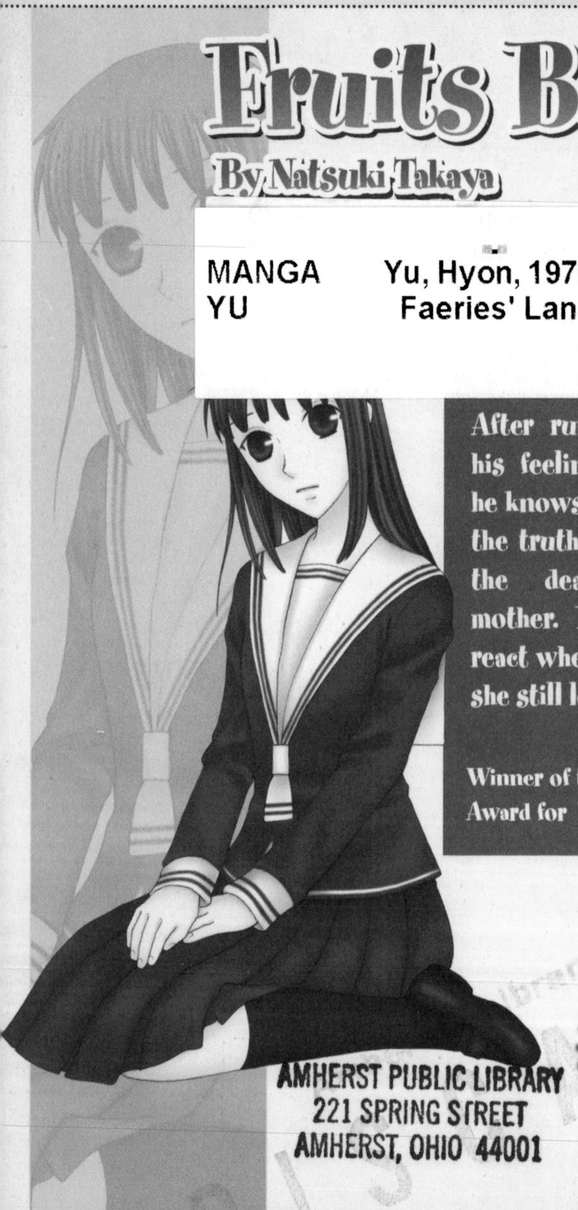